# Social Deviance
**Testing a General Theory**

# Social Deviance
## Testing a General Theory

## Howard B. Kaplan
*Texas A&M University*
*College Station, Texas*

and

## Robert J. Johnson
*Kent State University*
*Kent, Ohio*

## Kluwer Academic/Plenum Publishers
**New York, Boston, Dordrecht, London, Moscow**

*# 4693515*

Library of Congress Cataloging-in-Publication Data

Kaplan, Howard B.
    Social deviance: testing a general theory/Howard B. Kaplan and Robert J. Johnson.
      p.   cm.
    Includes bibliographical references and index.
    ISBN 0-306-46610-4
    1. Deviant behavior.   I. Johnson, Robert J., 1954–  II. Title.

HM811 .K36 2001
302.5′42—dc21

2001029877

ISBN: 0-306-46610-4

©2001 Kluwer Academic/Plenum Publishers, New York
233 Spring Street, New York, N.Y. 10013

http://www.wkap.nl/

10  9  8  7  6  5  4  3  2  1

A C.I.P. record for this book is available from the Library of Congress

To DSK, SCK, REK
—HBK

To LNT, EAJ, HJJ
—RJJ

# Preface

In this volume we report a series of analyses of panel data designed to test aspects of a comprehensive theoretical statement about the social and social–psychological processes that play a part in the onset and course (including cessation and continuation at increased, decreased, or constant levels) of deviant behavior. In Part I we outline our theoretical and methodological approach to the study of deviant behavior. Chapter 1 presents a comprehensive theoretical statement that has evolved over a period of more than two decades (Kaplan, 1972, 1975b, 1980, 1982, 1983, 1984, 1986, 1995, 1996) out of a consideration of the theoretical and empirical reports of others and in response to our own earlier tests of the general theory (Kaplan & Damphousse, 1997; Kaplan & Fukurai, 1992; Kaplan & Johnson, 1991; Kaplan, Johnson, & Bailey, 1986, 1987, 1988; Kaplan, Martin, & Johnson, 1986; Kaplan & Peck, 1992). The statement is organized as a response to four interrelated questions: What social and social–psychological factors (1) influence the social definition of deviant behavior; (2) motivate individuals to perform deviant behaviors; (3) facilitate the performance of deviant behavior independently of or in interaction with factors that influence motivation to engage in deviant behavior; and (4) influence the stability of deviant behavior, independently of or in interaction with factors that influence the initiation of deviant behavior? This statement provides a framework and rationale for the multivariate models we estimate and report in later parts of the volume. Chapter 2 provides details of the panel design and multivariate analytic techniques. The sample, a random half of the 1971 cohort of seventh graders in a large urban school district, was tested up to four times between early adolescence and young adulthood. The theoretically informed multivariate models are tested using the LISREL VI program (Jöreskog & Sörbom, 1986) to estimate the structural relationships among latent variables.

In Part II we estimate several models that account for variation in deviant behavior measured in the ninth grade in terms of constructs measured in the seventh and eighth grades. In Chapter 3 we estimate, for all subjects who provided data during the seventh, eighth, and ninth grade testings, a series of four increasingly elaborated models in which a new variable is added to the immediately preceding model as playing common antecedent and/or intervening explanatory roles. The most inclusive model has been published previously in its present form (Kaplan & Johnson, 1991); the three less inclusive models have appeared in somewhat different form (Johnson & Kaplan, 1987; Kaplan, Johnson, & Bailey, 1986, 1987; Kaplan, Martin, & Johnson, 1986). The present versions differ from the earlier versions in terms of exogenous variables, measurement variables, sample size, and inclusion of correlated disturbances in the models. The repetition of the most inclusive model and the reestimation of the other three models permit us to describe and easily communicate the effects of each successive theoretical elaboration and to discuss the results in greater detail than publication in the periodical literature generally permits. The reproduction of the most inclusive model also provides a base against which we can compare the models estimated in the next two chapters. In Chapters 4 and 5, respectively, we estimate this model for subgroups in order to test assumptions about the equivalence of measurement models and structural invariance between the different social groupings. In Chapter 4 we estimate the model for males and females. In Chapter 5 we estimate the most inclusive explanatory model for subgroups differentiated according to race/ethnicity.

In Part III we report analyses that address the validity of the model as an explanation of deviant behavior that is measured and expressed in young adulthood. In Chapter 6 the elaborated model as an explanation of deviant behavior in young adulthood is estimated for the most inclusive grouping available, white males and females considered together. When we were attempting to conduct subgroup analysis for groups differentiated according to race/ethnicity, it became apparent that—unlike the situation in predicting deviant behavior in early adolescence—the measures of deviant behavior used for the young adult analyses formed a valid construct only for the white subjects. The measures of the construct were not sufficiently valid or reliable to permit estimation in a sample of young black adults. Further, for Hispanic subjects the sample size simply was too small to provide stable estimates relative to the number of parameters in the most comprehensive model. Hence, in order to consider the differential explanatory power of the elaborated model in accounting for deviant behavior in young adulthood and early adolescence, respectively, we used the models for white subjects as points of reference. In Chapter 7 we apply the elaborated model to the explanation of deviance in young adulthood for males and females considered separately.

In Part IV we summarize the analyses and offer conclusions about the significance of this work. Chapter 8 considers the usefulness of the comprehensive theory in explaining some of the variance in deviant behavior at different points in the life cycle and specifying the nature of the relationships among explanatory variables. In closing, we offer illustrative subsequent studies that build on the earlier theory and analytic strategies.

# Acknowledgments

This work was supported in part by research grants R01 DA02497 and R01 DA04310 and by a Research Scientist Award (K05 DA00136) to the first-named author, all from the National Institute on Drug Abuse.

We are pleased to recognize the unwavering dedication of "Sam" McLean, Holly Groves, and Jefferson Rogers to the technical production of the manuscript.

Where we recognize the origins of our ideas, we acknowledge these sources by appropriate textual citations. However, many of our ideas—particularly as these are synthesized in our comprehensive theory of deviant behavior—are the products of lifetimes of scholarly activity and the precise sources or originality of these ideas can no longer be determined. Thus, often we must leave it to others to make judgments about the historical roots, originality, or independent creation of the theoretical statements in this volume.

# Contents

## PART III. DEVIANT BEHAVIOR FROM ADOLESCENCE TO YOUNG ADULTHOOD

## PART IV. SUMMARY AND CONCLUSIONS

# I ⸻

# THEORETICAL AND METHODOLOGICAL APPROACHES TO THE STUDY OF DEVIANT BEHAVIOR

Theoretically driven analyses, panel designs, appropriate multivariate techniques such as structural equations modeling with latent variables, consideration of multiple developmental phases, and the analysis of subgroups that address questions of structural invariance and equivalence of measurement models are appearing with increasing frequency in the literature on deviant behavior. However, studies (such as those reported in this volume) that are characterized by the confluence of these features are still quite rare. Even more rare are series of studies that build on earlier findings and engage in a continuing dialectic between theoretical formulation and estimation of models.

The series of studies reported here has been guided by, and generally has provided support for, our comprehensive theoretical formulation of the causes of deviant behavior. These studies are theoretically comprehensive because the general theory of deviant behavior tested here is an integrative framework. The integration is accomplished in two ways. First, more specific explanatory constructs are subsumed under more general constructs. Second, the theoretical framework includes a greater number of general explanatory constructs than had been included in the past (Kaplan, 1995). The integrative theoretical framework (outlined in Chapter 1) provides more finely drawn specifications of common antecedent, mediating, and moderating variables that influence the initiation and continuity of deviant behavior than were permitted in the past. Testing of the theoretically informed models was facilitated by the development of sophisticated analytical techniques that employ panel designs (described in Chapter 2) that permit the specification of temporal order among causal constructs and that incorporate insights from the developmental and life-course perspectives.

We accomplish our purpose, which is to test a general theory of deviant behavior, by systematically estimating a series of increasingly elaborated multi-variate models using a longitudinal data set obtained from several thousand adolescents tested up to three times at annual intervals during their junior high school years. The theory represents a synthesis of numerous theories that traditionally have been presented as competing explanations of deviant behavior rather than as separately contributing to a more complete multivariate explanation of deviant behavior (as in the present work). The analytic strategy rests on the techniques for estimating linear structural relationships among latent constructs. The increasingly elaborated causal models contribute to the explanation of deviance by: (1) increasing the amount of explained variance in deviant behavior, (2) decomposing direct effects through the interpolation of hypothesized intervening variables, (3) specifying the countervailing effects of putative causal variables via their direct positive effects on intervening variables that have opposing (facilitating versus inhibitory) effects on deviant behavior, (4) exposing suppressor effects, and (5) demonstrating that alternative explanations are untenable regarding the hypothesized and observed relationships in terms of common antecedent effects (that is, spurious relationships) or different specifications of causal linkages among the explanatory constructs. The general applicability of the causal processes is reflected in the success of the models in explaining a general measure of deviance, under specification of sociodemographic subcultures and gender effects. The general model is elaborated as special theories to account for sub-cultural variations and any observed idiosyncratic characteristics associated with specific models of deviance.

# 1

# Toward a General Theory of Deviant Behavior

The analyses reported in Chapters 3–7 are informed by a general theory of deviant behavior. The theory specifies mutually influential antecedents and consequences of motivations for deviant behavior, the acting out of deviant dispositions, and the continuity/discontinuity of deviant behavior. This first chapter describes the theory and places the theory in historical context. Points of overlap with the structured strain, opportunity, control, containment, subcultural, labeling, and other perspectives will be apparent to the informed reader as will differences between the general theory and more current attempts to synthesize multiple theoretical perspectives (Akers, 2000; Messner, Krohn, & Liska, 1989; Shoemaker, 1990).

## The Nature of Deviance

Although the behavior patterns that are the foci of the several analyses in this volume are widely recognized in the more inclusive society as examples of deviant behavior, the concept of deviance has more general applicability. The concept may refer to failure to conform to expectations in the context of a wide variety of interpersonal systems, including friendship groups, marital dyads, and work groups, as well as the general community. Indeed, the concept may refer to behaviors or attributes that conform to the expectations of one group but violate the expectations of another group from whose perspective the judgment of deviance is made. Deviance may refer to physical traits, social identities, experiences, behaviors, or a variety of other phenomena that describe a person.

Deviance, then, refers to behaviors or attributes manifested by specified kinds of people in specified circumstances that are judged to violate the normative

3

expectations of a specified group. "Shared normative expectations" refers to group evaluations regarding the appropriateness or inappropriateness of certain attributes or behaviors when manifested by certain kinds of people in certain situations.

Where deviant behavior is reflected in the presence of certain attributes or the performance of certain behaviors, the normative system expresses expectations in terms of prescriptions for particular attributes or behaviors. Being weak or sentimental might be proscribed for males, but not for females. Being gentle and courteous might be prescribed for females, but not for males.

The indication that certain patterns of behavior in certain contexts (i.e., manifested by certain kinds of people in certain situations) are socially defined as deviant is the administration of negative sanctions. Group members who are said to share a normative system impose these negative sanctions, which are responses that, according to the perceptions of the group, are intended to serve as punishment for the attributes or behaviors in question. The consistent application of relatively severe sanctions in response to particular kinds of behaviors serves as an indication that those behaviors are deviant according to the normative system that serves as a reference point. If the sanctions are applied only to certain kinds of people who perform the behaviors in question, then the implication is that the behaviors when performed by other kinds of people are not defined as deviant. If certain behaviors evoke negative sanctions regardless of the person's social characteristics and other situational contexts with perhaps very rare exceptions, then the implication is that the behavioral proscription is generally applicable except in extenuating circumstances. The ranking in the hierarchy of normative expectations of the evaluative standard that is violated by the behavior is reflected in the severity of the sanctions. Behaviors or attributes are deviant not only because they evoke negative sanctions but also because they would evoke negative sanctions if representatives of the socionormative system that defines the attributes or behaviors as deviant became aware of them.

A group that shares a normative system may evaluate the behaviors or attributes of individuals who do not belong to the group and may apply negative sanctions for behaviors or attributes that are judged to deviate from the normative expectations that are believed to be incumbent on even nongroup members. Depending on the group's access to sanctions that are meaningful to the nongroup members, the application of negative sanctions may have a great adverse impact on the outcomes of nongroup members.

In some cases, individuals whose behaviors or attributes appear to deviate from the normative expectations of a group to which they do not belong are not judged to be deviant. This is because the individuals (perhaps because of their perceived inferiority) are not expected to be capable of conforming to the normative expectations. These "barbarians" or "subhumans" are judged to be deviant by virtue of not belonging to the group that evaluates them, but are not otherwise punished for failing to conform to the specific normative expectations that define the shared normative system. At worst, the failure to conform to the normative expectations is taken to be a (further) indication of their primary deviation, that is, not being part of the group that shares the normative system.

In any case, the valuation of behaviors or attributes as deviant presumes that those making the judgment have taken into account the applicability of the normative expectations to the person and, more particularly, to the circumstances in which the person finds himself. It is not required that the deviant actor identify himself as a group member for the group to evaluate the actor's attributes or behaviors.

The judgment that certain behaviors or attributes deviate from the normative expectations may be made even if the deviant manifestations are beyond the individual's control. Every normative system offers examples of evaluative standards that stigmatize individuals for manifesting undesirable attributes or behaviors or for failing to manifest desirable attributes and behaviors that are beyond their control.

The de facto deviation from the expectations of specified normative systems may be motivated or unmotivated. Motivated deviance derives from either of two sets of circumstances. In the first set, the person is a member of a group that defines the attributes or behaviors in question as deviant. Because of his experiences in the group, the person loses motivation to conform to the normative expectations of the group in order to serve self-enhancing functions. The manifestation of the deviant attributes or behaviors is consciously or unconsciously intended to serve such functions. In the second set of circumstances, the person is a member of a group in which the attributes or behaviors under consideration are normatively prescribed. The person is motivated to conform to the normative prescriptions as one who has been socialized in the group. The person is either unaware or considers it to be irrelevant that another group judges the attributes or behaviors to be deviant. The behavior is motivated, but the fact that the behavior or attributes are deviant does not contribute to the motivation. Rather, the person's motivation stems from the need to conform to internalized group standards and to evoke approving responses from group members who share these standards for conforming to the group's normative expectations.

Unmotivated deviance refers to instances of failure to conform to the normative expectations of the person's membership or reference groups where the failure to conform is contrary to the person's volition. The person would conform if he were able to. The circumstances that contribute to unmotivated deviance are discussed in some detail below.

The patterns of deviance that are the subject of the analyses of this volume generally fall into the category of motivated deviance. Unmotivated deviance is relevant as an explanatory factor, rather than as a dependent variable. The involuntary possession of traits and the involuntary performance of behaviors that are defined as deviant influences judgment of deviance, the administration of sanctions and correlates of these phenomena that influence the onset of other deviant acts or the continuity of the deviant behaviors at the voluntary level.

## Motivation to Commit Deviant Acts that Violate Membership Group Norms

In this section, we consider the circumstances surrounding the development of dispositions to perform deviant acts that involve: (1) the person's earlier commitment to the normative system that judged such acts to be wrong and (2) the failure to achieve what was expected of the person according to the conventional standards. The person comes to see deviant patterns in general, or particular deviant patterns, as the only or most promising ways of satisfying his unresolved needs that, up to now, he tried to satisfy using more conventional response patterns.

### Conventional Failure and Deviant Dispositions

In the course of the normal socialization process, one learns to value the possession of particular attributes, the performance of certain behaviors, and particular experiences that are the outcome of purposive or accidental responses of others toward one. These attributes, behaviors, and experiences are the basis for the individual's feeling of self-worth. If the person is unable to evaluate himself positively, then the individual will be motivated to behave in ways that will gain attributes, enable the performance of behaviors, and increase the likelihood of the experiences that will increase feelings of self-worth and decrease the feelings of psychological distress that are associated with self-rejecting attitudes. If a person perceives an inability to achieve the attributes, perform the behaviors, and enjoy the experiences he has been taught to value as the basis for overall positive self-evaluation through conventional behavior, then he will be motivated to behave in deviant ways that offer the promise of gaining attributes, facilitating behaviors, and enjoying experiences that will permit him to gain a feeling of self-worth. The deviant behavior may involve using illegal means to achieve what the person has learned to value or engaging in deviant activities as a way of rejecting or avoiding the conventional standards by which he failed and substituting deviant standards by which he could more easily succeed and earn feelings of self-worth.

This brief formulation of the process by which individuals become disposed to perform deviant acts that violate the moral codes of the groups in which they were raised is a reflection of a theoretical and research tradition in which the motives to perform deviant acts are viewed as attempts to adjust to the psychological distress associated with failures to achieve specific values such as parental acceptance or occupational success. In the preceding synopsis and synthesis of this tradition, we subsume the various specific motives that are attributed to individuals (individually or collectively) as presumed antecedents of deviant response under a more general motive, namely, the need to avoid self-rejecting attitudes and to maintain or promote positive self-attitudes. Specific motives to attain consensually valued goals by illegitimate means are accounted for by the need to feel positively toward oneself, a prerequisite for which is the achievement of the consensually valued goals. Motivated acts that reflect contempt for the conventional value system and endorsement of values that contradict conventional value systems are intended to function in the service of the self-esteem motive by destroying the validity of the standards the person failed to meet and so evoked devaluing responses from self and others. Deviant patterns that appear to be motivated by the need to retreat (whether by decreasing contact with others or by changing one's psychological state) from contact with the conventional value structure function to enhance self-attitudes by: (1) avoiding further experiences of failure and rejection when measured against conventional standards or (2) avoiding recognition of such failure and rejection. The attraction of individuals who were socialized according to the conventional values to groups that endorse deviant values, in addition to serving any of the foregoing self-enhancing functions, provides a new set of (deviant) standards that the person can adopt or achieve and can therefore use as the basis for positive self-evaluation (Kaplan, 1972, 1975b, 1980, 1982, 1983, 1984, 1986, 1995, 1996).

## Social Determinants of Conventional Failure

The failure to approximate self-evaluative standards of membership/positive reference groups may be conceptualized as *unmotivated* deviance. The concept classifies instances of failure to conform to the normative expectations of specified groups in which the failure to conform is contrary to the person's will. The person wishes to conform but is unable to do so. Thus, in effect, he deviates from the expectations of others. The unmotivated deviance may take either of two forms: the failure to possess consensually valued traits or the failure to perform consensually valued acts. In the former case, the subject has been unable to display traits within an acceptable range of values as a result of the interaction between congenital and social circumstances. Independent of, or contrary to, his wishes, the subject comes to realize that he possesses physical or psychological impairments characterized in terms of undesirable race-, ethnicity-, religion- or socioeconomic-related social categories, or in terms of falling below acceptable levels of intelligence, physical appearance, strength, or other criteria that form the basis for invidious comparisons. Since the subject, along with other group members, has internalized these values and therefore wishes to approximate them, his failure to do so constitutes one class of unmotivated deviance. The other class of unmotivated deviance comprises instances of de facto failure to behave so as to conform to the normative expectations of the group members, assuming the subject's desire to conform.

Unmotivated deviance is a function of three general categories of circumstances. First, individuals will fail to conform to the expectations of others when they are unaware of, or mistaken about, the social identities of others with whom they interact, or when they are aware of the other's social positions but are unaware of, or are mistaken about, the role expectations defining their own social identity or that of those with whom they are interacting. In the former case, the person, not knowing the social positions of those with whom he is interacting, is unable to identify his own complementary position and therefore cannot play the appropriate role. Such circumstances are most likely to arise when a person is moved to a new set of interpersonal relationships and when situational cues are vague or ambiguous or both. Members of more mobile segments of our society would be more vulnerable to these circumstances. In the latter case, the subject may know both his identity and the other person's identity but have no expectations or erroneous expectations regarding the roles that the two of them should play. Such circumstances are most likely to arise during times of rapidly changing role definitions, as a consequence of improper role models of other inadequate socialization experiences, or following life events that require the playing of unfamiliar roles.

The second category of circumstances that influence the subject's unwilling failure to perform in accordance with the expectations of others relates to the subject's having status sets or role sets that impose conflicting expectations on him. Although the person wishes to conform to the expectations of all of the other parties with whom he is interacting, the nature of the conflicting expectations is such that he can conform to one set of expectations only at the cost of violating another set. In the case of the status set, the conflicting expectations are occasioned by the subject's simultaneously occupying two or more social positions and, in those capacities, engaging in two or more social relationships. In the case of the role set, the conflicting expectations are also occasioned by simultaneous participation in more than one relationship. In this case, however, the subject is expected to play different roles while acting in the same capacity, that is, occupying the same social position or status in each relationship. Such situations are likely to occur during periods of rapid and uneven rates of sociocultural change in diverse sectors of the more inclusive social system.

The third category of circumstances that influence unmotivated deviant behavior concerns the absence of instrumental resources to achieve legitimate goals. The absence of instrumental resources derives from: (1) congenital inadequacies, as in strength, dexterity, or intelligence, (2) the failure to acquire the skills and experience necessary for adapting to or coping with the environment as a result of faulty socialization experiences, or the disruption of already acquired adaptive/coping patterns by various life events, (3) placement in inadequate social support systems, (4) the occurrence of life events that impose legitimate requirements on an individual that cannot be met by his heretofore adequate resources, and (5) deviant attributions by other social systems. This last set of influences on legitimate instrumental resources relates to a concept of deviance other than that of motivated and unmotivated deviance. This concept takes into account the existence of more or less inclusive and interlocking social systems. As a result of the meshing among systems, it is possible for a subject to successfully conform to the expectations of the particular membership group in his own view and in that of other group members, and yet be judged deviant by other groups because the same behavior that conforms to the socionormative system of the membership group is judged to be deviant from the perspective of the other group's system of normative expectations. To the extent that the other group judges the subject's behavior to be deviant (and has the power to do so), it will implement negative sanctions. These negative sanctions will adversely affect the availability of legitimate instrumental resources that are required if the subject is to be able to conform to the expectations of his own membership group. In failing to conform to these expectations, against his will, the subject by definition manifests unmotivated deviance. Thus, unmotivated deviance is the indirect result of the attribution of deviance and the consequent administration of effective negative sanctions by a nonmembership reference group for behavior by a person that is motivated and normative in the context of that person's own membership/reference group.

## Motivation to Commit Deviant Acts that Conform to Membership Group Norms

The motivation to commit deviant acts is explained in part by the person sharing a deviant subculture with others. A deviant subculture is a set of normative expectations shared by segments of a more inclusive population that includes endorsements of behaviors that are defined by some specified group as deviant (whether or not the normative expectations also include prescriptions for nondeviant behaviors). In some deviant subcultures the deviant activities are closely bound up with other aspects of group life, including language, interpersonal life, and general style of living. In other deviant subcultures, including many youth gangs, deviant activities reflect a minor portion of the more inclusive set of norms that govern the person's activities. In fact, the activity itself may have no intrinsic value except as it reflects some basic value that could be illustrated as well by nondeviant activities. In groups that share deviant standards, the deviant behaviors may promise to meet the person's needs to gain the approval of group members and other rewards associated with such approval, to behave in ways that are consistent with personal values or to identify with a positively valued reference group.

The origin of deviant subcultures may be accounted for by the cultural diversity of groups living in the same society. The people who share a deviant subculture continue to endorse traditional values and activities, although the values and activities may have been defined as deviant by more politically influential groups. Alternatively, subcultures may develop as a collective solution to the failure to achieve conventional goals through conventional means. Individuals who share the circumstances that lead to failure as well as the fact of failure in the course of social interaction adapt to their situation by coming to accept shared values that endorse the use of deviant activities: (1) to achieve conventional goals, (2) as attacks on conventional values, (3) to permit withdrawal from conventional society, or (4) as substitute standards for the measure of self-worth. The solutions either permit the achievement of values or reduce the feelings of self-rejection associated with the failure to achieve them.

Regardless of the source of the deviant subculture, its persistence depends on the transmission of the normative expectations to those who do not yet share the subcultural standards and the appropriate sanctioning of responses by those who share the subculture. The individual internalizes the culture either by being born into and reared in a group that shares a deviant subculture or by later becoming attracted to such a group and becoming emotionally committed to the subcultural standards shared by the group. The person may become attracted to the group originally because of the deviant activities that promise gratification to the person and become committed to the group because of this gratification. Alternatively, the person may become attracted to the group independent of the deviant activities but adopt the deviant subculture as a means of evoking continued identification with the group whose approval he needs. In any case, over time the individual learns to conform to the deviant norms because such conformity is the conventional, right, fitting, or proper way to behave in the group that shares the deviant subculture.

## Acting Out Deviant Dispositions

The *motivation* to engage in deviant acts, whether generated by experiences in conventional or deviant groups, does not sufficiently explain why people *perform* deviant acts. Not all persons who are disposed or motivated to behave in deviant fashion actually engage in those behaviors. Other factors are at work to prevent them from behaving in ways that they are disposed to behave. In particular, whether or not a person acts out the disposition to commit deviant acts will depend both on the relative strength of the motives to commit the act and of those not to commit the act, and on the situational context and other opportunities to perform the act.

### Counteracting Motives

While a person may see the satisfaction of certain needs as being dependent on the performance of deviant acts and so be motivated to perform deviant acts, he may see the satisfaction of other needs as being dependent on not performing deviant acts. In the latter case, the projected deviant behavior poses a threat to the satisfaction of important needs, and the person is thus motivated to refrain from performing the deviant behavior. If the satisfaction of the needs that appear to be threatened by the performance of deviant behavior is more important to the person than the satisfaction of the needs that is expected to result from the deviant behavior, then the person is likely to refrain from the behavior.

Certain of an individual's needs are threatened by the mere *performance* of a particular deviant act. The need to obey the law, to do what one's parents and friends think is right, or to be a moral person are examples of needs that would be threatened by the performance of deviant behaviors and would be satisfied by refraining from deviant acts. Other needs will be threatened because of expected *consequences* of the act itself. For example, the need for the rewards granted to a person by group members might be jeopardized if the individual were known to have performed deviant acts, or the need to be in control of one's own emotions might be threatened by the use of psychoactive substances. The threats posed to the satisfaction of such needs influence the likelihood of acting out deviant dispositions. This being the case, if the processes by which the person is restrained from deviant behavior are to be understood, it is important to understand the origin of the needs that motivate the individual to restrain himself from yielding to impulses to perform deviant acts.

*Origin of Counteracting Motives.* The process by which a person comes to develop motivation to conform to the normative expectations of society—that is, the way in which one comes to need, for example, positive responses from parents, success in school, and (later) occupational success—is a complex one. The way that a person develops a commitment to the conventions of society is based on the infant's prolonged dependence on other human beings for the satisfaction of his biological needs. Since the adults in the child's immediate social circle satisfy his needs, he comes to value the presence of adults. However, as the circle of people in the child's world widens, he may note that need satisfaction is associated with certain persons and not others. By a process of association, the child comes to value those people and, less directly, the traits and behaviors associated with those people who satisfy his needs. Conversely, the child comes to disvalue the traits and behaviors that are associated in his mind with those persons who frustrate the satisfaction of his biologically given or acquired values.

A particularly important set of behaviors and attributes associated with people who ordinarily satisfy our needs are those traits and behaviors that are apparent on the particular occasions when those people satisfy our needs. Though a mother is ordinarily associated with satisfying the child's needs, there are occasions when she does not do so. Those behaviors and traits (smiles, soft words, and the like) that are associated with the occasions when the needs are satisfied come to be valued in their own right. The child is motivated to evoke those responses that he will later come to think of as approving responses. Conversely, those attributes or behaviors that are associated with the occasions when people who ordinarily satisfy the child's needs frustrate the satisfaction of those needs come to be regarded as undesirable in their own right. The child will be motivated to avoid such behaviors. Later, the child will come to think of such behaviors as disapproval. Thus, the person learns to value the positive and disvalue the negative attitudinal responses of others and the forms in which the attitudes are expressed—physical punishment, disapproving words, failure to reciprocate expectations.

Since people will display approving or disapproving responses depending on the individual's characteristics and behaviors, the child will come to associate certain of his traits and behaviors with approving responses and other traits and behaviors with disapproving responses. In this way, the child will come to evaluate behaviors and attributes as intrinsically worthy or unworthy because of their original association with approving or disapproving responses, respectively. Finally, having learned to value such traits and behaviors, the child comes to value in their own right any behavior patterns, resources, or relationships that he perceives to be instrumental to the achievement of these valued states. As the child's circle of significant others expands, he will come to invest with emotional significance others' traits and behaviors that are observed to evoke positive or negative sanctions.

In this way, in the ordinary course of socialization, the individual becomes emotionally attached to particular kinds of social relationships, particular attributes and behaviors that are associated with valued others, and personal attributes, behaviors, or experiences. The person has come to need the presence and approving responses of adults who have particular kinds of characteristics and behave in particular ways, and to possess the kinds of traits, perform the kinds of behaviors, and enjoy the kinds of experiences that are approved by these others. The satisfaction of these needs becomes the person's measure of self-worth. The person is motivated to behave in ways that will reflect or be instrumental in the satisfaction of these needs and, thus, to behave in ways that will evoke self-accepting attitudes. The person becomes emotionally invested in the image of self as one who has certain identities and conforms to the role expectations that are associated with those identities. If the social positions or identities are conventional ones and are defined in terms of conventional rules, then the person's self-conceptions will include images of self as not violating the law.

There are implications for both the development and the acting out of deviant dispositions in the processes by which a person: (1) becomes emotionally attached to the network of relationships and the expectations of the people in those relationships regarding appropriate traits, behaviors, and experiences, and (2) comes to evaluate himself in terms of conventional standards. To the extent that the person becomes attracted to and evaluates himself in terms of conventional values, he will forego engaging in deviant behaviors that threaten his needs to achieve those values. The extent to which the person evaluates himself in terms of conventional values, however, will be influenced by the degree to which he satisfies those needs by achieving conventional values. The consistent failure to achieve and to evaluate oneself positively according to conventional standards decreases emotional commitment to those standards and increases the likelihood that the person will develop dispositions to engage in deviant behaviors that promise to achieve conventional goals or to reduce the feelings of self-rejection.

*Varieties of Counteracting Motives.* Any of a number of motives may restrain a person from committing a deviant act that he is otherwise motivated to perform. The self-restraint might come from the anticipation that important needs might be satisfied by *not* performing the deviant act. For example, the person feels good when he does the "right thing." The person feels an ongoing need to be law abiding. This need is satisfied when the person resists temptations to violate the law. Alternatively, the person may be restrained from acting out deviant impulses because he anticipates that the performance of the deviant act will frustrate the satisfaction of important personal needs. The individual may have an ongoing need to be respected by others. He may anticipate that the satisfaction of this need (by being respected by others) will be frustrated if they find out he committed a deviant act.

The person's anticipation of the achievement or frustration of need satisfaction may be perceived by him as being more or less directly related to the nonperformance or performance of the act. The *direct* involvement of the deviant act is perceived when the fact of performing or not performing the deviant act frustrates or provides need satisfaction. The individual satisfies the need to be a law-abiding person or frustrates the need to conform to the expectations of family and friends by performing the deviant act. *Less directly*, the person perceives deviant behavior as having consequences that affect the satisfaction or frustration of his needs. It is not the deviant behavior itself, but the consequences of the behavior, that satisfies or frustrates strong needs. Thus, the person may perceive that conformity to the law will have consequences that satisfy needs (e.g., a good job and other rewards associated with conformity) and that deviant behavior will have consequences that frustrate needs (e.g., rejection by loved ones, going to jail).

To the extent that the anticipated satisfactions associated with the act or consequences of conformity and the anticipated frustrations associated with the act or consequences of deviant behavior outweigh the projected benefits of the deviant behavior, they will prevent the person from acting out any deviant dispositions he might experience.

*Moderating Factors.* The effectiveness of counteracting motives in forestalling the acting out of deviant dispositions is moderated by two general conditions. These conditions relate to emotional attraction to the conventional order and to the ability to define the deviant act as compatible with the conventional order.

Regarding the first condition, for a person to forego the performance of a deviant act because he believes it is wrong, because people he relates to think it is wrong, because it is inappropriate to his social identities, or because it will evoke informal and formal responses by others, it is necessary that the person have an emotional investment in the moral beliefs, social relationships and identities, and responses of others. If the person does not care about these things, they will not influence his behavior. The effectiveness of counterbalancing motives that prevent a person (who is motivated to commit a deviant act and who has the opportunity to commit a deviant act) from acting out those motivations to deviant behavior are tied up with his positive feelings about the conventional order. The individual is attracted to representatives of the conventional moral order and needs positive responses from them. Further, he respects the rightness of conventional rules and would feel guilty if he violated them. Finally, he gains gratification from his participation in social relationships and would not like to risk the loss of present and anticipated future satisfactions that might be forfeited as a consequence of his performing deviant acts.

Whether over the short term or longer term, any of a number of factors might reduce a person's emotional attraction to the conventional world. Over the short term, any factors that influence the person's emotional and cognitive states in general, and awareness of his conventional social identities in particular, might reduce the effectiveness of constraints against acting out deviant dispositions. The nature of some deviant activities is such that they may reduce the constraints that might ordinarily (in the absence of these acts) prevent the acting out of *other* deviant acts. For example, while under the influence of alcohol or other substances that affect emotional and cognitive states, the person might commit crimes against property or violent acts that he might not commit in more drug free states. Other circumstances allow the person to ignore his conventional social identities and therefore the emotional significance of conforming to the role expectations that define those identities. Such circumstances as being part of an anonymous crowd permit the individual to submerge his identity and with it the recognition that the deviant acts he is motivated to perform violate the role expectations that under less anonymous circumstances would be honored.

Over the longer term, the emotional attraction to the representatives, moral code, and activities of the moral order depend in part on how successful the person has been in achieving what he values within conventional society. The very same experiences of failure (such as feeling rejected by family, friends, or school and failing to attain other valued attributes such as getting good grades or being popular or good looking) that make a person ready to seek satisfactions through deviant acts influence the weakening of his ties to the conventional system. If the person experiences failure and associates that failure with the conventional order, then he will simultaneously become decreasingly attracted to the conventional society and increasingly attracted to the potential satisfactions of deviant behavior. In that event the motivation to deviance will be more likely to have actual deviant behavior as an outcome.

Yet common sense tells us that people who are disposed to perform deviant acts frequently do refrain from performing such acts for the aforementioned reasons. Thus, we must assume that the experiences of failure are rarely extreme enough to fully counteract the attachment to the social order that is associated with the individual's degree of experience with success. Although the strength of commitment to the social order may be weakened by failure, it still, in general, remains a potent force in forestalling the acting out of deviant motivations. It is only in extreme circumstances of near-total failure to achieve what is expected by conventional standards that the individual's attraction to the normative order ceases to restrain deviant impulses. Short of such extreme circumstances, a number of the person's satisfactions will continue to depend on conventional norms, identities, and relationships, and the individual will tend to restrain deviant impulses.

Regarding the second condition for effectiveness of counteracting motives in forestalling the acting out of deviant dispositions, it is not enough that a person be emotionally attracted to the conventional in order for deviant impulses to be restrained. A person attracted to the social order might be motivated to do the right thing, to behave appropriately in various social capacities, to do what those with whom he interacts think is right, to elicit approving responses from others, and to avoid social sanctions and still act out a deviant disposition. All that is necessary for this to occur is that the person who is committed to the conventional moral order justify performance of the act in terms that he thinks are consistent with the conventional moral code and are acceptable to the conventional groups to which he is attracted.

A person may be able to justify deviant acts in terms of the standards that apply specifically to particular social identities or in terms of standards that are more generally applied in society. An illegal activity may be justified in terms of doing it for kicks or because it is exciting or for other reasons that may be acceptable when applied to adolescent behavior. Other deviant activities such as violence are perhaps justifiable in terms of patterns that are endorsed informally in various social institutions. Violence in legitimated form is a prevalent pattern in recreational activities (television, sports) and global political strategy (war).

## Opportunities

Even if the person, on balance, expected satisfaction of important needs from the deviant behavior, he still might not perform the deviant act because of the absence of an opportunity to do so. The opportunity to perform the act includes physical, personal, and interpersonal resources as well as the situational context that provides the occasion and the stimulus for the deviant behavior. The current situation provides a number of features that may stimulate overt acts, given a predisposition to commit some form of deviant act. The opportunities presented by the person's current situation not only define the limits of what is possible but also stimulate latent dispositions, including dispositions to deviant acts. A person who is disposed to violence may be stimulated to commit a violent act at a particular time when cues for violence (e.g., a gun, television violence) are present. A person who is disposed to steal may do so when an appropriate object of value becomes accessible readily and there is little apparent risk.

The individual's current situation and motivation to perform deviant acts influence each other. A person disposed to commit a deviant act may seek out situational opportunities, and the situation in which a person finds himself may stimulate a preexisting disposition to commit a deviant act. A number of factors influence opportunities to perform deviant behaviors, including generality of deviant dispositions and involvement in the conventional order.

*Generality of Deviant Dispositions.* The range of opportunities that are available to the person who is motivated to perform acts defined as deviant depends in part on how general or specific the person's motives are. A person may be motivated to perform any of a range of illicit acts simply because they are illegal. The motive may stem from a history of experiences of failure and being rejected in the conventional world and from the consequent rejection of conventional morals. The motive is a general one in the sense that any of a range of deviant behaviors would satisfy the need. Thus, the opportunities to perform any of several patterns are greater than the opportunities to perform any one of them.

Similarly, the motivation to identify with and to be accepted by a group that endorses deviant patterns can be satisfied by performing any of a range of deviant behaviors. The opportunities to perform deviant behaviors multiply as the range of behaviors that can satisfy one's needs increases. Or, if acceptance by the group is dependent on conforming to a generally stated standard such as being daring, then any of a number of illicit activities that have a high associated risk might serve the purpose of securing group approval. Once again, as the number of deviant activities that may satisfy the person's needs multiply, so do the potential opportunities for engaging in deviant behavior. As the number of generally stated values increases, the opportunities to engage in deviant activities increase even further.

*Involvement in the Conventional Order.* The involvement of the person in conventional society is relevant to the availability of deviant opportunities in three ways. First, socialization in a group that shares homogeneous values may preclude conceptual awareness as well as observation of deviant adaptations. Second, such involvement increases the availability of normative response patterns that can serve the same functions as deviant patterns and so may forestall deviant behavior. If, for example, the failure to achieve the middle-class values to which one was committed leads to feelings of frustration, these feelings can be reduced by changing one's values to those of a less demanding set but one that is still acceptable within the conventional context. Third, which of a range of deviant patterns will be adopted when the person is disposed to perform deviant behavior (whether out of a need to conform to expectations that endorse deviant patterns or in response to the failure to conform to the standards of conventional society) will be affected also by the characteristic response patterns that the person learns in the course of socialization in his membership groups. Where the person is disposed to deviant responses, he is more likely to adopt those specific deviant responses that are compatible with his normal response disposition. Indeed, the deviant pattern frequently appears to be an extreme response that in a less extreme degree would be acceptable in the context of the person's membership groups. For example, certain deviant responses, particularly those involving aggressive behavior, are more appropriate as extensions of the masculine rather than the feminine role.

## Continuity of Deviant Behavior

Once a deviant response has occurred, what factors then account for the stability or increase, as opposed to the decrease, of antisocial behavior over time? Is it accounted for by reinforcing social responses or by the continuity of the same circumstances that led to the initial responses? Certain of the factors that determine whether early deviance will be continued or discontinued are related to the consequences of the early deviant behavior, while other influences reflect changes in the person's circumstances that are independent of the early deviant behavior (e.g., ongoing developmental processes).

Where the continuity or discontinuity of the deviant behavior is the result of consequences of the early performance of the deviant behavior, the relationship may be more or less direct. More directly, the individual may be motivated to continue or discontinue the behavior because of the immediate positive or negative consequences of the deviant behavior itself. For example, the use of illicit drugs may cause the person to feel good about himself or to feel ill. The physical abuse of another person or the destruction of property may increase the person's sense of power. Engaging in gang fights may result in physical injury. These outcomes may positively reinforce or extinguish motivation to continue the behavior. Less directly, the factors that influence continuation or discontinuation of the deviant response (whether by reinforcing or extinguishing motives to behave in this way or by influencing opportunities for deviant behavior) are mediated by other consequences of the earlier deviant behavior. Such consequences include the approving responses of deviant associates, the disapproving responses of conventional groups, and the stigmatizing effects of formal sanctions.

### Determinants of Continuation

Once a person has performed deviant acts, what circumstances will lead to the continuation, repetition, or escalation of the person's degree of involvement in deviant activity? The first set of circumstances includes those that provide positive reinforcement of the need to perform deviant acts. The positive reinforcement stems from the satisfaction of important needs experienced by the person as a result of the more or less direct consequences of the deviant behavior. The second set includes those circumstances that weaken the effects of motives that previously deterred the individual from performing deviant acts. The third set of circumstances increases or establishes ongoing opportunities for the performance of deviant behavior.

*Positive Reinforcement of Deviant Behavior.* Deviant behavior is self-reinforcing in two ways. First, the performance of deviant behavior may satisfy important needs for the person. Since the behavior satisfies the needs, as the needs continue or recur, the deviant behavior will continue or be repeated in the expectation that the need will still or once again be satisfied. Second, regardless of the motivation for the initial performance of the deviant behavior, the deviant behavior creates a need (specifically a need for self-justification) that is satisfied by continuation or repetition of the deviant act or by the structuring of the social environment in ways that facilitate the continuation or repetition of the deviant act. The difference between the two modes of self-reinforcement is that in the former instance a need precedes the deviant behavior that satisfies the need. In the latter case, the deviant behavior *creates* a need that is satisfied by repetition or continuation of the deviant behavior.

Regarding the self-reinforcement of deviant behavior, frequently the performance of deviant acts results in the satisfaction of the individual's needs. These satisfactions reinforce motives to perform the deviant act. The various needs that the person experiences are subsumed under the more general need for positive self-attitudes (Kaplan, 1975b, 1980, 1982). It has been argued that deviant acts can help to satisfy this need in any of three ways. Deviant behavior may permit the person to: (1) avoid the source of the self-devaluing attitudes, (2) attack the basis of the self-devaluing attitudes, or (3) substitute new sources of positive self-evaluation.

The *avoidance* of self-devaluing experiences as a result of deviant acts might occur through the enforced avoidance of the negative responses of people in the conventional environment. To the extent that the person spends more time with deviant peers, is incarcerated, or is otherwise excluded from interacting with conventional others, he will necessarily avoid negative reactions that he has experienced in the conventional environment in the past.

Deviant acts that involve *attacks* on conventional institutions or the representatives of these institutions have self-enhancing consequences by causing the individual to express his rejection of the values by which he in the past rejected himself. Deprived of self-acceptance by being unable to approximate conventional standards and, consequently, to earn group approval, the person would find rejection of the standards and of the group that rejected him to be gratifying. The deviant behavior would signify that he considers the standards by which he formerly rejected himself to be invalid.

Deviant acts provide *substitute routes* to positive self-evaluation. The deviant activity may involve associating with a group that endorses standards that are more easily attainable than those endorsed in the conventional environment. The individual thus gains gratification from achieving the new standards. Further, rejection by others in conventional groups sometimes stimulates the needs to be accepted by others. Toward the goal of being accepted by the group, the person behaves in ways (including deviant behavior) that he perceives the group as endorsing. Presumably, conformity to deviant group norms will result in acceptance by the group and will positively reinforce the value of the deviant behavior that earned the acceptance. It is not even necessary for deviants to share beliefs in the rightness of their behavior for the beliefs to influence individual behavior. As long as each person believes that the others think the behavior is correct and he is motivated to be accepted by the other members, he will continue to behave as if the group shared beliefs about the rightness of their behaviors.

In addition to the gratifications that stem from conformity to the standards of deviant associates, the deviant behavior may be positively reinforced as a result of any of a number of other consequences of the substitution of deviant sources of gratification for conventional ones. For example, deviant activities may give the individual a new sense of power or control over his environment that leads him to think of himself as a more effective individual.

Regarding the relationship between the need for self-justification and continuation of the deviant behavior, the initial performance of deviant acts is threatening to the satisfaction of important needs of people who were socialized in conventional society. Specifically, the person feels a need to conform to moral standards and to be accepted by the community as one who conforms to those standards. Once the person has performed deviant acts and thereby has threatened satisfaction of these needs, he is motivated to behave in ways that reduce the distress associated with the threat to need-satisfaction. Among the ways the person can reduce the distress are, first, by justifying the act in conventional terms, and second, by transforming his identity in ways that justify the behavior as appropriate to the new (deviant) identity. Both sets of self-justifying responses involve the continuation, repetition, or escalation of deviant involvement. In the first case, the justification of deviant behavior in conventional terms (often facilitated by the presence of collective justifications by deviant associates or the prevalence of the deviant pattern or both) reduces the barrier to repetition or continuation of earlier deviant acts. The repetition of the deviant behavior, in turn, testifies to the person's belief in the legitimacy of the act.

In the second case, being the object of negative social sanctions causes the deviant actor to positively value deviant behaviors and identities. The person becomes attracted to deviant behavior for reasons related to the reduction of self-rejecting feelings and the affirmation of self-worth. Primarily, deviant actors evaluate deviant behavior and identities positively to "regain their identity through redefining normality and realizing that it is acceptable to be who they are" (Coleman, 1986, p. 225). Negative social sanctions influence self-conceptions of being the object of negative social sanctions and of being one who experiences intrinsically and instrumentally disvalued outcomes such as loss of income and exclusion from conventional groups. Since positive responses from others and associated resources are among the standards for evaluation of self-worth, negative social sanctions lead the individual to judge himself negatively. Given the need to maintain one's self-esteem (Kaplan, 1986), the individual reevaluates the self-ascribed and other-ascribed deviant identities and behavior. The stigmatized social identity and the associated deviant acts are redefined as having positive value. At the same time, the person comes to value deviant patterns and identities because they reflect achievable standards for positive self-evaluation that replace conventional standards that cannot be achieved because the negative social sanctions exclude the deviant actor from conventional circles and restrict access to resources.

Having transformed the value of deviant behaviors and identities from negative to positive, the deviant actor is motivated to behave in ways that validate the deviant identity. Once he comes to value the identity, he is motivated to conform to its normative expectations in order to evaluate himself positively, that is, to perform deviant acts.

Loss of motivation to conform to, and acquisition of motivation to deviate from, normative expectations, as well as association with deviant peers, may facilitate the positive evaluation of deviant behavior. The individual's rejection of social conventions and the loss of motivation to conform to normative expectations reduce the costs of identifying with deviant roles. Insofar as conformity to social conventions and attractive positive responses from representatives of conventional society are no longer bases for positive self-evaluation, indeed, insofar as conventional others now constitute a negative reference group, the positive evaluation of deviant behaviors and identities does not pose a threat to one's self-esteem or to the possession of valued resources. Association with deviant peers facilitates the acquisition of deviant identities and conformity with deviant roles by providing social support for these identities and insulating the person from the experience and perception of conventional sanctions for such role performance.

*Weakening Social Controls.* Social controls are weakened by circumstances that either decrease expectations of adverse consequences or decrease attraction to conventional values. Decreased expectation of adverse consequences is accounted for directly by observation that few adverse consequences of initial deviance occurred and indirectly by the circumstances surrounding stigmatization of the deviant actor following initial deviance. In the latter case, when the initial deviance is observed and harshly responded to, the person is effectively expelled from conventional society and the interaction between the individual and representatives of conventional society is thereby markedly reduced. The person may be detained in an institution or simply be denied the privileges of informal interaction with family members, neighbors, or former friends. Paradoxically, these acts of expulsion that served as negative sanctions for earlier deviance effectively preclude the observation of further wrongdoing and therefore the administration of further punishments for deviant acts. In being expelled from society, the person is removed from the surveillance of those who might prevent him from future wrongdoing by punishing the deviant acts as they are observed.

The attraction to the values of conventional society and to membership in conventional groups as a basis for positive self-evaluation is weakened both by the very same processes that influenced the person's initial motivation to perform deviant acts and by the responses of society to the initial deviance. The person's inability to succeed by conventional standards leads to negative self-attitudes and to the disposition to perform deviant acts that might lead to more positive self-feelings. At the same time, the person's association, in his own mind, between the distressful self-rejecting attitudes and the conventional standards that are the measure of his failure decreases his attraction to these standards. Hence, any impulses to deviance that the individual experiences are less likely to be restrained, as they once were, by the attraction to the conventional standards.

In addition, the early performance of the deviant acts has consequences that more or less directly lead the person to reject conventional standards that ordinarily would help to restrain deviant impulses. The informal rejection by family or school, and the stigma associated with being the object of more formal sanctions such as being arrested, reflect intrinsically distressful experiences and barriers to the achievement of other emotionally significant goals. On one hand, the shame of being punished for certain infractions leads to a self-defensive rejection of the moral standards. The person, recognizing that the deviant behavior is an inescapable part of his public image, and over time, an accepted part of his self-image, is motivated by the need to evaluate himself positively to create personal justifications for the behavior and to ally himself with those who can offer collective justifications for the behavior. On the other hand, the rejection of the person by members of conventional society deprives the person of access to resources that, aside from being intrinsically valued, are means to the achievement of other valued ends. Such resources include a good job and the trust and respect of others. As a result, the person is decreasingly attracted to the normative order. Simply put, the individual no longer cares, or cares less, what the representatives of the conventional order think about his behavior. Since he does not care, the attitudes of others no longer constrain him from performing a deviant act that he otherwise is motivated to perform. Rather, he becomes increasingly dependent on deviant associates for standards of self-evaluation and for the resources for achieving those standards.

*Opportunities for Deviance.* The early performance of deviant acts frequently has consequences that increase the individual's opportunity to perform deviant acts. As a result of the person's rejection of and by the conventional society, he becomes increasingly attracted to deviant associates and increases the amount of social interaction with other deviants. Some of this interaction with deviant associates is the necessary result of periods of detention in custodial institutions. The increased interaction increases the opportunities to observe and learn deviant patterns and additionally provides numerous occasions that call for the enactment of the deviant behavior. With increasing interaction comes the motivation to conform to the expectations of deviant associates on whom the person depends for satisfaction of day-to-day needs. As the individual becomes symbolically and physically separated from conventional society, he depends on deviant associates for an increasingly greater proportion of the opportunities to satisfy his needs.

### Determinants of Discontinuation

Just as different factors influence the continuation, repetition, or escalation of deviant activity, so may any of a variety of circumstances influence the discontinuation of or decreased involvement in deviant activity.

*Absence of Positive Reinforcement.* Just as people may adopt deviant values and perform deviant acts because of failure to achieve conventional values, so may people who were socialized to accept deviant behavior as proper be disposed to *reject* deviant values if they are not able to be successful according to these standards. Just as we might predict that individuals who were not successful in achieving conventional values would be more likely to commit deviant acts than those who were successful, so would we predict that individuals reared in subcultures that endorse deviant acts would be less likely to be motivated to continue performance of the deviant acts if they were unsuccessful in achieving the values. Given the opportunity to succeed according to another set of values, they would be good candidates for disengaging from the deviance-endorsing subcultures.

However, as in the instance of people who become disposed to reject conventional values, continuation of the newly adopted behavior would be at risk, since the earlier set of values continues to exert some influence on the person and mitigates the tendency to continue violating the earlier set of values.

*Adverse Consequences.* Not only might a person discontinue deviant behavior because he was unable to satisfy the needs (e.g., for self-esteem, to be accepted by other group members) that he anticipated would be satisfied through performing such behavior, but he might also be moved to cease deviant behaviors because of consequences that threatened the satisfaction of other needs. Among the needs that are awakened by the consequences of initial performance of the deviant acts are the discomfort experienced by the violation of conventional values to which the person continues to remain committed. A major source of motivations that counteract or mitigate the disposition to deviance is the early adoption of conventional values in the course of the socialization process. We noted earlier that individuals who have failed to achieve the values they learned in the course of the socialization process may adapt in any of a number of ways, including using deviant behaviors to achieve conventional values, withdrawing from the conventional world, and rejecting the validity of the values. However, these adaptations are potentially unstable because the actors have great difficulty in totally ridding themselves of the standards of behavior by which they were taught to evaluate themselves. It is precisely the strength of these values that makes the deviant responses unstable. As long as the person continues to feel strongly about the values he is apparently rejecting, he will feel some discomfort while performing deviant acts. Given the opportunity to successfully pursue conventional values, he is likely to cease being attracted to and performing deviant acts.

*Changes in Needs and Opportunities.* Since deviant behavior frequently reflects attempts to satisfy needs, it is to be expected that changes in the person's needs or the opportunities to meet those needs will make deviant behavior unnecessary. Often, the individual will experience an increase in perceived personal resources as a result of deviant behavior that might render such behavior obsolete. The successful completion of such acts might lead the individual to have faith in his own ability to achieve more conventional goals through the use of conventional means. Alternatively, a deviant act such as dropping out of school might remove the person from salient sources of self-rejection and so obviate the need for deviant responses to assuage feelings of self-rejection.

Purposive interventions may take the form of providing conventional resources to deviance-prone individuals thereby reducing their motivation to perform deviant acts in order to satisfy their needs. Further, the normal process of maturation provides persons with new age-appropriate needs and the conventional means to satisfy these needs that render deviant adaptations unnecessary.

This outline is provided only as a brief review of the complex integrative theory of deviant behavior that guides the analyses to be reported in Chapters 3–7. The reader is referred to other sources for more detailed coverage (Kaplan, 1972, 1975b, 1980, 1986, 1995, 1996). This theory effectively integrates a large number of special theories that address particular aspects of explanations of deviant behavior. Our intention was not to integrate these theories. However, following the implications of our initial premises it was inevitable that our general theory would encompass these other perspectives and in effect create our own integrative theory. For present purposes it is not necessary to highlight areas of overlap with perspectives such as social control, labeling, subcultural, social learning, and numerous other orientations. Each of these frameworks offers important insights. Again, the points of overlap will be apparent to the reader.

# 2

# Method

## Sample and Data Collection

Data were obtained from a longitudinal study of seventh grade students tested up to three times at annual intervals during the junior high school years (Time 1 through 3) and once as young adults (Time 4). The panel is a random half of all seventh grade students in the Houston Independent School District in 1971. The total sample size of this panel cohort is $N = 9335$. The entire panel data set consisted of over 200 self-report items over each of the first three waves and nearly 2000 primary self-report items with a potential of an additional 2158 contingency items at the fourth wave.

The first wave of the panel (Time 1) generated a baseline of 7618 respondents representing 82% of the cohort. Two follow-up administrations of the repeated measures questionnaire were executed in the two subsequent year periods, generating the original 3-year three-wave panel.

The second wave of data (Time 2) was collected 1 year later, in 1972. At this time, many of the respondents had left school, moved to another school, were absent on the day of the questionnaire administration, or provided unusable questionnaires. Only students who provided usable questionnaires from the first wave were identified and surveyed for this second wave of the panel.

The third wave of data (Time 3) was collected in 1973. Again, by this time, many of the respondents had left school, moved to another school, were absent on the day of the questionnaire administration, or provided unusable questionnaires. Only students who provided usable questionnaires from the second wave were identified and surveyed for this third wave of the panel. Of the original wave 1 respondents, 41.3% ($N = 3148$) participated in all three panel waves.

A fourth administration of the repeated measures plus a substantially expanded questionnaire began in 1980. In-household personal interviews were completed over a 7-year period (1980–1987) for 6084 of the original 9335 sample respondents, a 65.2% response rate. Where in-person interviews were not feasible, mail or telephone interviews were substituted.

## Analysis

The estimation of the theoretically based relationships that purport to explain deviant behavior was accomplished using latent variable models with recursive and nonrecursive simultaneous equations. We used the LISREL program (Jöreskog & Sörbom, 1986) for computer implementation of the structural equation model. The LISREL program uses variable correlations and standard deviations to estimate specified model parameters using both iterative and noniterative techniques. The analytic strategy involves the estimation of successive theoretically informed, increasingly elaborated models. Through the addition of theoretically indicated latent constructs the understanding of the causal processes at work is increased by increasing the amount of variance in deviant behavior that is explained and/or by clarifying the mechanisms through which exogenous and endogenous variables exert their effects on the dependent variable. Thus, increasingly elaborated models: (1) define the variables that intervene in the previously hypothesized and observed direct effects of explanatory variables, (2) specify the opposing indirect effects of antecedents of deviant behavior, and (3) identify suppressor effects of independent variables. At the same time, alternative models are tested to examine the tenability of arguments that specification of common antecedents or different causal paths would fit the data as well as the theoretically informed model. The influence of sample attrition is evaluated by comparing within-wave models for subjects who were present only at Time 1 with those who were present at all of the test administrations.

Subsequent analyses examined the invariance of structural models across subgroups at any point in time and over time, and so considered the moderating influence of sociodemographic variables and stage in the life course.

## Measurement Model

The measurement model in a LISREL model refers to four matrices: (1) the parameter matrix of factor loadings called "lambda-$y$" ($\lambda_y$) or "lambda-$x$" ($\lambda_x$), also referred to as reliability coefficients; (2) the variable matrix of observed variables, also referred to commonly as measurement variables, indicator variables, or $x$ and $y$ variables; (3) the matrix of latent variables designated as eta ($\eta$) or xi ($\chi$), and also referred to as latent constructs, theoretical constructs, or unobserved variables; and (4) a parameter matrix of error estimates called epsilon ($\varepsilon$) or delta ($\delta$). The parameters themselves are referred to as residuals, residual variance, unique variance, or error variance. The distinction between $\eta$ and $\chi$, $y$ and $x$, or $\varepsilon$ and $\delta$ is, respectively, endogenous versus exogenous specification in causal path models. In our models, we rely mostly on endogenous model parameters and variables. The reader should be aware that we will discuss the models in terms of $y$, $\lambda_y$, $\eta$, and $\varepsilon$. The reader should recognize that most of what is said can be equally applied to $x$, $\lambda_x$, and $\delta$. However, causal effects between $\chi$ are not allowed, as will be discussed in connection with $\eta$.

### *Factor Loadings*

There are two general ways in which $\lambda_y$ factor loadings can be specified. One way is to use a theory to specify a particular pattern of factor loadings. Another way is to specify no pattern of factor loadings, but rather to estimate them all and determine which are indicators of one or another factor. These two approaches are referred to, respectively, as confirmatory factor analysis (CFA) and exploratory factor analysis (EFA). Exploratory versus confirmatory factor analyses have implications for the models and matrices that will be estimated when using LISREL. Some of the distinctions can be made if we consider the equations for estimating the measurement model. The first equation is in matrix form and expresses the relationships between the measurement variables and the latent variables:

$$Y = \Lambda\eta + \varepsilon \tag{2.1}$$

where
$Y$ is an $n$ by 1 matrix of $n$ observed variables
$\Lambda$ is an $n$ by $p$ matrix of $\lambda_y$ coefficients representing the pattern of effects of $p$ latent variables on $n$ observed variables
$\eta$ is a $p$ by 1 matrix of $p$ latent variables
$\varepsilon$ is an $n$ by 1 matrix of residuals or error terms

In an EFA, the coefficient matrix $\Lambda$ has parameters in every row and column position, so that for a model with $n$ = six observed variables and $p$ = two latent variables, there are $n \times p$ coefficients in six equations:

$$y_1 = \lambda_{11}\eta_1 + \lambda_{12}\eta_2 + \varepsilon_1 \tag{2.2a}$$
$$y_2 = \lambda_{21}\eta_1 + \lambda_{22}\eta_2 + \varepsilon_2 \tag{2.2b}$$
$$y_3 = \lambda_{31}\eta_1 + \lambda_{32}\eta_2 + \varepsilon_3 \tag{2.2c}$$
$$y_4 = \lambda_{41}\eta_1 + \lambda_{42}\eta_2 + \varepsilon_4 \tag{2.2d}$$
$$y_5 = \lambda_{51}\eta_1 + \lambda_{52}\eta_2 + \varepsilon_5 \tag{2.2e}$$
$$y_6 = \lambda_{61}\eta_1 + \lambda_{62}\eta_2 + \varepsilon_6 \tag{2.2f}$$

In a CFA, the coefficient matrix $\Lambda$ has parameter estimates in each latent variable column only for the rows that represent the hypothesized observed variable, so that fewer than 12 parameter estimates are made in six equations. For example, if each observed variable is a unique indicator for only one latent variable, and the first latent variable has two indicators while the second has four, the following equations would be generated:

$$y_1 = \lambda_{11}\eta_1 + \varepsilon_1 \tag{2.3a}$$
$$y_2 = \lambda_{21}\eta_1 + \varepsilon_2 \tag{2.3b}$$
$$y_3 = \lambda_{32}\eta_2 + \varepsilon_3 \tag{2.3c}$$
$$y_4 = \lambda_{42}\eta_2 + \varepsilon_4 \tag{2.3d}$$
$$y_5 = \lambda_{52}\eta_2 + \varepsilon_5 \tag{2.3e}$$
$$y_6 = \lambda_{62}\eta_2 + \varepsilon_6 \tag{2.3f}$$

In all of the analyses that are reported we used confirmatory factor analyses when we specified the pattern of $\Lambda$.

### Error

Error in the measurement model is sometimes referred to as residual variance, unique variance, or measurement error. Each term actually assumes something different about the nature of the variance that is not accounted for by the latent variable. And each assumption about that variance is probably partially correct. Remember that the measured variable is dependent on the latent variable and its variance is explained by the proportion of variance in common to the latent variable (standardized $k$) plus the residual variance ($e$) that is left unaccounted for by the latent variable.

The term *residual variance* makes the least meaningful assumption about the meaning of $e$. Residual variance refers simply to that variance that is left over, not accounted for by the latent variable. In order for residual variance to remain meaningless, we must assume that it is completely random. Residual variance that takes on a nonrandom dimension becomes substantively or methodologically meaningful.

*Error variance* attributes a different meaning to this parameter. If it is assumed that the measurement variable is meant to measure the latent variable and have no other meaning, then any variance unaccounted for by the latent variable must be an error in measurement. The measurement variable was unable to perfectly indicate the latent variable, and the degree of imperfection is attributable to that error. Such measurement error is also least important when it is random with respect to the other variables in the model. However, it may be nonrandom when methodological procedures generate a common response, such as in repeated measures or response sets. In such cases, steps must be taken to account for these nonrandom measurement errors.

Finally, *unique variance* attributes another meaningful dimension to the measurement variable, independent of its meaning as an indicator of the latent variable it "loads on." The unique variance may "load" on another latent variable or may be uniquely related to the unique variance in other measurement variables. In either case, the meaning attributable to this parameter is now substantive rather than methodological. We believe any of these meanings is appropriate for interpretation of the error parameters and we offer interpretations in accordance with the context of each model in which they appear.

### Fixed Reliability of Single Indicators

Single-indicator latent variables do not provide enough information to estimate $e$ parameters. Sometimes this poses no problem, for example, when the measurement variable can be assumed to be a "perfect" indicator of the latent variable. Such an assumption is warranted when the researcher believes little or no measurement error exists in the variable and/or the variable is completely uni-dimensional. For example, in a clean data set the interviewer-recorded sex of the subject may fit these criteria as well as other observed sociodemographics. However, even if the assumption is not warranted, the researcher who is limited to a single indicator must "fix" the $e$ parameter. The parameter can be "fixed" or set equal to zero if the measurement properties of the single measurement variable are assumed to be "perfect" or at least very good. In other situations the researcher may have a priori evidence of the amount of variance in the measured variable that should be attributed to the latent variable and the amount that should be attributed to unique, error, or residual variance. With such knowledge, $e$ can be "fixed" or set equal to some nonzero value. We have used both strategies in this volume, and when using a nonzero fixed estimate of error variance, we will give the theoretical and empirical justification for doing so.

### Correlated Error

In many research situations, the researcher makes the assumption that even if there is error in the measurement variables, the error is random and unrelated to the error in other measurement variables. In some of these research situations the assumption is unwarranted. Correlated error exists when such an assumption is wrong and the residual variance in one measurement variable is related to the residual variance in another measurement variable. The LISREL model includes two matrices, theta-epsilon ($\theta\varepsilon$) and theta-delta ($\theta\delta$), that allow specification of these correlated error parameters. The matrices correspond to correlations among endogenous and exogenous measurement variable residuals, respectively. Correlations between endogenous ($y$) and exogenous ($x$) residuals are not incor-porated in the standard LISREL model, although models can be specified using nonstandard procedures to do so (see Hayduk, 1987).

We routinely specify correlated error terms to be estimated in our models for measurement variables that are repeated in multiple waves of the panel. These are referred to as autocorrelated error terms. Autocorrelated error may exist because of systematic biases in these repeated measures. Thus, without controlling on potential autocorrelated error, the cross-wave stability of latent variables that these measurement variables represent may be enhanced or similarly biased. In addition, these autocorrelated error terms control on the tendency for typical overestimates of the relationships between the repeated latent variables and inter-vening latent variables. Such overestimates weaken the fit of the model, and thus autocorrelated error terms often improve the fit of the model.

We also examine ill-fitting models for other possible correlated error terms, although on an ad hoc basis. These parameters are specified in final models when they are significant, improve the fit of the model, we can provide a meaningful substantive or methodological interpretation, or when we believe they may pro-vide a challenge to weak structural effects.

## Structural Model

### *Latent Constructs*

A true advantage to the LISREL model is that it allows the researcher and theorist to find common ground. This common ground is the latent construct, latent variable, unobserved variable, structural variable, or factor. The many names applied to the latent construct intend to convey the meaning that the variable lies at a level of abstraction removed from measured or empirical observations. And because our models are all CFA models, the latent constructs we specify also have important a priori theoretical implications. Unfortunately, the latent construct can-not be directly observed or perfectly measured. Latent construct modeling does enable the researcher and theorist to overcome these traditional disadvantages. "While latent variables cannot be directly observed, information about them can be obtained indirectly by noting their effects on observed variables" (Long, 1983, p.11). The more the effects on observed variables conform to our expectations regarding the nature and dimensions of the latent variable, the more trustworthy our model becomes. The latent construct is thus ideally formed by multiple indi-cators. Each indicator or measurement variable provides some information about the latent construct that is presumed to underlie the observation.

In covariance structure models, one indicator or measurement variable provides information about the scale of the latent construct. This is accomplished by "fixing" the factor loading to unity. Although alternative methods are avail-able, such as assuming unit variance in the latent variable, we employ the fixed factor loading method in our models. This method is more readily transported to subgroup analyses and comparison of unstandardized effects across groups for models we report in later chapters. The other variables each contribute a common, shared substantive interpretation to the latent variable.

## *Causal Modeling*

Causal modeling, also referred to as path modeling, is a method of specifying a system of equations that represent the causal effect of one variable on another. The independent variable is a causal variable that influences the dependent variable. The nature of this causal influence is determined by estimates of coefficients and their significance. Several methods of estimation are possible including ordinary least squares regression (OLS), two-stage least squares regression (TSLS), and many types of maximum likelihood estimations (MLE). We use MLE in the LISREL models we report in our models. The MLE structural parameter is a regression-type estimate of the magnitude and significance of the effect of a causal latent variable on a dependent latent variable. For the system of endogenous equations we estimate these parameters constitute elements of the Beta (B) matrix. The element of the Beta (B) that lies below the diagonal in the third row and second column represents the effect of the second latent variable on the third latent variable and is designated $\beta_{32}$. The matrix notation for an entire system of structural equations is written

$$\eta = B_\eta + f \qquad (2.4)$$

where
$\eta$ is a $p$ by 1 matrix of $p$ latent variables
B is a $p$ by $p$ matrix of $p$ latent variables
$f$ is a $p$ by 1 matrix of $p$ residual variance

In a fully recursive system of equations, B is a subdiagonal matrix with fixed zero element along and above the diagonal. This system of equations is represented in path models with direct, one-way causal effects between latent variables. An untrimmed model is one in which all theoretically indicated or interesting beta ($\beta$) coefficients are estimated. For a system of six latent variables, for example, there are potentially 15 subdiagonal elements in B for the untrimmed model. These equations can be written as

$$\eta_6 = \beta_{61}\eta_1 + \beta_{62}\eta_2 + \beta_{63}\eta_3 + \beta_{64}\eta_4 + \beta_{65}\eta_5 + f_6 \qquad (2.5a)$$
$$\eta_5 = \beta_{51}\eta_1 + \beta_{52}\eta_2 + \beta_{53}\eta_3 + \beta_{54}\eta_4 \qquad + f_5 \qquad (2.5b)$$
$$\eta_4 = \beta_{41}\eta_1 + \beta_{42}\eta_2 + \beta_{43}\eta_3 \qquad + f_4 \qquad (2.5c)$$
$$\eta_3 = \beta_{31}\eta_1 + \beta_{32}\eta_2 \qquad + f_3 \qquad (2.5d)$$
$$\eta_2 = \beta_{21}\eta_1 \qquad + f_2 \qquad (2.5e)$$

A trimmed model is one in which some theoretically indicated or otherwise interesting $\beta$ coefficients are set equal to zero. This is called "fixing" a parameter and represents one type of constraint that can be imposed on a model prior to estimation of remaining parameters. For example, if the effect of the latent variable

$\eta_1$ on latent variable $\eta_5$ is trimmed from the model represented by Equations (2.5a) through (2.5e), then Equations (2.5a), (2.5c) through (2.5e) remain unchanged while Equation (2.5b) becomes

$$\eta_5 = \beta_{52}\eta_2 + \beta_{53}\eta_3 + \beta_{54}\eta_4 \qquad + f_5 \qquad (2.5f)$$

A nonrecursive system of equations is represented by nonzero above-diagonal elements in the B matrix. The symmetrical specification of above- and below-diagonal elements in the B matrix is the way reciprocal causal effects are represented in these models. Reciprocal causal effects are specified in these analyses only to the extent to which no a priori theoretical statement leads us to prefer one causal priority over another and some alternate hypotheses can be generated to warrant testing of reciprocal effects. These effects are confined entirely to within-panel-wave latent variables.

### Elaboration Strategy

The elaboration strategy that we have been applying in the analysis of previous structural equation models is based on the postulate that the relationship observed between theoretical constructs that do not share both temporal and theoretical synchronicity actually represents a causal process that can partially be explained by the introduction of intervening variables. These intervening causal processes that lack temporal synchronicity are distinctly obvious in the estimation of multivariate models drawn from panel studies in which variables from earlier panel waves indirectly affect variables from later panel waves via variables drawn from panels subsequent to the earlier variables and antecedent to the later variables. Within-wave effects assumed to reflect causal processes are more equivocal. However, in addition to the hypothesized causal process based on theory there are other methods that can be applied to support the model. For example, the instrumental variable technique (see Kessler & Greenberg, 1981) or use of cross-lagged effects to estimate causal priority between sets of related variables (see Duncan, 1969; Goldberger, 1971; Rozelle & Campbell, 1969; and particularly for warnings of potential problems see Rogosa, 1980) can be used for additional support. However, even these methods may be somewhat equivocal and the reader should be cautioned that these techniques may be misapplied to the extent that, as Rogosa terms it, the researcher is looking for a "causal winner" in determining the specification of these processes. Indeed, we recognize other possibilities including misspecification of models based on unidentified common causal antecedents or consequences of observed relationships. For this reason, we stress that the elaboration strategy is particularly appropriate in the sense that no observed relationship is considered as empirically verified and exists only to the extent that it represents processes of common causal antecedents, intervening explanatory or common consequences of the variables under consideration. The only exception to these postulates is the unique instance or general class of relationships that are or can be considered to share both theoretical and temporal synchronicity. In such instances the reciprocal effects, sometimes referred to as feedback or simultaneous effects, can be explicitly modeled given certain assumptions and empirical requirements. Kessler and Greenberg (1981) again may be consulted for a technical presentation of the issues, although we do not explicitly deal with simultaneous reciprocal effects in this series of models.

In this series of models we deal specifically with the elaboration of the simple causal chain first presented as a baseline model (Kaplan, Martin, & Johnson, 1986). To this model, extended over three panel waves, we add two variables in sequence: one common antecedent (earlier deviance) and one intervening explanatory variable (deviant peer associations) are added to form the second and third model. In the fourth model in the series, we add a variable that plays both a common antecedent and an intervening explanatory role in the elaboration of a model that attempts to explain deviant behavior. This variable, the negative social sanctions applied by authorities, is modeled so as to intervene between the first and second panel wave and serve as a common antecedent cause of the remaining second and third wave variables.

The distinction between an intervening explanatory variable and a common antecedent cause is that in the first case only one dependent variable need be specified and the effect of the variable need only be to significantly attenuate previous observed effect (without adding significantly to overall explained variance). However, a common antecedent cause must both increase our understanding of the more than one consequence and thereby account for some of the previous observed covariation. We expect, as stated earlier, that negative social labeling will function in both respects, intervening between earlier deviance and later disposition to deviance as well as contributing independently to later disposition to deviate, becoming aware of and seeking out deviant peers, and engaging in deviant behavior.

The practical aspects of the elaboration strategy are such that they allow for increasingly complex structural models. At each step of the elaboration process, the models are reexamined for stable measurement properties and robustness of the findings. As the models become more complex, it may become obvious that certain measurement variables are not well suited to the construct validity of the latent variables. These measurement variables may be abandoned in later models. In very complex models, a large number of measurement variables that could or should be abandoned may prevent the estimation of the model. The practical ease of estimating simpler models, eliminating problems one by one as they arise, and then moving to a more complex model are reasons to recommend this strategy. The strategy also "forces" the researcher to clearly specify the theoretical rationale not only for including new variables, but also for specifying them at one point in the model instead of another.

The pitfall of the strategy is that it admits to the estimation of ecologically incomplete models, each one being replaced by a more complete model. The admission of this pitfall, however, is the major caveat that serves as a defense of the strategy. Each model, as it is introduced, specifies the precise test intended for an admittedly complex process, a test that the researcher expects will support the theory, but one that the researcher also recognizes does not prove the theory. In addition to the general caveat, there are other ways to avoid mistakes given the shortcoming of the approach. The measurement model should always be examined from one model to the next with the expectation that the factor loadings will remain quite stable. If factor loadings change dramatically with the introduction of new latent variables, then perhaps either the measurement variables or the newly introduced constructs are more complex than originally hypothesized. If minor accommodations to the measurement model do not "fix" the problem, the hypotheses regarding the entire theoretical specification should be reexamined: the new latent variable may be misspecified as to its placement in the model, the characteristics of its measurement variables may have been misjudged, or the construct itself may be theoretically weak or inappropriate. As more and more constructs are added to increasingly complex theoretical models, and as each piece "fits" without major disturbances to earlier specified measurement and structural parameters, the researcher can take increasing confidence in the notion that an accurate model of the phenomena investigated has been developed. In this sense, overcoming the pitfalls of the methodology at each step of the model building process leaves the researcher with a model that provides a better understanding.

## Assessment of Fit

Every latent class structural equation model can be evaluated in terms of several criteria, most of which relate to an assessment of the goodness-of-fit criteria. Some goodness-of-fit assessments can be made for the overall model. We routinely employed criteria such as an overall chi-square or the goodness-of-fit index (GFI). Other assessments of fit can be made of individual parameters in the model. For these assessments we routinely examined indicators such as the modification index (MI) or the normalized residual.

The overall chi-square goodness-of-fit statistic is based on the overall difference between the observed covariance matrix of the measurement variables and the reproduced covariance matrix that would be produced if some common underlying latent structure could theoretically be assumed to be causing these observed relationships. The chi-square statistic is distributed over $m$-$q$ degrees of freedom, where $m$ is the number of observed variances and covariances (the number of known values in the system) and $q$ is the number of parameter estimates in the model (the number of unknown values in the system of equations). The objective is to specify models that adequately reproduce the observed covariance structure so that chi-square is small. The overall chi-square statistic is sensitive to sample size, however, and very large samples can generate chi-square values that are large and significant. Some have recommended that in such cases a ratio of chi-square to degrees of freedom be used in assessing models rather than the actual significance level of the chi-square. Wheaton, Muthen, Alwin, and Summers (1977) suggested this ratio should be about 5:1 for very large samples. We use this criterion for judging the adequacy of preliminary or embryonic models. Our goal, however, is always to specify models that can reproduce covariance matrices that do not differ significantly from those we observed.

The GFI has a value close to 1 for good-fitting models. In our experience, we have found that "close to 1" can be defined as greater than a range of values between 0.90 and 0.95. GFI values that fall below 0.90 almost always are obtained for models that have at least one very serious flaw and often many serious flaws. Thus, since the statistical distribution of this index is unknown, it can be misleading for evaluation of the specified model. It does, however, have the advantage of being independent of the sample size, unlike the chi-square value. We used the GFI as a secondary assessment for the goodness-of-fit determination, and were very satisfied if it was greater than 0.95.

The delta statistic ($\Delta$) proposed by Bentler and Bonett (1980) is a difference in chi-square values distributed by the difference in degrees of freedom between the models. An assessment of the adequacy of the theoretical model can be made employing the application of a form of the statistic by comparing the chi-square value for a model that assumes mutual independence among observed variables to the specified theoretical model. Additionally, $\Delta$ can be used to assess improvements in the model through a hierarchical or stepwise modification process. Estimation of additional model parameters decreases the degrees of freedom associated with the model. If the decrease in chi-square is significant in relation to the decrease in degrees of freedom, the model is significantly improved. We have used this technique more often for making assessment of improvements in the second application than in the first.

Modification indices are optional output for LISREL models. They univariately indicate the expected size of decrease in the overall chi-square value if the specified parameter is freely estimated rather than constrained. Thus, parameters with values of 3.84 (the value of chi-square that is significant at $p = 0.05$ for 1 $df$) or greater should provide a significant improvement in fit for the model if specified. The index should be used with caution, however, because it tends to favor specification of additional factor loadings over correlated error. Caution is warranted also because a significant improvement in a model using a sample with very large number of subjects can be obtained by the specification of a nonsignificant coefficient. We tend to favor the specification of correlated error rather than complex factor loadings in our models, and we tend to favor models "trimmed" of nonsignificant coefficients. For these reasons we do not rely solely on the modification index when making the decision of whether to trim or specify a particular parameter.

Normalized residuals are also optional output that allow assessment of specific portions of the model. These residuals do not refer to specific parameters estimated by the model, however, as do modification indices. The normalized residuals are a standardized assessment of the corresponding fit between the observed covariance and the estimated covariance. A positive normalized residual greater than 2 in magnitude indicates that the model is significantly underestimating the actual variance or covariance observed between a pair of measurement variables. A negative normalized residual less than 2 (e.g., $-3.4$) indicates that the model is significantly overestimating the observed variance or covariance. The normalized residuals do not indicate specific parameters, but do give valuable clues as to where the model could be modified. Note also the distinction between the normalized residual (a measure of the amount of difference in fit between observed and estimated measurement variable variance or covariance) and the residual variance (a measure of the amount of variance in the measurement variable that is unaccounted for by the latent variables). The first is an assessment criterion for goodness of fit between an observed and predicted variance or covariance. The second is a measurement model parameter (epsilon or delta) that appears in the diagonal of the theta matrices.

## Subgroup Comparisons

We use subgroup comparisons in the analyses of the models in order to test assumptions about equivalent measurement models and structural invariance between groups of subjects who represent sample attrition or presumed sociodemographic conditional effects.

### Hierarchical Model Restrictions

Hierarchical model restrictions are imposed so that in subgroup comparisons certain parameter matrices or particular parameters are constrained in hierarchical fashion. The general procedure we follow is to estimate a model in which the covariance matrices of two or more groups are compared. This null hypothesis model is then used as a baseline model. We compare the subsequent model, which usually imposes a similar factor structure for each subgroup, to the null model. If a significant improvement in fit is obtained by the specifications of this theoretical structure, further restrictions are imposed and compared to the model in which the restrictions did not exist. Again, usually the pattern of restrictions followed include restrictions of equivalent factor loadings, relaxation of these restrictions for individual factor loadings for which invariance seems unwarranted by goodness-of-fit criterion and restrictions on structural parameters (zero, nonzero, or invariant across groups). When stable measurement and structural models are obtained, the final comparison of unstandardized coefficients across groups and the separate estimate of standardized effects are reported. At each hierarchical step correlated error terms are estimated if they seem appropriate according to goodness-of-fit criterion.

### Conditional Effects and Measurement Scales

In subgroup comparisons of model parameters, a conditional effect on the measurement scales means that the factor loading is significantly different in one group than it is in another. The significance of this difference is determined by $\Delta$ for two models, one in which the factor loading is constrained to be equivalent in both groups and the second in which this assumption is relaxed. If relaxation of the assumption of equivalent measurement scales provides a significant $\Delta$, the group variable has a conditional effect on the measurement model. Either individual parameters or entire matrix of parameters can be tested in this manner.

### Conditional Effects and Structural Invariance

Once subgroups are shown to have equivalent measurement parameters, or once significant differences in measurement parameters are accounted for by conditional effects, we can compare unstandardized structural parameters between groups. Again, using hierarchical $\Delta$ statistics, individual parameters or pattern matrices can be compared. Structural invariance exists when a structural parameter can be constrained to be equal in both groups without decreasing the fit of the overall models.

### Separate Model Estimates

After comparisons between unstandardized measurement and structural parameters are made, the MLE of the best-fitting model are input as pattern matrices in separate models. The matrices are constrained to equal the MLE estimates and the estimates are separately standardized. We standardize the parameters separately because LISREL uses pooled variance and covariance matrices to standardize in subgroup analyses. Since we did not always find measurement or structural invariance for each parameter, the separate estimates were the only way to provide accurate standardized effects.

# II

# DEVIANT BEHAVIOR IN ADOLESCENCE

In Part II we report a series of analyses dealing with the explanation of deviance over the junior high school years. In Chapter 3 we report on a series of systematically elaborated causal models for the entire example. In each model a new construct is added to the previous model. The construct partially decomposes previous linear relationships and/or increases the amount of variance explained for the dependent variable (deviant behavior). In the first model we estimate the indirect influence of seventh-grade self-rejection on ninth-grade deviant behavior via the influence of self-rejection on intervening (eighth grade) disposition to deviance (loss of motivation to conform to, and motivation to deviate from, conventional expectations). In the second model the relationship is estimated net of the common association of these three constructs with antecedent (seventh grade) deviant behaviors. In addition, we specify a theoretically informed countervailing direct inverse effect of self-rejection on deviance. In the third model deviant association with peers is specified as mediating the inverse effect of self-rejection and the positive effects of early deviance and disposition to deviance on later deviance. In the most inclusive model, being the object of negative social sanctions is modeled as mediating the direct and indirect effects of early deviance on later deviance. Early deviance evokes negative social sanctions that indirectly affect later deviance by affecting disposition to deviance and deviant peer associations, and directly affects later deviance as well.

In Chapter 4 the most inclusive model specified in Chapter 3 is estimated separately for male and female subgroups. Of the nine structured parameters that were significant in the most inclusive model estimated for the full sample, all but two parameters remained significant, and in the same direction for the male and female subgroups although the strength of the effects varied in some instances by gender. In two instances, the stability of deviance between the seventh and ninth grades and the inverse effect of self-rejection on deviant peer associations, the significance of the effect was gender specific. In any case, for the most part the specified models were consistent with the guiding theoretical framework but were not consistent with many contemporary interpretations of the relationship between gender and deviant behavior. The nature of the gender-specific findings regarding significance and magnitude of effects, however, did suggest hypotheses regarding the mechanisms through which gender moderates structural effects.

In Chapter 5 we estimated the most inclusive model developed on the full sample for subgroups differentiated according to race/ethnicity in order to evaluate, as in the case of the estimation of gender-specific effects, both measurement and structural invariance across demographic subgroupings. While several structural parameters were invariant across groups in terms of statistical significance and direction of effects, the magnitudes of the effects varied by race/ethnicity. For other parameters the effects were significant for one or two groups but not the other(s). The findings sensitize us to the scope conditions under which the general theoretically informed models hold.

# 3

# An Elaboration Strategy for the Study of Deviant Behavior

We estimate four models specifying aspects of an increasingly more inclusive multivariate explanation of deviant behavior. The practice of including additional constructs in each sequential model is an elaboration strategy we adopted for several reasons. First, the elaboration strategy begins with baseline models that are relatively simple, which permits us to simultaneously conduct a confirmatory factor analysis (CFA) of the latent structure of key theoretical constructs in the context of an explanatory model. This was important in the early development and specification of the model because most of the previous research did neither. If CFA was performed, it was often done on a battery of items selected and tested in isolation from other constructs. Once valid and reliable constructs were identified, they were scaled and entered into ordinary least squares (OLS) regression equations, and no further attention was given to the factor structure. However, as we discovered early in the process, the factor structure was often not isolated from the context of the explanatory model, and as many have discovered (Elliott, Huizinga, & Ageton, 1985), it is often not possible to estimate large complex explanatory models without first obtaining stable latent variables. Some researchers have mused that this is a problem with latent variable analyses. We maintain, however, that it is, instead, a problem with failing to properly construct the theoretical model. The elaboration strategy is an approach we advocate because it permits the researcher to use the methodology and theory in synergism, accomplishing both stable measurement models and meaningful explanatory models. To accomplish this, the elaboration strategy does not seek simply to add more constructs. Rather, each construct is first specified as to its measurement properties, and then specified a priori to operate at a unique point in the explanatory process. The models we present are estimated using the LISREL program for analyses of the linear structural relations among latent constructs in a three-wave panel data set.

For the baseline model, an earlier analysis is replicated using refined measurement variables. The refinement in the measurement model was necessitated by the circumstances specified above: adding additional explanatory constructs can influence the factor structure of baseline constructs. In this case, one measurement scale was eliminated from the latent construct "self-rejection" (modeled in terms of global self-derogation, and experiences of rejection and failure in family and school) at Time 1 because the addition of early deviance (the first step in the elaboration) revealed that, in the context of this more complex model, one scale had properties more unique than in common with self-rejection. For similar reasons, the measurement scales for "disposition to deviance" were revised. Nonetheless, the refined constructs were expected to retain their strong positive effects in the model: self-rejection on the latent construct "disposition to deviance" (measured in terms of indices of disaffection with and readiness to adopt antisocial alternatives to conventional school and laws) at Time 2, which, in turn, has the same anticipated strong positive effect on the latent construct "deviance" (reflecting the commonality underlying the adoption of any of a range of deviant behaviors in three different groupings based on probability of occurrence) at Time 3.

In the second model, we account for the influence of earlier involvement in deviance as an explanation of later deviance. To accomplish this, "deviance" is included at Time 1. It is modeled as a control construct to determine if self-rejection continues to operate as hypothesized in the context of earlier deviance. In addition to the hypothesized indirect positive effect of self-rejection on deviance via disposition to deviance, we hypothesize a direct inverse effect of self-rejection on later deviance. Further we hypothesize direct positive effects of early involvement in deviance on self-rejection, disposition to deviance, and later deviance. The predicted effects of the simpler model are again observed. In addition, the hypothesized direct negative effect of Time 1 self-rejection on Time 3 "deviance," and the theoretically indicated direct positive effects of Time 1 "deviance" on Time 1 "self-rejection," Time 2 "disposition to deviance," and Time 3 "deviance" are observed.

In the third model, we investigate the influence of association with deviant peers on the individuals' involvement in subsequent deviant behavior. To accomplish this, a construct reflecting association with "deviant peers" is included at Time 2, modeled to intervene between "disposition to deviance" and Time 3 "deviance." This construct is hypothesized to have a direct effect on later deviance, mediating the influences of disposition to deviance and early deviance. This elaboration permits the construct of deviant peers to explain how dispositions to certain behaviors are enacted. It also permits a test of whether such associations sustain deviant behavior over time, as when the construct intervenes between earlier and later deviance.

In the fourth model (Model IV), we are interested in specifying the role that negative social sanctions play in explaining the continuity or discontinuance of deviant behavior. This construct, "negative social sanctions," is measured at Time 2, but modeled prior to Time 2 disposition to deviance and deviant peer associations. It intervenes between these constructs and earlier deviance. As such, it intervenes between earlier deviance and disposition to deviance, between earlier deviance and deviant peer associations, and between earlier and later deviance.

The increasingly elaborated models are each discussed in more detail, and the results for each are presented. Before proceeding to the next model, these results are discussed in view of the hypotheses derived from the general theory of deviant behavior. Ultimately, all of the observed models are interpreted as providing strong support for the general theory. We begin with a brief background sketch of the theoretical and historical basis of the theory, and its relevance for the models to follow.

The theoretical basis of the models is a multivariate framework that overlaps with several theoretical traditions (Kaplan, 1980, 1982, 1984; Wells, 1978). Elements of the structured strain perspective (Cloward & Ohlin, 1960; Merton, 1938), the subcultural perspective (Cohen, 1955; Miller, 1958), control theories (Briar & Piliavin, 1965; Hirschi, 1969; Polk & Halferty, 1966), containment theories (Reckless, 1967; Reckless, Dinity, & Murray, 1956; Voss, 1969), and labeling perspective (Becker, 1963; Kitsuse, 1962; Lemert, 1951) all are apparent in our approach. This integration of multiple theoretical orientations is part of a growing recognition that deviant behavior cannot be accounted for satisfactorily by only one or a few of the earlier theoretical perspectives. The impetus to the development of integrative frameworks coincided with trends in multivariate analysis that render the estimation of complex models more feasible than in earlier times. However, these techniques have not precluded a continuing tradition of pitting one special theory against another (Matsueda's 1982 analysis of the relative merits of control theory and differential association theory is a case in point).

Other illustrations of the tendency toward integrative explanations of deviance include: Johnson's (1979) attempt to integrate features of strain, subculture, and control theory; Clayton and Voss's (1981) representation of aspects of differential association, social control, anomie, containment, and opportunity theories, along with the labeling perspective; and the integration of strain, control, and learning theories by Elliott et al. (1985). Several integrative explanations, including our own, are described by Akers (2000).

# Model I: Self-Rejection in the Explanation of Deviance

The theoretical framework that guides these analyses is most clearly distinguished from other multivariate frameworks in the pivotal role played by self-referent responses (self-conception, self-evaluation, self-feeling). The special processes that are featured in other theoretical approaches to deviance in general are viewed here as related to deviant behavior by virtue of being antecedents, moderators, or consequences of self-referent responses. The congruence with the more inclusive general theory that guides these analyses and other theoretical approaches to delinquency is described elsewhere (Kaplan, 1980, 1982, 1984). Here we discuss only those aspects of the theory that underlie the separate elements of the models to be estimated.

As stated earlier, the first model is a replication of an analysis by Kaplan, Martin, and Johnson (1986) of the structural relationships among self-rejection, disposition to deviance, and deviance. As in the earlier analysis we hypothesize an indirect positive effect, through disposition to deviance, of self-rejection on deviance. However, due to the influence of earlier deviance when specified in the second model, and thus as a direct consequence of the elaboration strategy we advocate, we use refined measurement models for self-rejection and disposition to deviance.

The first model is illustrated in Figure 3.1. Self-rejection is hypothesized to increase later disposition to deviance. Disposition to deviance, in turn, is expected to increase subsequent deviant behavior. The theoretical basis of the hypothesized indirect effect of self-rejection on deviance has been characterized as "the esteem enhancement model of delinquency."

Beginning with Cohen's (1955) description of delinquency as a response to status deprivation, the delinquency-as-esteem-enhancement model has been successively elaborated and clarified by Cohen and Short (1966), Gold (1978), Gold and Mann (1972), Hewitt (1970), and especially Kaplan (1975b, 1980). According to this model, delinquency is an adaptive or defensive response to self-derogation (Wells & Rankin, 1983, p. 12). The threat to self-esteem stems from a failure to perform or achieve according to conventional group standards.

Past statements of Kaplan's model have been described (Wells, 1978, p. 190) as reflecting a rapprochement between the viewpoints of structural interactionism and socialization-control analyses that in the 1960s were the "dominant perspectives on the use of the self-concept in the study of deviance." According to Kaplan (1972, 1975b, 1980, 1982), central to this approach is the postulate of the self-esteem motive. That is, people characteristically behave so as to minimize the experience of self-rejecting attitudes and to maximize the experience of positive self-attitudes. Self-rejecting attitudes may be reflected in the perceived evaluations

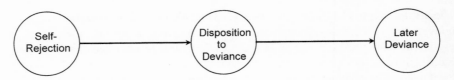

**Figure 3.1.** Model of deviant behavior.

of significant others, such as parents and teachers, or in the reflective attitudes an individual develops through self-comparisons with group standards.

In both instances, attitudes of self-rejection are the end result of a history of membership group experiences in which the person was unable to defend against, adapt to, or cope with circumstances having self-devaluing implications. In the first instance, these circumstances include disvalued attributes and behaviors resulting from negative evaluations of the person by valued others. For example, the subject might report experiences such as feeling rejected by his teachers. Additionally, there may be actions of others that are interpreted as rejection, as when the subjects report that their parents do not pay attention to them. In the second instance, these circumstances include disvalued attributes and behaviors resulting from self-reflective negative evaluations in relationship to real or imagined group standards. These may be generalized feelings such as feeling useless or that one is without worth. Though this is the conceptualization that dominates in these measures, it is also possible that such self-reflective negative evaluations may result from specific feelings of worthlessness, such as being unattractive, unskilled in a particular behavior, or lacking highly valued status attributes like wealth or power or a dominant group identity.

When self-devaluing experiences in membership groups affect the development of intrinsically distressful negative self-attitudes, the individual begins to recognize the association between these experiences and the genesis of derogatory self-attitudes. Consequently, the person loses motivation to conform to the normative patterns that in the past were ineffective in facilitating the achievement of valued attributes, and the performance of valued behaviors, and in mitigating the resultant experience of self-rejecting attitudes. Furthermore, since these and other related normative patterns are subjectively associated with the genesis of emotionally distressful self-rejecting attitudes, these patterns come to be experienced as highly distressing in their own right. To continue to conform to these patterns would be to continue to engage in activities that not only were unrewarding in the past, but also are now intrinsically distressing. The individual not only loses motivation to conform to normative expectations, but also becomes motivated to deviate from these distressful patterns.

Concurrent with these processes, the individual becomes increasingly motivated to behave in ways that minimize the experience of negative self-attitudes and maximize the experience of positive self-attitudes. Continued exposure to the same normative environment that led to self-derogating attitudes leads to the exacerbation of the self-esteem motive. Because normative patterns are no longer motivationally acceptable responses, deviant patterns represent alternative responses by which the person can act effectively to subserve the intensified self-esteem motive.

Given this motivation to deviate from the normative expectations of the individual's membership group(s) and the need to find alternative patterns that will enhance self-esteem, the person is increasingly likely to become aware of and adopt any of a range of deviant patterns. Which particular patterns are adopted is a function of situated opportunities and indications of potential self-enhancing/self-devaluing outcomes of the deviant behavior.

In the present analysis, this theory is modeled as two direct positive effects: (1) self-rejection on disposition to deviance and (2) this disposition to deviance on deviance. "Self-rejection" is the subject's cognitive association between self-derogation and prior self-devaluing experiences in conventional membership groups. Disposition to deviance is conceptualized as the analytically distinct, but contemporaneous, loss of motivation to conform to conventional patterns of behavior and acquisition of motivation to deviate from these patterns. Deviance is conceptualized as the occurrence of any behavior that violates conventional normative expectations and is therefore represented by the broad range of alternatives that are present in the subject's social environment.

In a series of separate analyses, using three-wave panel data and employing partitioning and mean residual gain scores to control on earlier observations of the dependent variables, Kaplan observed the theoretically expected linkages between: (1) experiences of rejection by and failure according to the standards of conventional groups and self-derogation (Kaplan, 1976a), (2) self-derogation and disposition to deviance (Kaplan, 1975c), and (3) disposition to deviance and adoption of each of a wide range of deviant responses (Kaplan, 1977a). Kaplan (1975a, 1976b, 1977b) also reported observation of the direct effects of self-derogation on subsequent adoption of each of a range of deviant behaviors among subjects who had reported no recent occurrence of the deviant responses. However, a second group of analyses (Bynner, O'Malley, & Bachman, 1981; Rosenberg & Rosenberg, 1978; Wells & Rankin, 1983) using data from the Youth in Transition panel study (Bachman, 1970; Bachman, O'Malley, & Johnston, 1978), and a longitudinal study of students in Catholic and public schools in two middle Atlantic cities (McCarthy & Hoge, 1984) failed to find consistent or strong support for the hypothesized association between self-rejection and deviance.

Kaplan, Martin, and Johnson (1986) argued that these studies did not operationalize the theory appropriately in that: (1) the effect of self-derogation was examined net of, rather than in association with, the putative sources of self-derogation, (2) disposition to deviance was not specified as an intervening variable, and (3) deviance was not measured in a way that represented the commonality underlying the adoption of one or a few particular deviant behaviors. In addition these studies tended to assume infallible measurement. In an analysis that purported to overcome these limitations, Kaplan, Martin, and Johnson (1986) reported strong support in a three-wave panel study for the hypothesized indirect positive effect of self-rejection (via disposition to deviance) on deviance. In this analysis the LISREL program for analysis of the linear structural relations among latent constructs was used. This analysis is replicated here on the same data set with some differences in the nature of the multiple indicators of the "self-rejection" and "disposition to deviance" constructs.

## Model II: Continuity of Early Deviance

The second model specifies relationships among four latent constructs as summarized in Figure 3.2. Self-rejection (the perceived association between negative self-feelings and self-devaluing experiences in family and school) is modeled as having an indirect positive effect via disposition to deviance (loss of motivation to conform to conventional standards and motivation to adopt deviant response patterns) on deviant behavior. These were the relationships specified in the baseline model, and are represented here by the broken arrows. The elaboration is expressed by inclusion and specification of the solid circles and arrows.

The recognition by the subject that his self-rejecting feelings derive from self-devaluing experiences in the family and school leads to the loss of motivation to conform to conventional patterns of behavior because these patterns do not

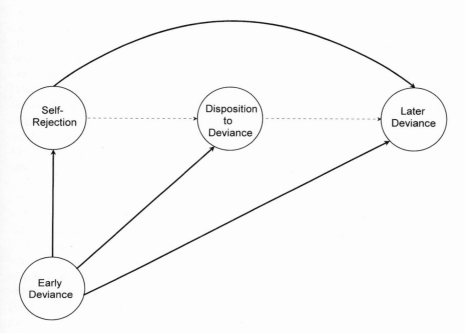

**Figure 3.2.** First elaboration (solid lines) of the general model of deviance: controlling on early deviance.

appear to contribute to the satisfaction of the person's needs. Indeed, this recognition increases the person's need to adopt deviant patterns of behavior because: (1) the association of distressful self-feelings with conventional patterns leads to the experience of conventional patterns as intrinsically distressing and, consequently, to the need to avoid or violate these patterns, and (2) deviant patterns of behavior represent the only alternatives to conventional patterns (that are now motivationally unacceptable) that might function to reduce the experiences of self-rejecting feelings or increase the experience of self-enhancement. Given the motivation to deviate from the normative expectations of the groups that are perceived as the sources of self-rejecting feelings and the need to find alternative patterns of behavior that might enhance self-esteem, the person is increasingly likely to become aware of and adopt any of a range of deviant behaviors.

Net of the indirect positive effects of self-rejection (via disposition to deviance) that further the likelihood of deviant behavior, the model specifies a direct negative effect that mitigates the likelihood of later deviant behavior. This effect is posited on three theoretical grounds. First, individuals who experience self-derogating attitudes associated with perceptions of negative responses from others and/or of having failed are expected to be motivated to so behave as to evoke positive responses from the group members and to approximate the standards of these individuals. If the person were not motivated to so behave, the perceived failure to evoke the positive responses and to approximate the standards would not be associated with derogatory self-attitudes. Individuals who perceive themselves as more distant from these goals would be more desirous of behaving in ways that would achieve these goals. Such behavior would preclude the acting out of deviant impulses. Second, the person's perceived persistent inability to forestall self-devaluing experiences or to foster self-enhancing outcomes in the context of conventional membership group experiences influences self-perceptions of being ineffective, powerless, or lacking in control over his own destiny. The person thus ceases to engage in purposive behavior. The sense of helplessness, initially associated with futility of conventional behavior, generalizes to deviant responses as well. The person, anticipating that the deviant responses will also fail to evoke desirable outcomes, (and may even have adverse outcomes) chooses not to respond with purposive behavior, deviant or otherwise. Passive resignation to unwelcome circumstances becomes the substitute for efficacious action. Third, the person's experience of self-derogating attitudes in conjunction with self-perceptions of devaluing membership group experiences presumes effective socialization and the internalization of group standards, including those that proscribe the performance of acts labeled as deviant. These internalized proscriptions inhibit the acting out of deviant impulses. Over the same time period the person is influenced by dispositions to deviate and internalized proscriptions that inhibit deviant behavior.

Finally, this model specifies direct effects of early deviant behavior on self-rejection, disposition to deviance, and later deviant behaviors. These effects are hypothesized to show that deviant behaviors significantly increase each of the constructs. Early deviance is expected to increase self-rejection because deviant behavior reflects a violation of internalized values and evokes negative responses from other group members. Early deviance has indirect positive and negative effects through self-rejection on later deviance. Early involvement in deviance is expected to have a direct effect on disposition to deviance since it implies a number of related phenomena that reflect the weakening of emotional investment in the normative order and the expectation of gratifying outcomes including: (1) negative sanctions by conventional others that negatively condition attitudes toward the conventional others and (2) social exclusion that attenuates the significance of informal sanctions for the person. Early involvement in deviance is expected to have a direct effect on later deviance by virtue of maintaining or increasing opportunities to learn deviant activities from others who engage in the act and with whom the subject affiliates, by decreasing the effects of sanctions by conventional others, and by increasing the need to justify the earlier deviant responses.

## Effects of Self-Rejection that Mitigate Deviant Responses

As noted earlier, the inverse direct effect of self-rejection on later deviant behavior, net of the indirect positive effect of self-rejection on deviant behavior (via disposition to deviance), is posited on three theoretical grounds. These relate to: (1) the need to conform to group standards, (2) internalized constraints against acting out deviant impulses, and (3) self-attributions of inefficacy. Each of these is considered in turn.

*Need to Conform to Group Standards.*   Overlapping the period during which the person loses motivation to conform to and acquires motivation to adopt deviant patterns of behavior is a time during which the person experiences an intensification of the need to conform to the expectations that the others hold of the individual. Individuals who experience self-derogating attitudes associated with perceptions of negative responses from others and/or of having failed, are expected to be motivated to so behave as to evoke positive responses from the group members and to approximate the standards of these individuals. If the person were not motivated to so behave, the perceived failure to evoke the positive responses and to approximate the standards would not be associated with derogatory self-attitudes. Individuals who perceive themselves as more distant from these goals would be more desirous of behaving in ways that would achieve these goals. Such behavior would preclude the acting out of deviant impulses. The need to evoke positive responses from other group members and to approximate their expectations would lead to attempts to conform rather than to deviate. To deviate would be to increase the risk of evoking negative responses and of distancing oneself further from valued standards. If disposed to deviate, the person will likely behave in a deviant fashion. However, during a period of intensified need to conform, and independent of disposition to deviate, deviant behavior is precluded. Which of these processes will be more influential with regard to the inhibition or acting out of deviant dispositions may be contingent on such factors as the person's expectations that the anticipated conforming or deviant behavior will be successful and rewarded. In the absence of knowledge of which contingencies are operative, both countervailing influences are anticipated.

*Internalized Constraints.*   Again, overlapping the period in which the subjective recognition of a relationship between self-derogation and self-devaluing membership group experiences disposes the person to reject normative standards and to adopt deviant responses is a time during which residual dispositions to inhibit acting out of deviant impulses are operative. Just as a person learns to value being the object of positive attitudes from socializing agents and approximating their expectations, so does the person learn to disvalue those behaviors that the membership group labels as deviant. The person's experience of self-derogating attitudes in conjunction with self-perceptions of devaluing membership group experiences presumes effective socialization and the internalization of group standards, including those that proscribe the performance of acts labeled as deviant. These internalized proscriptions inhibit the acting out of deviant impulses. Over the same time period the person is influenced by dispositions to deviate and internalized proscriptions that inhibit deviant behavior. Which of the two influences, disposing or inhibitory, will prevail may be a function of such factors as the continuing physical presence in the person's environment of conventional socializing agents. Without specifying whether or not such factors in fact characterize the person's situation, both countervailing influences are to be expected.

*Self-Attributions of Inefficacy.*   We expect that self-derogation in conjunction with self-perceptions of self-devaluing membership group experiences will inhibit deviant behavior because there is, we believe, an unmeasured mediating effect of generalized feelings of inefficacy or powerlessness. The person's perceived persistent inability to forestall self-devaluing experiences or to foster self-enhancing outcomes in the context of conventional membership group experiences influences self-perceptions of being ineffective, powerless, or lacking in control over one's own destiny. The person thus ceases to engage in purposive behavior. The sense of helplessness, initially associated with the futility of conventional behavior, generalizes to deviant responses as well. The person, anticipating that the deviant responses also will fail to evoke desirable outcomes (and may even have adverse outcomes), chooses not to respond with purposive behavior, deviant or otherwise. Passive resignation to unwelcome circumstances becomes the substitute for efficacious action.

In summary, we expect that, net of its effect on disposition to deviance, self-derogation in conjunction with self-perceptions of self-devaluing membership group experiences would be inversely related to later deviant behavior. The association of self-derogating attitudes with perceptions of self-devaluing membership experiences should: (1) increase the need to conform to conventional standards and (2) increase feelings of powerlessness to avoid adverse outcomes and to foster desirable outcomes through one's own efforts. Each of these two variables, in turn, should decrease the likelihood of subsequent deviant responses, in the one case out of a need to conform, and in the other case because such behavior would not be expected to have desirable consequences. In addition, the association of self-derogating attitudes with perceptions of self-devaluing membership group experiences presumes the earlier internalization of conventional standards, including those that proscribe the performance of behaviors that the group labels "deviant." The expected inverse relationship between self-rejection and deviance, then, is to be accounted for in part by the common association of these variables with antecedent socialization experiences. Socialization into conventional society leads both to negative self-attitudes in the face of failure to approximate conventional standards and to inhibitions of acting out deviant dispositions.

In the models to be tested, however, the increased need to conform, feelings of powerlessness, and internalization of proscriptive standards are not measured. They are discussed here only as the theoretical rationale for the expected inverse relationship between self-rejection and deviance, net of the hypothesized indirect (via disposition to deviance) positive effect of self-rejection on deviance.

## Effects of Early Deviance

We consider in turn the hypothesized direct or indirect effects of early deviant behavior on or via self-rejection, dispositions to deviance, and later deviance.

*Effects on Self-Rejection.* Early deviance is expected to have a direct positive effect on self-rejection since deviant behavior reflects a violation of internalized values and evokes negative responses from other group members. Within the first wave of the panel, deviance is modeled as causally prior to self-rejection. This decision is made on methodological grounds. It does not preclude the theoretical expectations that the relationship between the constructs is actually reversed, as represented in the full panel, or reciprocal within waves (i.e., instantaneous effects). To model this effect any other way would, first, force us to assume the within-wave intervening effect of disposition to deviance. Second, it would not allow us to test the possibility of spurious effects between self-rejection and disposition (i.e., earlier deviance accounting for both self-rejecting feelings and commitment to a contranormative orientation).

Through its effects on self-rejection early deviance has indirect positive and negative effects on later deviance. The effect of early deviance (via self-rejection) on later deviance is positive insofar as self-rejection increases disposition to deviance. The indirect effect of early deviance (via self-rejection) is negative insofar as self-rejection: (1) intensifies the need to approximate conventional values and evoke positive responses from others, (2) presumes internalization of norms that proscribe deviant behavior, and (3) increases expectations of negative outcomes of one's own behavior and a low sense of self-efficacy.

The presence of early deviance in the model is expected to facilitate the observation of the direct negative effect of self-rejection on later deviance that would otherwise be suppressed. The putative inhibitory effects of self-rejection presume normal participation in the conventional socialization process. If the person did not invest conventional group membership, values, and sanctions with affective significance (if, for example, the person was influenced by subcultural standards that endorsed the deviant behaviors), then the negative effects of self-rejection should not be observed. The presence of early involvement in deviance (insofar as this to some extent reflects deviant subcultural involvement) in the model permits controlling on such influences that would (to the degree they were present) suppress the expected effects.

*Effects on Disposition to Deviance.*   Early involvement in deviance is expected to have a direct effect on disposition to deviance in addition to the indirect effect via self-rejection. Early involvement in deviance implies a number of related phenomena that reflect the weakening of emotional investment in the normative order and the expectation of gratifying outcomes: negative sanctions by conventional others that negatively condition attitudes toward the conventional others; social exclusion that attenuates the effects of informal sanctions on the person; and experiences of gratification from the activity or from significant others who endorse the activity. These are hypothetical constructs and are unmeasured in the model. They are, however, the theoretical basis of the prediction of a direct path from early deviance to disposition to deviance.

*Effects on Later Deviance.*   Early involvement in deviance, net of its indirect effects (via disposition to deviance), is expected to have a direct effect on later deviance by virtue of maintaining or increasing opportunities to learn deviant activities from others who engage in the act and with whom the subject affiliates. The analytic distinction is made between the effect of early deviance on the attitudes toward conventional/deviant norms and the awareness of and learning how to perform the deviant activities, that is, between affective and cognitive dimensions. The affiliation with others is presumed to be the result of the need for positive reinforcement, the attractiveness of the subject to others who perform deviant activities, and the exclusion of the subject from competing normative activities as a result of negative social reactions to the initial deviance. Again, these are hypothetical explanatory constructs that are unmeasured in the present model but serve as the theoretical basis for predicting a direct effect of earlier on later deviance. These effects are expected to operate through the stability represented in the structural coefficients, independent of autocorrelated error representing response bias and related phenomena.

In addition to enhancing the explanation of later deviance the presence of earlier deviance in the model permits the test of whether the earlier model is spurious, that is, whether the indirect effect of self-rejection (via disposition to deviance) on later deviance is independent of the direct effects of early deviance on self-rejection, disposition to deviance, and later deviance.

Finally, the addition of earlier deviance in the model has the effect of making more explicit the nature of the deviance variable. Without the inclusion of early deviance in the model the dependent variable is interpreted as "engaging in deviant behavior." With early deviance represented in the model the dependent variable is interpretable as change in deviant behavior.

The theoretical basis of all of the foregoing relationships is discussed in greater detail in earlier reports (Kaplan, Johnson, & Bailey, 1986; Kaplan, Martin, & Johnson, 1986). The analysis under consideration and subsequent analyses in this series are intended to test the theoretical assumptions that purport to account for these relationships as well as to increase the explanatory power of the model. The methods differ slightly from the earlier reported studies in that each of the subsequent elaborations of the model is based on earlier models that incorporate the later refinements in measurement variables, such that in these analyses, each model is appropriately nested in the following models. This allows for direct comparisons between models of the effect that each elaboration has on earlier relationships among constructs, giving a clear indication of the exact explanation attributable to the elaboration construct as it appears in the theoretically specified process.

## Methods

### Sample and Data Collection

The subject sample represents a 50% sample of junior high students in the 36 junior high schools of the Houston Independent School District in 1971. The survey is a three-wave panel study beginning in 1971 (Time 1) and repeated in 1972 (Time 2) and 1973 (Time 3). The questionnaires generally were completed in class. Students were guaranteed confidentiality and were given a code number paired with a separate cover sheet to permit matching with later waves of the panel. Usable questionnaires were returned by 7618 students (82%) at Time 1.

A total of 3148 students were present for all three administrations, constituting 41% of the usable sample interviewed at Time 1. Of these, 2561 subjects provided data for all measures used in the analyses.

A number of differences in mean levels were noted between those who were present at all three points in time and those who were present only at the first test administration. Analyses of these differences were presented in an earlier study (Kaplan, Johnson, & Bailey, 1986). For present purposes the most meaningful differences were those relating to self-reports of deviant behavior. Those subjects who did not continue in the study were more likely to report any of a wide variety of deviant acts. In the previous study, we conducted comparative analyses of the interrelationships among the Time 1 variables for subjects who were present at all three points in time and for subjects who were present at the first data collection only. The nature and implications of these analyses for generalization of the results obtained for the former group to the entire Time 1 sample were presented. We concluded that the overall similarity of measurement parameters and structural relationships between groups is sufficient to accept the hypothesized structure. Any biases in the estimated relationships when using the "present" sample appear to be, at worst, conservative and underestimated. Nevertheless, the cross-wave relationships might be biased and we always remain cautious regarding generalizability to the full panel.

### Data Analysis

The causal models were estimated using the correlation matrices and standard deviations of the measured variables as input to LISREL (Jöreskog & Sörbom, 1984). This program provides maximum-likelihood estimates of all identified model parameters. It also evaluates the degree to which an overidentified model reproduces the observed variance–covariance matrix in terms of a chi-square goodness-of-fit statistic.

For each of the causal analyses the measurement model and the structural relations model were estimated simultaneously. The measurement model described the hypothesized relationships between a number of measured variables and the latent or unobserved constructs that are presumed to underlie the multiple indicators. The relationships between the measurement (observed) variables and the latent construct that is indicated by the measurement variables are expressed as factor loadings. The structural relations model expresses the hypothesized causal relationships among the latent constructs as regression coefficients.

### Measurement Models

The structural relations model specifies relationships among three latent constructs: "self-rejection," "disposition to deviance," and "deviance." The multiple indicators of these constructs are scales developed within the three waves of the panel. First measures of self-rejection and deviance were drawn from the panel at Time 1; measures of disposition to deviance were drawn from the panel at Time 2; and measures of deviance (identical to those from Time 1) were drawn for the panel at Time 3. Within waves these measures were examined as multiple-item-additive scales. Scale items and reliabilities are reported in the Appendix.

"Self-rejection" at Time 1 is conceptualized as the person's subjective association of self-derogating attitudes with self-devaluing experiences in conventional membership groups. This construct is represented by three measurement variables: (1) a 13-item measure reflecting global feelings of self-derogation (e.g., At times I think I am no good at all; All in all, I am inclined to feel that I am a failure), (2) a 4-item measure of perceived rejection by teachers (e.g., My teachers are not usually interested in what I say or do; By my teachers' standards I am a failure), and (3) a 3-item measure of perceived rejection by parents (e.g., As long as I can remember, my parents have put me down; My parents do not like me very much). It might be argued that self-rejection should be modeled as an interaction between self-derogation and perceived rejection by others, reasoning that self-derogation only has an effect on deviance at high levels of rejection by conventional others. However, we argue here that self-rejection is appropriately modeled as a latent construct representing the commonality underlying both self-derogating attitudes and felt rejection by conventional others. An interaction effect implies that the two variables are perfectly measured independently occurring events and that the existing mean level of the other alters the effect of one of these. However, the subject's perception of his self-derogation and of being the object of others' devaluing attitudes are not independent of each other. Nor are these assumed to be perfect measures. They are, as argued here, measures of a common underlying construct—one that we interpret as the subjective recognition of an association between self-rejecting attitudes and rejection by conventional others.

In an earlier analysis (Kaplan, Martin, & Johnson, 1986) the measure of self-derogation consisted of only seven items. The present expanded version includes items that reflect perceived changes in self-attitudes (e.g., I do not like myself as much as I used to) as well as nature of self-attitudes. In the earlier analysis a fourth measure was included in the measurement model. However, it showed unique and significant effects with the multiple indicators of deviance and, therefore, was excluded from the present analysis.

"Disposition to deviance" at Time 2 is conceptualized in terms of attenuated motivation to conform to, and the genesis of motivation to deviate from, conventional group norms. This construct is reflected in two scores: (1) a six-item measure reflecting the use of antisocial defenses and (2) a six-item measure reflecting disaffection with the conventional order. The first score expresses the readiness to respond to self-devaluing circumstances with the avoidance of, attacks on, or manipulation of others, and to expect gratification from these responses (e.g., If someone insulted me I would think about ways to get even; If you want people to like you, you have to tell them what they want to hear even if it is not the truth). The disposition to deviance is expressed in the second instance in terms of the readiness to avoid or blame conventional institutional structures (family, school, the law) that are associated with self-derogating attitudes, and to anticipate gratification from patterns of behavior that contravene the conventional norms (e.g., I would like to quit school, I have a better chance of doing well if I cut corners than if I play it straight).

"Disposition to deviance" was measured differently in the earlier analysis (Kaplan, Martin, & Johnson, 1986). The two measures used in the earlier analysis were incorporated into the measure of disaffection with the conventional order in the present analysis. Further, certain items that on a face-valid basis appeared to reflect perception of self-devaluing experiences in conventional membership groups as well as motivation to engage in deviant behavior were excluded. This was done to preclude the possibility that the previously observed strong relationship between Time 1 self-rejection and Time 2 disposition to deviance was not spuriously enhanced. Finally, in the present analyses we included another measure of a general tendency to employ antisocial responses to forestall or assuage the effects of self-devaluing circumstances.

"Deviance," measured at Time 3 only in the first model and at both Time 1 and Time 3 in the elaborated model, is conceptualized as any of a range of behaviors that reflects violation of conventional norms. Deviance is modeled as a latent construct indicated by three measures. Each of the measures reflects self-reports of engaging in one or more of several deviant responses that have prevalence rates falling within a narrow range (as defined by frequencies observed at Time 3). Self-reports of deviance at Time 3 refer to behavior during the preceding year with the exception of using wine, beer, or liquor more than two times which refers to the last week. At Time 1 self-reports of deviant behavior refer to behavior during the preceding month with the exceptions of alcohol use (which, again, refers to the last week) and failing grades (which refers to the preceding 9-week period).

The grouping of least prevalent behaviors had prevalence rates between 5 and 9%. This grouping consisted of seven self-report items (e.g., took things worth $50 or more that did not belong to you; breaking and entering; participation in gang fights; vandalism). The grouping of moderate prevalence items had prevalence rates ranging between 12 and 17%. This grouping consisted of six items (e.g., carried a weapon; started a fistfight; stole things from a desk or locker at school; used drugs). The grouping of most prevalent patterns had prevalence rates ranging between 24 and 28%. This grouping consisted of six items (e.g., stole things worth less than $2; smoked marijuana; skipped school without an excuse).

The three measures were created as dichotomies. In the case of moderate and severe forms of deviance the occurrence of at least one incident is taken as indicative of deviant behavior. However, where behaviors are more prevalent, it is reasonable to think of an occasional performance as being incidental to deviant motivation. For this reason, in the prevalent modes of deviance index we used two as the cutting point for indicating deviant behavior.

Modeling the deviance construct in this fashion offers several advantages. First, each measure reflects engaging in some form of deviance (as opposed to none) rather than the amount or continuity of deviance (i.e., the number of acts over time). This is appropriate in a test of a model that purports to explain some form of deviant behavior from among the range of deviant acts that constitute violations of the normative expectations of specified membership groups. Second, each measure is defined in terms of behaving in any of a number of heterogeneous deviant ways. Again this is appropriate in the test of a theory that recognizes that deviant dispositions in a given social context may be expressed in any of a number of ways, the common defining element being the contravention of the group norms. Which of the several theoretically available deviant acts is adopted in fact is a function of more specific personal and situational constraints. To measure deviance in terms of more homogeneous indices (e.g. stealing, violence) would decrease the likelihood of observing the expression of deviant responses (perhaps because of existing constraints against the acting out of these particular behaviors). Third, since the prevalence of deviant behaviors in each measure is roughly equal, the likelihood that any measure will be unduly weighted in favor of more prevalent items is precluded. This is important since either a successful or an unsuccessful test of the theory might be conditional on the unique features of the more prevalent deviant patterns. Finally, insofar as the differential prevalence rates are interpretable in terms of severity of deviance, it is possible to consider the applicability of the general theory to engagement in one or more deviant behaviors of differential severity whether these specific acts be points of entry or way stations on a progressive scale.

In the elaborated model the deviance construct appears at Times 1 and 3. The error terms of the three measures at the two points in time are expected to be correlated because of systematic response bias and other related measurement biases. They are therefore so specified in the initial test of the elaborated model.

### Structural Relations Model

Two structural relations models are specified. The first model (see Figure 3.1) is a validation of the model reported earlier (Kaplan, Martin, & Johnson, 1986). Three measures of perceived self-rejection are modeled as a latent construct in the first panel wave. Two measures of disposition to deviance are modeled as a latent construct in the second wave, and the latent construct of general deviance is modeled with three measures in the third wave. This model represents a simple causal chain that tests a general theory of the explanation of deviance in which Time 1 self-rejection leads to disposition to deviance at Time 2, and Time 2 disposition to deviance influences deviant behavior at Time 3.

The second model (see Figure 3.2) elaborates this causal model by including the latent construct of deviance at Time 1. The causal sequence specified in the first model is expected to hold net of the hypothesized effects of Time 1 deviance on Time 1 self-rejection, Time 2 disposition to deviance, and Time 3 deviance. In addition, net of the positive indirect effect of Time 1 self-rejection (via Time 2 disposition to deviance) on Time 3 deviance, Time 1 self-rejection is expected to manifest a direct inverse effect on Time 3 deviance.

# Results

The means, standard deviations, and intercorrelations of the 14 measurement variables used in the estimation of the causal models are presented in Table 3.1. Only 8 variables are used in the baseline model, 11 in the first elaboration of the model, 13 in the second elaboration, and finally all 14 measurement variables are used in the final elaboration. The variables added to the last two elaborations are discussed below along with the presentation of these models. The estimations of the first two theoretical models are presented in three sections: (1) the specification of the measurement model, (2) the estimation of effects between latent constructs, and (3) an assessment of fit. The third section also includes specification of correlated error terms and a discussion of their implications for the relevant structural models.

## *Measurement Model*

The estimated unstandardized (U) and standardized (S) lambda coefficients and their associated T values (T) for both models are reported in Table 3.2. We consider each of the latent constructs in turn.

*Self-Rejection, Time 1.* The three indicators of the latent construct "self-rejection" include self-reports of: (1) felt rejection by teachers (RJTT), (2) felt rejection by parents (RJTP), and (3) self-derogation (SDRG). To identify this latent construct the scale was set to the metric of self-derogation (i.e., unstandardized lambda coefficient set equal to 1.0). The three measurement variables have large and significant loadings on the construct. This latent construct reflects the current feelings or self-attitudes of the subject in association with perceived rejection by representatives (parents, teachers) of the conventional order.

*Disposition to Deviance, Time 2.* The two indices of the latent construct we substantively identify as "disposition to deviance" include: (1) antisocial defenses (ASD) and (2) disaffection with the conventional order (DSCO). The scale of this

Table 3.1. Correlations, Means, and Standard Deviations for the Variables Included in the Structural Model

| | MOST1 | MOD1 | RARE1 | SDRG | RJTT | RJTP | NSS | ASD | DSCO | KASDEV | FRNDEV | MOST3 | MOD3 | RARE3 |
|---|---|---|---|---|---|---|---|---|---|---|---|---|---|---|
| PREV1 | 1.000 | | | | | | | | | | | | | |
| MOD1 | 0.376 | 1.000 | | | | | | | | | | | | |
| RARE1 | 0.309 | 0.409 | 1.000 | | | | | | | | | | | |
| SRJT | 0.236 | 0.188 | 0.133 | 1.000 | | | | | | | | | | |
| RJTT | 0.279 | 0.288 | 0.231 | 0.359 | 1.000 | | | | | | | | | |
| RJTP | 0.189 | 0.188 | 0.202 | 0.292 | 0.336 | 1.000 | | | | | | | | |
| NSS | 0.319 | 0.307 | 0.256 | 0.110 | 0.248 | 0.137 | 1.000 | | | | | | | |
| ASD | 0.165 | 0.208 | 0.228 | 0.188 | 0.217 | 0.171 | 0.231 | 1.000 | | | | | | |
| DSCO | 0.236 | 0.241 | 0.232 | 0.211 | 0.266 | 0.240 | 0.305 | 0.400 | 1.000 | | | | | |
| KASDEV | 0.162 | 0.182 | 0.159 | 0.127 | 0.167 | 0.092 | 0.210 | 0.231 | 0.277 | 1.000 | | | | |
| FRNDEV | 0.291 | 0.262 | 0.172 | 0.142 | 0.225 | 0.141 | 0.344 | 0.220 | 0.403 | 0.378 | 1.000 | | | |
| PREV3 | 0.283 | 0.261 | 0.192 | 0.127 | 0.195 | 0.104 | 0.333 | 0.236 | 0.301 | 0.262 | 0.355 | 1.000 | | |
| MOD3 | 0.255 | 0.244 | 0.207 | 0.126 | 0.212 | 0.126 | 0.316 | 0.235 | 0.296 | 0.245 | 0.337 | 0.516 | 1.000 | |
| RARE3 | 0.208 | 0.229 | 0.217 | 0.095 | 0.137 | 0.100 | 0.266 | 0.254 | 0.231 | 0.185 | 0.225 | 0.383 | 0.431 | 1.000 |
| Mean | 0.179 | 0.257 | 0.159 | 4.100 | 0.663 | 0.248 | 0.423 | 1.191 | 1.137 | 3.970 | 0.649 | 0.359 | 0.364 | 0.216 |
| SD | 0.383 | 0.437 | 0.367 | 2.689 | 1.053 | 0.599 | 0.694 | 1.312 | 1.328 | 2.377 | 1.001 | 0.494 | 0.493 | 0.432 |

$N = 2561$.

Table 3.2.   Measurement Model Parameters for Models I and II

| | Model I | | | Model II | | |
|---|---|---|---|---|---|---|
| | U | S | T | U | S | T |
| Early deviance | | | | | | |
| PREV | | | | 1.00 | 0.58 | |
| MOD | | | | 1.34 | 0.67 | |
| RARE | | | | 0.96 | 0.57 | |
| Self-rejection | | | | | | |
| SRJT | 1.00 | 0.54 | | 1.00 | 0.53 | |
| RJTT | 0.47 | 0.66 | 16.78 | 0.49 | 0.67 | 18.07 |
| RJTP | 0.21 | 0.52 | 16.14 | 0.22 | 0.52 | 16.69 |
| Disposition to deviance | | | | | | |
| DSCO | 1.00 | 0.69 | | 1.00 | 0.69 | |
| ASD | 0.82 | 0.58 | 17.72 | 0.82 | 0.58 | 18.38 |
| Later deviance | | | | | | |
| PREV | 1.00 | 0.69 | | 1.00 | 0.69 | |
| MOD | 1.08 | 0.74 | 24.31 | 1.08 | 0.74 | 24.94 |
| RARE | 0.73 | 0.57 | 22.30 | 0.74 | 0.58 | 22.83 |
| Chi-square, *df* | 44, 17 | | | 111, 35 | | |
| GFI | 1.00 | | | 0.99 | | |
| AGFI | 0.99 | | | 0.99 | | |

construct is fixed to DSCO. The loadings of both measures are large and highly significant. The measures clearly reflect a disposition to respond in a deviant fashion to perceived source of self-devaluing experiences, particularly when the perceived occasions of self-devaluing circumstances are representatives of the conventional order.

*Deviance, Time 1, Time 3.*   Within the first and third waves of the panel we developed three measures of general deviance. The latent construct is fixed to the index of most prevalent deviant behaviors. Within both panels the three indices of most (MOST), moderate (MOD), and rare (RARE) prevalence have large and highly significant loadings. There is an overall pattern of increased reliability of these measures from the first to the third panel. It is not unreasonable to expect that self-reports of involvement in deviance do become more reliable during this period. However, the differences in Time reference between Times 1 and 3 might also be implicated.

Small but significant autocorrelated error terms between MOST and RARE deviance are observed. The error correlation is not significant for self-reports of moderate deviance (MOD) which has the highest loading on the deviance construct. The latent construct is interpretable in terms of a violation of conventional norms, which may be expressed in any of a wide variety of ways depending on situational and personal contingencies.

## *Structural Relations Models*

We consider in turn the simple (Model I) and elaborated (Model II) causal models.

*Model I.* The postulated causal chain whereby self-rejection influences disposition to deviance, and disposition to deviance influences deviant behavior finds strong support in this analysis. The standardized structural coefficients are reported in Table 3.3. Both effects are large and statistically significant beyond the 0.001 level of probability. Substantial portions of the variance are accounted for in "disposition to deviance" ($R^2 = 0.35$) and "deviance" ($R^2 = 0.36$).

These results confirm those of an earlier analysis although a somewhat different measurement model was employed. In this analysis one of the multiple indicators of self-rejection in the earlier analyses (Kaplan, Martin, & Johnson, 1986) was omitted since it shared unique and significant effects with all three indicators of Time 3 deviance. In addition, in the present analysis items were removed from the indicators of disposition to deviance because it appeared that they might reflect self-rejecting feelings as well as motivation to deviate, and thus might inflate the relationship between self-rejection and disposition inappropriately. These changes were expected to attenuate the relationships between self-rejection and deviance and between self-rejection and disposition, respectively, observed in the earlier analysis. Nevertheless the observed relationships in the present analyses remain strong and significant.

*Model II.* The elaborated model, in addition to specifying the indirect effects of self-rejection (via disposition to deviance) on deviance, specifies a direct negative effect of self-rejection on Time 3 deviance. Further, deviance at Time 1 has direct positive effects on self-rejection at Time 1, disposition to deviance at Time 2, and Time 3 deviance. The standardized structural coefficients and correlations among constructs are reported in Table 3.4. All structural coefficients are significant beyond the 0.001 level of probability.

Because Time 1 deviance is specified as causally prior to the three remaining constructs in the model, two tests of the simple causal chain are made. First, if the effects had been so attenuated as to prove nonsignificant, the model would have to be rejected on the grounds that it was a spurious explanation of later deviance. The results do not allow the rejection of the model on these grounds.

**Table 3.3.   Structural Parameters for Model I – Standardized (Unstandardized)**

|                          | Self-rejection | Disposition to deviance | $R^2$ |
|--------------------------|----------------|-------------------------|-------|
| Disposition to deviance  | 0.59 (0.37)    |                         | 0.35  |
| Later deviance           | 0.02 (0.01)    | 0.58 (0.21)             | 0.36  |

Table 3.4.  **Structural Parameters for Model II – Standardized (Unstandardized)**

|                          | Early deviance | Self-rejection | Disposition to deviance | $R^2$ |
|--------------------------|----------------|----------------|-------------------------|-------|
| Self-rejection           | 0.62 (4.04)    |                |                         | 0.39  |
| Disposition to deviance  | 0.31 (1.31)    | 0.39 (0.25)    |                         | 0.41  |
| Later deviance           | 0.39 (0.60)    | −0.15 (−0.04)  | 0.47 (0.17)             | 0.44  |

Only modest attenuation of the magnitude of the effects in the simple causal chain model is observed. Second, this model tests the applicability of the general theory to predict change in deviance (Time 3 deviance net of Time 1 deviance) as well as an explanation of level of general deviant behavior. The results confirm the model as a predictor of change in deviance.

The inclusion of Time 1 deviance in the model permits observation of the expected direct negative relationships of Time 1 self-rejection on Time 3 deviance. And finally, deviance at Time 1 has the expected direct effects on Time 1 self-rejection, Time 2 disposition to deviance, and Time 3 deviance. The inclusion of deviance at Time 1 increases the overall explained variance of Time 3 deviance by 8% (from $R^2 = 0.36$ to $R^2 = 0.44$).

### Assessment of Fit

One method for assessing the fit of the models to the observed data is chi-square, which is an indicator of goodness of fit. In Models I and II the values with their degrees of freedom are 44, 17 df and 110, 35 df, respectively. Considering the large sample size we judge these values to be adequate. In addition, the GFI is extremely large for Models I and II; 1.00 and 0.99, respectively. As others have pointed out, this overall measure is independent of sample size (Jöreskog & Sörbom, 1984) and in both models is at or very near its maximum value of 1.0.

These values refer to the overall fit of the model. However, a more detailed assessment can be made by examining the normalized residuals (Jöreskog & Sörbom, 1984). On closer inspection of these residuals we note that of the 36 variances and covariances estimated by Model I only 2 are significantly different from their observed values. The covariances between moderate deviance and self-derogation is overestimated and the covariance between antisocial defenses and rare deviance is underestimated. In Model II, of the 55 variances and covariances, 4 of the estimated values are significantly different from their observed values. Moderate and rare deviance at Time 1 with self-derogation is overestimated, moderate deviance at Time 3 with self-derogation is overestimated, and self-derogation with Time 3 rare deviance is underestimated. When these relationships are tested, by specifying correlated error terms between pairs of measurement models, none obviate the structural parameters. Thus, we do not believe the model has been misspecified.

# Discussion of Models I and II

The estimation of the models provided strong support for the theoretically predicted relationships. On the assumption that they are generalizable the results have important implications for the general theory of deviant behavior that informs the analyses. However, because of sample attrition and other considerations the generalizability of the results is problematic. We consider the extent to which the results may be generalized, and then the theoretical implications of the findings on the assumption of generalizability.

## *Generalizability of Findings*

Perhaps the major barrier to generalizing the findings stems from the possibility that strong biases were introduced into the analyses as a result of sample attrition. The analyses of the theoretical models were based on 3148 subjects who were present in all three waves of the panel data. Listwise deletion of missing values for those present reduced the overall sample size to 2561. Subjects not present in all three waves ($N = 3965$) represent those who were absent during subsequent interviewing at either the second, third, or both of the later administrations. Since data for both groups, "present" and "missing," are available at Time 1, within limits the possibility of bias may be examined by comparing the covariance matrices of the study variables using multisample analysis described in Jöreskog and Sörbom (1984). The correlation matrices for both groups were examined in an earlier analysis (Kaplan, Johnson, & Bailey, 1986). All of the correlations in both groups were significant, roughly of the same magnitude, and had the same sign. In all but three instances, however, the strengths of the relationships were greater within the "missing" sample.

We tested nine hypotheses regarding differences between present and missing samples (see Table B-2, Kaplan, Johnson, & Bailey, 1986). First, we tested the hypothesis (H1) that observed differences in correlations are not significant, assuming that both groups have identical covariances for all variables. The hypothesis was rejected. Assuming the equality of individual covariance for each and every variable overestimated the strengths of associations for the "present" sample and underestimated the strengths of associations in the "missing" sample. These differences were significant.

Such differences in individual covariances between groups do not necessarily imply different factor structures. In fact, with such large sample sizes it would be surprising if small differences in these many relationships did not prove to be significant. The second hypothesis (H2), regarding similarity of factor structures, was also rejected by conventional standards (i.e., the chi-square is large and significant). However, comparing H1 with H2 it is apparent that assumptions about a common factor pattern were clearly more reasonable than assuming no factor pattern (see Table B-2, Kaplan, Johnson, & Bailey, 1986). That is, the difference in the chi-square test showed a significant improvement in the fit of the data to the hypothesized model under the assumption of the hypothesized factor structure (see Bentler & Bonett, 1980). Indeed, subsequent tests of hypotheses (H3–H9) demonstrated that two of the six factors' variances/covariances are essentially equal in both groups.

However, two of the covariances (H5, H6) were significantly different. In order to examine the implications for these statistically significant differences, we estimated both the measurement models and structural relationships (correlations among factors) in both groups assuming a common population variance for all three factors. Although we already knew the factor variances were different for disposition and deviance (H4, H8), such a comparison could be meaningful only under such an assumption. (Under the assumption of different variances, any differences in relationships might be attributable to the former.) In any case, the comparison was made for substantive implications only. The findings were presented in Table B-3 (Kaplan, Johnson, & Bailey, 1986). The most important distinction observed was that among the more deviant "missing" sample, disposition to deviance was more strongly related to deviance. In the other two relationships virtually no substantive differences were observed.

We concluded that the overall similarity of measurement parameters and structural relationships between groups was sufficient to accept the hypothesized structure. Any biases in the estimated relationships when using the "present" sample appeared to be, at worst, conservative and underestimated. Speculations about the stronger relationships in the more deviant "missing" sample suggest that the latter subjects are less lacking in normative inhibitions and are less subject to normative social controls. Therefore, these subjects will be more likely to translate deviant dispositions into behavior. In addition, the more deviant "missing" subjects may be assumed to have had more opportunities to act out deviant dispositions. The observed stronger relationship between disposition to deviance and deviant behavior among subjects who are presumed to be less subject to personal and social controls and to have greater opportunities to enact deviant dispositions is consistent with the general theory that guides these analyses (Kaplan, 1984). Future analyses among the "present" subjects will test the assumptions that personal inhibitions and social constraints as well as increased opportunities intervene in the relationship between disposition to deviance and deviant behavior.

In any case the comparisons between the present and missing samples must be considered conservatively since we may not easily assume that within-wave comparisons between "present" and "missing" subject groupings would be replicated for cross-wave relationships. Further, at best these analyses speak to the generalizability of results to the subjects who responded at Time 1. We cannot estimate any bias in the structure of relationships among variables for the 18% of the sample who did not respond at Time 1. Nor may we, without some risk, generalize to other cohorts. The possibility remains that the structure of relationships is unique to those who were in the seventh grade in 1971.

## Theoretical Implications

Insofar as the results reflect general processes the findings have clear implications for the general theoretical statement that stimulated the analyses. The replication of an earlier analysis using a refined measurement model provided further support for the theoretical propositions that the subjective association between self-derogation and perceived sources of self-devaluing experiences leads to the loss of motivation to conform to and the readiness to respond in ways that deviate from the normative expectations endorsed by the perceived sources of self-devaluing experiences. The disposition to deviate from the normative expectations in turn increases the likelihood of acting out the disposition to deviate, that is, to behave in ways that contravene the normative expectations of the perceived sources of self-devaluing experiences.

The results of the analysis may not be accounted for in terms of the common association of self-rejection, disposition to deviance, and later deviance with earlier deviance. When the simpler model is elaborated by including earlier deviance, a noteworthy indirect effect of self-rejection (via disposition to deviance) on later deviance continues to be observed.

The theoretically indicated countervailing effects of the subjective association of self-derogation with perceived sources of self-devaluing experiences on deviant outcomes were also observed in the elaborated model. Net of the indirect positive effects (via disposition to deviance) of self-rejection on deviance, self-rejection was observed to have the expected direct negative effect on deviance. The theoretical basis for the negative effect was the putative intervening exacerbation of: (1) the need to conform to membership group standards and (2) feelings of inefficacy. These consequences of perceptions of self-devaluing membership group experiences were expected to inhibit deviant behavior. In addition, the observed negative effect of self-rejection on deviance was expected on the grounds that prior internalized proscriptions against deviant responses, implied by the experience of negative self-attitudes in conjunction with self-devaluing membership group experiences, inhibit acting out of deviant dispositions. However, in the present analysis the hypothesized intervening increased need to conform to conventional standards and the sense of personal inefficacy as well as the presumed prior internalization of proscriptive norms were not operationalized. While the observed relationships were consistent with theoretical expectations, future elaborations of the model will determine whether the inclusion of indicators of these constructs will serve to reduce or obviate the direct negative effect of self-rejection on later deviant behavior and, thereby, lend support to the theoretical premises.

In like manner the processes that were presumed to underlie the hypothesized and observed direct positive effects of Time 1 deviance on Time 1 self-rejection, Time 2 disposition to deviance, and Time 3 deviance were not operationalized. Future elaborations of the model will determine if the inclusion of indicators of the putative intervening processes effectively decomposes the direct effects. These processes include the association with deviant others and the rejection by conventional others that are expected to intervene between early involvement in deviant behavior and disposition to deviance (via satisfaction or frustration of needs) and between early deviance and later deviance (via the increased provision of occasions and opportunities for deviant responses, and the decreased opportunities for normative responses). For the moment, however, we conclude that the analyses: (1) reaffirm the theoretical position regarding the indirect (via disposition) positive effects of self-rejection on later deviance and (2) are compatible with theoretical assertions regarding the direct negative effects of self-rejection on deviance, and the direct positive effects of early deviance on self-rejection, disposition to deviance, and later deviance.

## Model III: Deviant Peer Associations and Deviant Behavior

In the analysis presented above we estimated a model in which later deviant behavior was explained in terms of the direct positive effects of disposition to deviance and early deviance, the direct negative effect of self-rejection, and the indirect positive effects of self-rejection and early deviant behavior. The next phase in the analysis estimates an elaborated model in which, in addition to the above effects, association with deviant peers has a direct effect, and mediates the influence of early deviance and disposition to deviance on later deviance. The model is estimated using the LISREL VI program for analyses of the linear structural relations among latent constructs on other wave panel data set. The results are consistent with the general theory that guides the analyses. The addition of association with deviant peers to the model increases the explained variance and partially decomposes the effects of earlier deviance and disposition to deviance on later deviant behavior.

The present analysis is the third model in a projected series of estimates of increasingly elaborated theoretically informed models that explain deviant behavior. Each of the successive elaborations adds a construct to the explanatory model that specifies linear structural relations among latent variables. The elaborated model is intended to increase the explained variance of the dependent variable (deviant behavior) and/or to specify in greater detail the nature of the structural relationships. The more detailed specification is accomplished by: (1) decomposing direct effects through the interpolation of hypothesized intervening variables, (2) specifying the countervailing effects of putative causal variables via their like effects on intervening variables that have opposing (facilitative versus inhibitory) effects on deviant behavior, or via their opposing effects on intervening variables that have like effects on deviant behavior, and (3) exposing suppressor effects. For each elaboration we evaluate the tenability of alternative explanations of observed relationships (that are contrary to the theoretically informed explanations) in terms of common antecedent effects (that is, spurious relationships) or different specifications of causal linkages among the explanatory constructs.

In the present analysis the explanatory model is further elaborated by the inclusion of interaction with deviant peers as an explanatory construct. Deviant peers is expected to increase the efficiency of the explanation of deviance and to account, in part, for the earlier observed direct effects of self-rejection, disposition to deviance, and early deviant behavior on later deviant behavior.

# Theory

The successive elaborations are guided by a general theory of deviant behavior that reflects a synthesis of several theoretical traditions including the structured strain (Cloward & Ohlin, 1960; Merton, 1938), subcultural (Cohen, 1955; Miller, 1958), social control (Briar & Piliavin, 1965; Hirschi, 1969; Polk & Halferty, 1966), containment (Reckless et al., 1956; Voss, 1969), labeling (Becker, 1963; Kitsuse, 1962; Lemert, 1951), and social learning perspectives (Akers, 1977). In synthesizing these traditional approaches to the study of deviant behavior, special emphasis is given to the subjective recognition of the source of self-rejecting/self-accepting feelings as motivating deviant behavior. The integration within a single framework of diverse theoretical positions that in the past have been presented as competing, rather than complementary explanations of deviant behavior is becoming an increasingly common practice (see, for example, Clayton & Voss, 1981; Elliott et al., 1985; Johnson, 1979) as is the use of appropriate multivariate techniques to estimate theoretically informed models.

The theory that guides this series of analyses and the points of overlap with other theories of deviant behavior has been described elsewhere in detail (Kaplan, 1980, 1982, 1984). Here we review, briefly, only those aspects of the theory that inform the earlier models and, in greater detail, the present model that elaborates the earlier models.

## *Elaborated Model with Deviant Peer Associations*

The elaborated model is summarized in Figure 3.3. The person's association with deviant peers is modeled as having a direct effect on deviant behavior and as mediating the effects of self-rejection, disposition to deviance, and earlier deviant behavior on later deviant behavior. Once again, the solid construct and effects

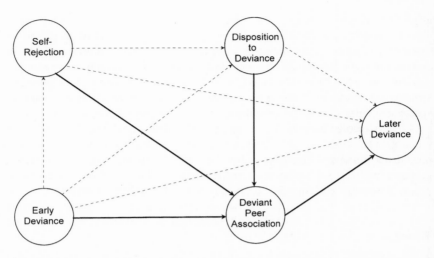

**Figure 3.3.** Second elaboration (solid lines) of the general model of deviant behavior: the role of deviant peers.

represent the elaboration of the base model, which is presented as broken arrows. We consider in turn the theoretical basis of, and the results of other studies relating to, the direct and mediating influence of association with deviant peers.

*Direct Effects of Deviant Peers on Later Deviant Behavior.* That association with deviant peers influences deviant behavior is implicit or explicit in a number of theories of deviant behavior. The focus on this construct is most apparent, perhaps, in Sutherland's (1947) differential association theory and in a later revision that incorporated concepts from operant conditioning theory (Akers, Krohn, Lanza-Kaduce, & Radosevich, 1979; Burgess & Akers, 1966). In the context of groups that provide the major social contexts for learning, behavior is differentially reinforced by the social and nonsocial rewards and punishments of the behavior and through modeling of others' behavior. In the social context the person learns to evaluate behavior in positive or negative terms. These evaluative definitions serve as cues for behavior. Deviant peers represent one potential social context for the learning and positive evaluation of deviant behavior. As these positions are incorporated in the general theory of deviant behavior that informs the present analysis, association with deviant peers is expected to have an impact on deviant behavior at a later point in time because such associations: (1) facilitate the performance of deviant acts under conditions in which the person is motivated to perform such acts, (2) motivate the person to engage in deviant behavior, and (3) decrease the effectiveness of social control mechanisms that, in the absence of association with deviant peers, might inhibit the acting out of deviant dispositions.

Association with peers who engage in deviant behavior facilitates the acting out of deviant dispositions in three ways. First, deviant peers teach the person how to engage in deviant behaviors. The teaching may be by direct and intended instruction or by serving as role models for the subject. Second, association with deviant peers provides the means (where such are necessary) to engage in the deviant behavior. If the deviant behavior, for example, demands access to drugs, deviant peers may provide the drugs that permit an individual who is so disposed to use drugs illicitly. Third, association with deviant peers facilitates acting out deviant dispositions by defining the interactive situation as an appropriate one for the performance of the deviant behavior. The interactive situation provides the symbolic stimuli that evoke the deviant behavior as appropriate for the situation.

Association with deviant peers affects the person's motivation to engage in deviant behavior. Assuming that the deviant peers represent a positive reference group for the individual, the person will learn to value behaviors that are endorsed by the positive reference group. Over time the person comes to intrinsically value those behaviors because of their initial endorsement for its own sake and/or because the pattern reflects a more basic value. Thus, a person may engage in illicit drug use because of the intrinsic gratification associated with the pattern or because the pattern reflects conformity to another value such as risk-taking behavior.

Association with deviant peers may lead to motivated deviant behavior even where the behavior does not come to be intrinsically valued. Again, assuming that the deviant peers represent a positive reference group, the individual may engage in deviant behavior that carries with it no intrinsic gratification in order to evoke intrinsically gratifying positive responses from one's peers or in order to obtain resources that are controlled by the deviant peers.

Association with deviant peers provides the individuals with experiences that function to place limits on the extent to which personal and social controls inhibit the acting out of deviant dispositions. These limitations are accomplished through three mechanisms. First, deviant peers offer a system of justifications for engaging in deviant behavior that obviate the effect of normative proscriptions against engaging in the deviant behavior. Second, association with deviant peers decreases the amount of interaction with representatives of the conventional environment who might otherwise offer informal sanctions occasioned by deviant behavior. To the extent that interaction with conventional others is decreased, the others will be less aware of the deviant behavior, on the one hand, and the deviant actor will be less aware of any informal sanctions associated with the deviant behavior, on the other hand. The informal sanctions may take the form of disapproving attitudes or deprivation of other intrinsically or instrumentally valued resources. Third, even where informal sanctions are applied and recognized by the person, the emotional significance of the sanctions may be attenuated since alternative sources of expressive and instrumental gratifications are available to the deviant actor from the deviant peers.

Generally, the empirical literature is compatible with the theoretical basis for anticipating a positive relationship between association with deviant peers and deviant behavior. Research reports in recent decades have reinforced earlier findings that involvement with peers who engage in and/or endorse deviant behavior increases the likelihood of performance of deviant behavior (Brennan, Huizinga, & Elliott, 1978; Conger, 1976; Ginsberg & Greenley, 1978; Jensen & Eve, 1976; Jessor & Jessor, 1977; Johnson, 1979; Kandel, 1978a,b; Matsueda, 1982; Meier & Johnson, 1977; Thompson, Smith-DiJulio, & Matthews, 1982; West & Farrington, 1977). In fact, involvement with deviant peers is generally reported to be the strongest single predictor of deviant behavior in multivariate studies, whether using cross-sectional or longitudinal data (Kandel, 1978a,b; Kornhauser, 1978). As this literature has been summarized:

> The consistency of findings involving different populations, different measures of theoretical constructs, and different forms of analysis is impressive. In addition, the convergence of findings from studies of the relationships between delinquent peer bonding and delinquent behavior with those from studies of selection and socialization influences on behavioral congruence in adolescent peer group provides rather compelling evidence for the claim that bonding to deviant groups is a major cause of delinquency and drug use. The evidence is indirect but substantial. (Elliott et al., 1985, p. 89)

Relatively few studies attempt to decompose the observed relationship between deviant peers and deviant behaviors in order to test theoretical assumptions regarding the processes that are thought to underlie the relationship. Among these are studies of smoking behavior. For example, Krohn, Skinner, Massey, and Akers (1985) observed that friends' reactions and perceived effects intervened between differential association and smoking. Further, the relationship between awareness of friends' smoking behavior and/or perceived approval of smoking behavior by friends, on the one hand, and initiation of smoking, on the other hand, was mediated by anticipated reaction by friends and neutralizing (justifying) attitudes.

For the most part, however, hypotheses regarding the mechanisms by which association with deviant peers influences deviant behavior remain untested in the empirical literature. In the present analysis as well, tests of the theoretical assumptions underlying the hypothesized effect of deviant peer associations on deviant behavior are reserved for future analyses. Rather, in addition to testing the hypothesized direct effect of deviant peer associations on deviant behavior, theoretical assumptions regarding the mediating role of deviant peer associations are examined.

*Mediating Role of Deviant Peers.* Association with deviant peers is modeled as a consequence and mediator of the effects of early involvement with deviant behavior, self-rejection, and disposition to deviance on deviant behavior. The previous hypothesized and observed effects of these variables on later deviance are expected to be explained in part by their effects on association with deviant peers, which in turn influences later deviant behavior.

Early deviant behavior is expected to increase the likelihood of association with deviant peers for three reasons. First, the performance of deviant behavior increases the attractiveness of the deviant actor to others who endorse the deviant behavior. To the extent that the deviant actor was already involved in a network of deviant peers, the behavior reinforces the ongoing interaction. To the extent that the deviant actor was not part of the deviant network, the deviant behavior brings the actor to the attention of deviant peers. Second, the performance of deviant behavior increases the person's need (particularly where the person was raised in a conventional environment) for social support for the activity. The need for social support attracts the individual to those who endorse the activity. Third, deviant behaviors evoke negative sanctions from conventional others including exclusion from ongoing interaction with the conventional others. This serves to decrease the opportunities for conventional interactions and increases the opportunities for interaction with deviant peers who offer greater promise of accepting responses. At the same time the opportunities for being the object of conventional social controls and the salience of conventional controls that might preclude deviant peer associations are reduced.

This model that posits an effect of early deviant behavior on later peer association, as well as an effect of deviant peer association on later deviant behavior, is consistent with a number of studies in the literature. Although Elliott et al. (1985) did not specify an effect of prior self-reported delinquency on strong bonding to delinquent peers in their test of an integration of strain, control, and learning theories, they did note that their review of studies addressing the two causal orderings of delinquent peers and delinquency suggests support for a reciprocal causal relationship. Thus, they propose incorporating the reciprocal relationship into their integrated model by including a causal path from earlier delinquency to involvement with delinquent peers. On theoretical grounds we hypothesized and (to anticipate) observed such a reciprocal effect that is consistent with findings from studies in which the nonrecursive relationship between deviant behavior and association with deviant peers was supported (Cohen, 1977; Ginsberg & Greenley, 1978; Kandel, 1978a,b).

Deviant peer association is expected to mediate the direct inverse effect of self-rejection on deviance by the same reasoning that led to the prediction of the direct countervailing effect. Exacerbation of the need to conform to conventional group standards reduced feelings of self-confidence, and preexisting internalized conventional standards would be expected to mitigate the willingness and/or ability to associate with deviant peers.

Disposition to deviate (the loss of motivation to conform to and the acquisition of motivation to deviate from conventional norms) is expected to increase the likelihood of association with deviant peers since such relationships represent: (1)

repudiation of the conventional norms that were the source of self-perceived rejection and failure and/or (2) the opportunities to achieve gratifications (e.g., social acceptance) that they felt deprived of in conventional groups. The loss of motivation to conform and the motivation to deviate from conventional norms results primarily from the person's recognition that his self-rejecting feelings were associated with experiences of failure and rejection in conventional membership groups. In addition, earlier involvement in deviant activity which contributes to the experience of self-rejection evokes negative sanctions that further alienate the individual from the source of those sanctions (that is, conventional others) and increases the need to seek gratification from alternative sources (that is, from deviant peers).

This formulation is consistent with other multivariate models such as that proposed by Elliott et al. (1985) in which high levels of strain and weak bonding to conventional groups and activities are identified as conditions leading youth to develop bonds to delinquent groups. The expectation that strain and weak bonding to conventional groups and activities would influence association with delinquent peers is represented in the present model in the expectation that the subjective association of self-derogation with perceived failure and rejection in conventional groups (self-rejection) would influence disposition to deviance that, in turn, would have a direct effect on delinquent peer associations. However, we do not posit a direct positive effect of self-rejection on delinquent peers. This association is expected to have an effect only through dispositions to engage in deviant behavior. Rather, as noted previously, we anticipated a countervailing inverse effect of self-rejection on deviant peer associations.

The proposed relationship between disposition to deviance and association with deviant peers is compatible with a broad range of research findings that report an inverse relationship between attachment to conventional groups, on the one hand, and association with deviant peers, on the other (Jensen, 1972; Jessor & Jessor, 1977; Johnson, 1979). Elliott et al. (1985, p. 58) cite Johnstone's (1983) study of gang recruiting among black adolescents in the Chicago area. Johnstone (1983, p. 297) concluded:

> The data suggests that boys that fail at school and are rejected at home eventually come to see themselves as heading for failure as adults. It may be at this point that gangs become meaningful as alternative sources of attachment and commitment.

In short, the generally observed pattern is that "bonding to delinquent groups mediates a substantial part of the total influence of ... conventional bonding on delinquent behavior" (Elliott et al., 1985, p. 84).

To summarize, in the context of the more inclusive explanatory model, association with deviant peers is modeled as having a direct effect on deviant behavior, and as a consequence and mediator of the influence of early deviant behavior, self-rejection, and disposition to deviance on later deviant behavior. These relationships are in addition to those specified in the earlier model presented in Figure 3.1.

## Methods

### Sample

The same subjects of junior high students in the Houston Independent School District in 1971 were used in this analysis. The survey is a three-wave panel study beginning in 1971 (Time 1) and repeated in 1972 (Time 2) and 1973 (Time 3).

### Data Analysis

The causal models were estimated using the correlation matrices and standard deviations of the measured variables as input to LISREL (Jöreskog & Sörbom, 1984). This program provides maximum-likelihood estimates of all identified model parameters. It also evaluates the degree to which an overidentified model reproduces the observed variance–covariance matrix in terms of a chi-square goodness-of-fit statistic.

For each of the causal analyses the measurement model and the structural relations model were estimated simultaneously. The measurement model described the hypothesized relationships between a number of measured variables and the latent or unobserved constructs that are presumed to underlie the multiple indicators. The relationships between the measurement (observed) variables and the latent construct that is said to be indicated by the measurement variables are expressed as factor loadings. The structural relations model expresses the hypothesized causal relationships among the latent constructs as regression coefficients.

### Measurement Models

The structural relations model specifies relationships among five latent constructs: self-rejection, disposition to deviance, deviant peer association, early deviance, and later deviance. The multiple indicators of these constructs are scales developed within the three waves of the panel. Measures of early deviance and self-rejection were drawn from the panel at Time 1. Measures of disposition to deviance and deviant peer association were drawn from the panel at Time 2, and measures of later deviance (identical to those from Time 1) were drawn for the panel at Time 3. Within waves these measures were examined as multiple item additive scales. Scale items and reliabilities are the same as those reported in earlier models and can be found in the appendix.

The measurement items for four of the five latent variables in this model are the same as reported in Model II. These include self-rejection at Time 1, disposition to deviance at Time 2, and deviance, measured at both Time 1 (early deviance) and Time 3 (later deviance). To reiterate, self-rejection is conceptualized as the person's subjective association of self-derogating attitudes with self-devaluing experiences in conventional membership groups. Disposition to deviance at Time 2 is conceptualized in terms of attenuated motivation to conform to, and the genesis of motivation to deviate from, conventional group norms. The additional construct is deviant peer associations.

Deviant peer associations measured at Time 2 is conceptualized as affiliation with and knowledge of deviant peers. The involvement of a person with deviant peers is reflected in two measurement variables indicating deviant behavior by friends, and by peers at school, respectively. Deviant behavior by friends consists of three items (my friends get in trouble a lot, my friends use drugs, my friends use marijuana) that reflect a peer reference and membership group that provide the support mechanisms that enable engagement in deviant acts and the source of approval for doing so. Awareness of deviant behavior among peers at school consists of several items (kids at school carry weapons, damage or destroy property, break and enter, beat up others, engage in social protest, take narcotic drugs, smoke marijuana, and engage in petty theft). These items reflect the awareness of deviant opportunities and occasions to learn and enact deviant responses. The two indicators of association with deviant peers imply both recognition of the performance of deviant behavior by people in one's more or less intimate peer network and relatively sustained (particularly in the case of friends) interaction with those peers who are recognized as performing deviant acts. This construct, then, encompasses what in other studies guided by the social learning perspective have been discriminated as peer definition of deviance, peer imitation, and differential association with deviant peers (see, for example, Krohn et al., 1985).

### *Structural Relations Model*

In addition to the relationships hypothesized in an earlier analysis (see Figure 3.2), the latent construct of deviant peer associations at Time 2 is modeled as an intervening effect between Time 2 disposition and Time 3 deviance, as well as between Time 1 deviance and Time 3 deviance, and between Time 1 self-rejection and Time 3 deviance. The effects of Time 1 deviance and self-rejection and Time 2 disposition to deviance on Time 3 deviance (Kaplan, Johnson, & Bailey, 1986) are thus expected to be attenuated due to this intervening influence of deviant peer association. In essence, this construct is expected to decompose the stability of the deviance parameter and the direct effects of self-rejection and disposition to deviance on later deviance, as well as to increase the explained variance in Time 3 deviance. Involvement with deviant peers is expected to be the outcome of early involvement in deviance (and of associated social support for deviant affiliations and behavior, concomitant with attenuation of ties to the social order) and the genesis of deviant dispositions (stemming primarily from perceived relationships between self-derogation and self-devaluing membership group experiences), as well as of the countervailing inhibiting influence of self-rejection.

# Results

The means, standard deviations, and intercorrelations of the 14 measurement variables used in the estimation of the causal models are presented in Table 3.1. The theoretical models are presented in three sections: (1) the specification of the measurement model, (2) the estimation of effects between latent constructs, and (3) an assessment of fit. The third section also includes specification of correlated error terms and their implications for the structural model.

### Measurement Model

The estimated unstandardized (U) and standardized (S) lambda coefficients and their associated T values for the model are reported in Table 3.5. We examined each of the latent constructs in turn to assure ourselves that the measurement characteristics were similar between the constructs in the earlier model and those in the elaborated model. Deviant peer associations is the new construct and its measurement characteristics also appear in Table 3.5.

The two indices of the latent construct we substantively identify as Time 2 deviant peer associations include (1) deviant friends (FRNDEV) and (2) deviant peers at school (KASDEV). The scale of this construct is fixed to FRNDEV. The loadings of both measures are large and highly significant. The measures reflect associations with peers who are deviant and are able to provide emotional support for deviant behavior, and awareness of opportunities for further engagement in deviant activities.

### Structural Relations Models

The current investigation introduces a fifth latent construct (deviant peers) into a four-construct model that has been reported elsewhere (Kaplan, Johnson, & Bailey, 1986). In order to evaluate the influence of the fifth construct on the developing model, we present the structural model without the deviant peers construct (reported earlier by Kaplan, Johnson, & Bailey, 1986) as a basis for

**Table 3.5.   Measurement Model Parameters for Model III with
Unique Associations**

|                           | Model III | | |
|---------------------------|-----------|------|-------|
|                           | U         | S    | T     |
| Early deviance            |           |      |       |
| PREV                      | 1.00      | 0.58 |       |
| MOD                       | 1.36      | 0.67 | 20.35 |
| RARE                      | 0.96      | 0.57 | 19.29 |
| Self-rejection            |           |      |       |
| SRJT                      | 1.00      | 0.53 |       |
| RJTT                      | 0.50      | 0.67 | 17.59 |
| RJTP                      | 0.21      | 0.52 | 16.27 |
| Disposition to deviance   |           |      |       |
| DSCO                      | 1.00      | 0.75 |       |
| ASD                       | 0.80      | 0.57 | 18.93 |
| Deviant peer associations |           |      |       |
| KASDEV                    | 1.71      | 0.52 | 18.74 |
| FRNDEV                    | 1.00      | 0.73 |       |
| Later deviance            |           |      |       |
| PREV                      | 1.00      | 0.70 |       |
| MOD                       | 1.05      | 0.74 | 26.48 |
| RARE                      | 0.72      | 0.57 | 23.00 |
| Chi-square, *df*          | 75, 44    |      |       |
| GFI                       | 1.00      |      |       |
| AGFI                      | 0.99      |      |       |
| RMSEA                     | 0.02      |      |       |

comparison with the elaborated model. Using the reestimated four-construct model as a basis for comparison we are able to present clearly the effect of the additional construct on the increased explanatory efficiency of the model as well as the nature of the causal paths. The clarification of the causal mechanisms is permitted by observing changes in the direct effects of one variable on another as another construct is added to the model.

We review the structural model for the relationships among the four latent constructs (this time excluding race as an exogenous variable), present the latent structure for the model in which deviant peers was added as a fifth latent construct, and evaluate the effect of adding the fifth construct to the model with regard to both explained variance of later deviance and decomposition of the previously observed direct effects of early deviance and disposition to deviance on later deviant behavior.

*Earlier Model.*   The structural relationships among self-rejection at Time 1, deviant behavior at Time 1, disposition to deviance at Time 2, and deviant behavior

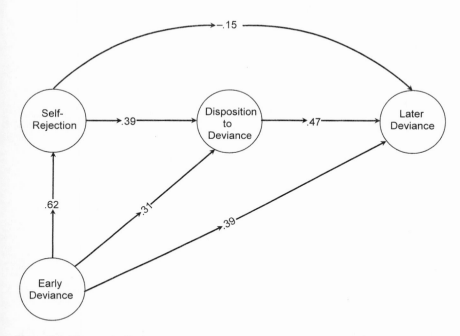

**Figure 3.4.** The standardized structural effects for the first elaboration of the general model of deviance: controlling on early deviance.

at Time 3 are summarized in Figure 3.4. The observed relationships were as expected according to the general theory that guided the analysis. Deviant behavior at Time 1 and disposition to deviance at Time 2 had direct positive effects, and self-rejection at Time 1 had a direct negative effect on deviant behavior. Self-rejection at Time 1 and deviant behavior at Time 1, in addition, had indirect positive effects (via Time 2 disposition to deviance) on Time 3 deviance. The $R^2$ for Time 3 deviant behavior is 0.44.

*Elaborated Model.* The structural relationships among the four constructs that comprise the earlier model and the fifth construct (deviant peers) that is added to this elaborated model are summarized in Figure 3.5. All of the effects observed in the earlier model are again observed. In addition, as expected, deviant peers at Time 2 has a direct positive effect on Time 3 deviant behavior and is positively influenced by Time 1 deviant behavior and Time 2 disposition to deviance. The $R^2$ for deviant peers is 0.63. The $R^2$ for Time 3 deviance is 0.51.

The addition of deviant peers obviates one of the relationships observed in the earlier model. However, as expected, deviant peer association partially

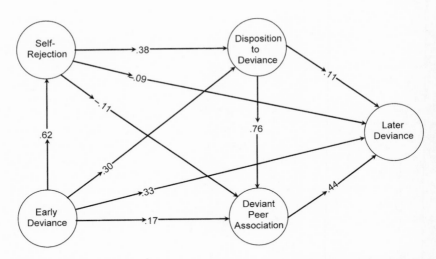

**Figure 3.5.** The standardized structural effects for the second elaboration of the model of deviant behavior: the role of deviant peers.

decomposes both direct effects of deviance at Time 1 (from 0.39 to 0.33) and disposition to deviance at Time 2 (from 0.47 to 0.11) and the countervailing inverse effect of self-rejection at Time 1 on Time 3 deviance (from 0.15 to 0.09). In addition, this construct increases the overall explained variance of Time 3 deviance by 7% (from 0.44 to 0.51).

### Assessment of Fit

Again, one of the methods we used for assessing the fit of the models to the observed data is the chi-square statistic. In the elaborated model with eight unique error terms, the value is 75 with 44 *df*. Considering the large sample size, we judge these values to be adequate. In addition, the GFI is extremely large for both models, 1.00. As others have pointed out, this overall measure is independent of sample size (Jöreskog & Sörbom, 1984) and in both models is at its maximum value of 1.0.

These values refer to the overall fit of the model. However, we also made a more detailed assessment by examining the normalized residuals (Jöreskog & Sörbom, 1984). In an earlier analysis (Kaplan, Johnson, & Bailey, 1986) it was determined that the small unique association among measurement variables did not obviate the structural parameters when these relationships were tested by specifying correlated error terms between pairs of measurement models. In the present analysis as well, when the eight correlated error terms are specified, none obviate the structural parameters.

These eight correlated error terms were between the measure of most prevalent deviance and the measures of self-rejection (0.05) and deviant friends (0.07), between the measure of rare deviance and the measures of self-rejection ($-0.04$) and antisocial defenses (0.05), between the measure of rejection by parents and disaffection with the conventional order (0.05), between the measure of antisocial defenses and the measures of deviant friends ($-0.10$) and rare deviance (0.07), and between the measures of deviant friends and rare deviance ($-0.04$).

These unique associations, when specified in the models, considerably improve the overall fit of the models. Specifying such relationships is reasonable when sound theoretical reasons exist for including them in the model. Because the first objective of this paper was to test the theoretically informed general model, initially we reported only the original model. We report the results of the better-fitting model because the unique associations do not alter significantly the theoretical model when we reestimated it with specified correlated error terms.

# Discussion of Model III

The estimation of the models provided strong support for the theoretically predicted relationships. On the assumption that they are generalizable the results have important implications for the general theory of deviant behavior that informs the analyses. However, because of sample attrition and other considerations the generalizability of the results is problematic. We first consider the extent to which the results may be generalized. We then consider a number of theoretical implications of the results.

## Generalizability of Findings

One major barrier to generalizing the findings stems from the possibility that strong biases were introduced into the analyses as a result of sample attrition. The analyses of the theoretical models were based on 3148 subjects who were present in all three waves of the panel data. Listwise deletion of missing values for those present reduced the overall sample size to 2561. Subjects not present in all three waves ($N = 4263$) represent those who were absent during subsequent interviewing at either the second, third, or both of the later administrations. Since data for both groups, "present" and "missing," are available at Time 1, the possibility of bias may be examined by comparing the covariance matrices of the study variables using multisample analysis described in Jöreskog and Sörbom (1984). All of the correlations in both groups are significant, roughly of the same magnitude, and have the same sign. In 36 out of 45 of the relationships, the strengths of the relationships are greater within the "missing" sample.

We tested nine hypotheses regarding differences between present and missing samples. First, we test the hypothesis (H1) that observed differences in correlations are not significant. This involves assuming that both groups have identical covariances for all variables. The hypothesis is rejected. Assuming the equality of individual covariance for each and every variable generally overestimates the strengths of associations for the "present" sample and, except for KASDEV with SDRG, RJTT, ASD, and DSCO, underestimates the strengths of associations in the "missing" sample. These differences, excluding the exceptions, are significant.

Such differences in individual covariances between groups do not necessarily imply different factor structures. In fact, with such large sample sizes it would be surprising if small differences in these many relationships did not prove to be significant. The second hypothesis (H2), regarding similarity of factor structures, can also be rejected by conventional standards (i.e., the chi-square is large and significant).

Results of the comparison of measurement models for "present" and "missing" samples show that the factor loadings on the self-rejection construct are very similar. We hesitate to draw any substantive conclusions based on these minor differences. The factor loadings on the remaining three constructs are, however, moderately larger among the "present" sample. The largest difference between the two groups is the factor loading of KASDEV on deviant peer associations (0.62 for "present," 0.39 for "missing"). The fact that subjects in the "missing" sample (those who were not present in the surveyed schools during the next 2 years) were older, from more mobile families, and predisposed to leave school, led to an earlier conclusion that these subjects were less integrated into the peer structure at school (Kaplan, 1980, pp. 20–24). This substantially smaller loading (and therefore influence) of the deviant peer subculture of the more inclusive school environment supports the earlier conclusion. Other major substantive differences in the factor loadings might be problematic if the measurement model indicated different factor structures, rather than simply different relative loadings on the same factors. This does not appear to be the contributing effect in these observed differences, however. Moreover, comparing H1 with H2 it is apparent that assumptions about a common factor pattern are clearly more reasonable than assuming no factor pattern. That is, the difference in the chi-square test shows a significant improvement in the fit of the data to the hypothesized model under the assumption of the hypothesized factor structure (see Bentler & Bonett, 1980). Indeed, subsequent tests of hypotheses (comparing H3 with H4–H9) demonstrate that four of the six factors' covariances are essentially equal in both groups.

However, two of the covariances (H8, H9) are significantly different. In order to examine the implications for these statistically significant differences, we estimate both the measurement models and structural relationships (correlations among factors) in both groups assuming a common population variance for all three factors. The most important distinction to be made is that among the more deviant "missing" sample, disposition to deviance and self-rejection are more strongly related to deviance. In the other four relationships (including those in which "deviant peers" is implicated), virtually no substantive or significant differences are observed.

We conclude that the overall similarity of measurement parameters and structural relationships between groups is sufficient to accept the hypothesized structure. Any biases in the estimated relationships when using the "present" sample appear to be, at worst, generally conservative and underestimated. Speculations about the stronger relationships in the more deviant "missing" sample suggest that the latter subjects are less lacking in normative inhibitions and are less subject to normative social controls. Therefore, these subjects will be more likely to translate deviant dispositions into behavior. The observed stronger relationship between disposition to deviance and deviant behavior among subjects who are presumed to be less subject to personal and social controls is consistent with the general theory that guides these analyses (Kaplan, 1984). In addition, the more deviant "missing" subjects may be assumed to have had more opportunities to act out deviant dispositions. The stronger relationship between deviant peer associations and deviance, although not significant, lends some support to this assumption. The more convincing evidence, however, is not found in the differences between these two groups but rather in the results of the test of the model in which this factor plays an intervening role between the dispositions and deviance constructs. Future analyses among the "present" subjects will test the assumptions that personal inhibitions and social constraints as well as increased opportunities intervene in the relationship between self-rejection and deviant behavior.

In any case the comparisons between the present and missing samples must be considered conservatively since we may not easily assume that within-wave comparisons between "present" and "missing" subject groupings would be replicated for cross-wave relationships. Further, at best these analyses speak to the generalizability of results to the subjects who responded at Time 1. We cannot estimate any bias in the structure of relationships among variables for the 18% of the sample who did not respond at Time 1. Nor may we, without some risk, generalize to other cohorts. The possibility remains that the structure of relationships is unique to those who were in the seventh grade in 1971.

## Theoretical Implications

The results of the analyses provide strong support for the guiding general theory that in effect integrates a number of theoretical perspectives. The results elaborate the meaning of earlier empirical observations and have implications for the several competing theories that purport to explain theories from one perspective (to the exclusion of other perspectives). Among the findings that have noteworthy implications are: (1) the observation of the direct effects of deviant peers on later deviance, (2) the effects of early deviance, self-rejection, and disposition to deviance on deviant peer associations, (3) the independent effects of early deviance and disposition to deviance on later deviance, and (4) the absence of effects of deviant peer association on disposition to deviance.

*Direct Effect of Deviant Peers.* As expected, deviant peer association had a direct positive effect on delinquent behavior. This direct effect of association with deviant peers on later deviant behavior cannot be accounted for by the common effects of alienation from the conventional order (that is, disposition to deviance) on both deviant peers and deviant behaviors. While such effects are in fact observed, a noteworthy effect of deviant peers on later deviant behavior continues to be observed.

In an analysis to be reported below it was also observed that the effect of deviant peers on later deviant behavior (although in somewhat attenuated form) continues to be observed after controlling on earlier coming to the attention of the authorities. Although this variable has direct effects on both deviant peers and deviant behavior (and so attenuates the effect of deviant peers on deviant behavior), deviant peers continues to have a significant effect on later deviant behavior.

The observation of a direct effect of association with deviant peers on later deviant behavior is congruent with both cross-sectional and diachronic studies that report deviant peer association to be a powerful predictor of deviant behavior. It is precisely because it appears to be so significant that it is necessary to understand the causal processes leading to deviant peer association.

*Antecedents of Deviant Peer Association.* The findings support the expectations that deviant peer association is influenced by both the disposition to deviance and (to a lesser but still significant extent) the early involvement with deviant behavior. These findings are compatible also with empirical support from other studies suggesting that the frequently observed association between earlier deviant behavior and later deviant behavior (Ghodsian, Fogelman, Lambert, & Tibbenham, 1980; Loeber & Dishion, 1983; Robins, 1966, 1978; Werner & Smith, 1977; West & Farrington, 1973) is a reciprocal one. As Elliott et al. (1985, p. 88) summarize the literature:

> The data ... support the position that bonding to delinquent groups and delinquent behavior, are mutually reinforcing variables with approximately equal influence on each other. The association between bonding to delinquent peers and delinquency/drug use as established in cross-sectional studies thus reflects socialization and selection processes, both causes and effects of delinquency. It is reasonable to assume, therefore, that these cross-sectional associations overestimate the causal influence of bonding to delinquent peers. At the same time, the traditional causal claim cannot be rejected on the grounds that the association is entirely or even primarily the result of the

delinquent behavioral influences on bonding patterns. Those studies that control the temporal order of these variables indicate that bonding to deviant peers continues to be the best predictor of delinquency.

Elliott et al. (1985), indeed, proposed a modification of the explanatory model that they tested on the basis of a review of the empirical evidence indicating a reciprocal causal relationship between these variables. The expectation by Elliott et al. (1985) of an appreciable increase in the explained variance of bonding to delinquent peers resulting from adding earlier delinquency to the model is warranted on the basis of our own hypothesized and observed relationship between early involvement in deviance and later association with deviant peers.

The mediating role of deviant peer association in the countervailing inverse effect of self-rejection on deviance is consistent with the theoretical premises offered earlier. Exacerbation of the self-esteem motive by experiences of rejection and failure would lead to increased conventional responses including eschewing deviant associations. Further, the social anxiety that accompanies self-rejection would inhibit entering new relationships, including deviant peer associations. Finally, preexisting internalized normative expectations would mitigate any dispositions to associate with deviant peers.

The mediating role of deviant peer association with regard to the effects of disposition to deviance and early deviance is compatible with any of a number of theoretical orientations. From the differential association perspective the effects of early deviance and disposition to deviance might reflect circumstances that attract the person to, and make the person attractive to, deviant peers. From the social control perspective these variables might imply the absence of internalized moral proscriptions and/or the failure to perceive the potential force of negative sanctions by conventional others in response to real or fancied deviant responses. From the labeling perspective, early deviant behavior in particular may lead to societal reactions that function to channel social interactions toward peer associations. From the point of view of the theoretical structure that guides this analysis, all of these processes are operative.

*Direct Effects Net of Deviant Peers.* The independent effects of early deviance, self-rejection, and disposition to deviance (net of their direct or indirect effects on deviant peers) on later deviance strongly suggest that neither deviant peer association (as differential association theory would have it) nor disposition to deviance (as either social control or differential association theory might imply) is a final common pathway to deviant behavior. Either position might imply that disposition to deviance reflects definitions favorable to deviant behavior and/or the absence of definitions unfavorable to deviant responses.

The direct effect of disposition to deviance on deviance net (although not significant) of its indirect effect via association with deviant peers is compatible with the reports of others that attachment to conventional others has an effect on deviance independent of the effect of deviant peers (Hirschi, 1969; Jensen, 1972; Jensen & Eve, 1976). However, as in other data sets (Jensen, 1972) the inclusion of deviant peer associations in the model appreciably attenuates the effect of alienation from conventional others on deviant behavior.

Other recent studies report independent effects of variables conceptually related to our construct "disposition to deviance" net of the effect of deviant peers on later deviant behavior. However, these studies tend to find that deviant peer associations may be a much stronger predictor than the indicators of bonding to the conventional order (Johnstone, 1981; Meade & Marsden, 1981; Simons, Miller, & Aigner, 1980). In contrast, although the present analysis agreed with these other analyses in finding independent effects of a construct akin to that of absence of conventional social bonding and of deviant peer associations on later deviance, it found that these effects were roughly equivalent. The comparable effects of deviant peers and disposition to deviance observed in the present study corroborate the observation of similar effects of attraction to conventional sources and attraction to deviant peers on self-reported delinquency reported by Elliott and Voss (1974). In any case, the observed direct effects of early deviance, self-rejection, and disposition to deviance on later deviance testify to the inadequacy of deviant peer associations as a sufficient explanation of these effects. Additional intervening theoretical constructs remain to be specified.

*Deviant Peers and Disposition to Deviance.* In the present analysis we specified a recursive effect of deviant peer association on disposition to deviance. A within-wave effect of deviant peer association on disposition to deviance was not specified since it was reasoned that deviant peer association presumes the prior alienation from conventional definitions and/or the social separation that would render conventional definitions irrelevant. However, as we will describe below, from other theoretical perspectives a within-wave effect of deviant peers on disposition to deviance might be expected. Therefore, we tested the viability of models that specified a positive effect of deviant peer association on disposition to deviance, employing two strategies: the use of an instrumental variable to estimate within-wave effects, and the estimation of lagged effects.

In the instrumental variable approach (Kessler & Greenberg, 1981), it was hypothesized that self-rejection at Time 1 should have its total effect on deviant peers at Time 2 only indirectly through increased disposition to deviate at Time 2. Under this assumption, a structurally just-identified system of simultaneous equations can be estimated in which within-wave reciprocal effects between Time 2 disposition to deviate and Time 2 deviant peers are specified. If the model fits the observed covariance structure, the relative significance of causal influence within this wave can be determined. Given the theoretical model we tested, the presence of significant direct effects from Time 1 self-rejection to Time 2 disposition, and from Time 2 disposition to Time 2 deviant peers, and the absence of a significant reciprocal (reverse) effect of Time 2 deviant peers on Time 2 disposition to deviate would confirm our hypothesized structure.

This model adequately accounts for the total effects among the three latent variables. In addition, the reciprocal (reverse) effect of deviant peer associations at Time 2 on disposition to deviance at Time 2 was not significant. These findings provide one basis for accepting the causal order as specified in the full model.

According to the second strategy, the absence of a causal influence of deviant peers on disposition to deviance should be expected, given our model, if cross-lagged effects of Time 2 deviant peers on Time 3 disposition to deviance were spurious and could be accounted for by their common dependence on the earlier hypothesized causally prior effects of Time 3 disposition to deviance.

Both direct and indirect effects of Time 2 disposition to deviance through Time 2 deviant peers and a direct effect of Time 2 deviant peers were specified. The estimated covariance of the latent constructs Time 2 deviant peers and Time 3 disposition to deviance was demonstrated to be spuriously dependent on the hypothesized causal latent variable Time 2 disposition to deviance. That is, the direct lagged effect of deviant peers at Time 2 on Time 3 disposition to deviance was nonsignificant. Both Time 2 deviant peers and Time 3 disposition to deviance are evidenced to be causally dependent on Time 2 disposition to deviance. These findings provided a second basis for accepting the causal order as originally specified in the full theoretical model.

In view of the positions taken from other theoretical perspectives, one of the more significant findings of the present analysis is the absence of a mediating effect of disposition between deviant peers and deviant behavior. It is frequently assumed if not explicitly modeled (see, for example, Matsueda, 1982) that peer influence affects delinquency via a balance of definitions favorable to deviance over definitions favorable to nondeviance. Unlike the present analysis where it is clear that deviant peers has an effect on deviant behavior that is not mediated by definitions favorable to deviance (a construct that is comparable to our disposition to deviance construct), Matsueda (1982) found that number of friends picked up by the police has a large positive total impact on definitions favorable to delinquency. However, in the present study disposition to deviance, far from mediating the effect of deviant peers on deviance, appears to be causally prior to deviant peers. The influence of deviant peer associations on later deviant behavior apparently does not operate by increasing alienation from conventional norms and increasing attraction to deviant norms. Rather, deviant peers is likely to provide the mechanism for facilitating the enactment of deviant dispositions by decreasing the negative sanctions associated with acting out deviant dispositions and by increasing the opportunities to enact such dispositions.

The differences in findings between Matsueda's (1982) model and the present analysis may be accounted for by the cross-sectional nature of the Matsueda analysis. Matsueda did not report the alternative specification whereby definitions favorable to criminal activity influenced having close friends who have been picked up by the police. If the causal direction were reversed in Matsueda's study so that definitions favorable to deviance had a direct effect on having friends who were picked up by the police, then the latter variable would have had a direct effect on delinquency as in the present cross-wave analysis. Matsueda (1982, p. 500) does note that "the causal ordering of the variables could be incorrect, since the data are cross-sectional." Thus, serious biases in the parameter estimates might exist.

### A Research Agenda for Deviant Peers

On the basis of a general theory of deviant behavior, association with deviant peers was expected to have a direct positive effect on later deviant behavior. Although we have provided a number of hypothetical constructs that are presumed to intervene between deviant peer associations and deviant behavior, we did not test for the existence of these intervening constructs in the present analysis. Rather we modeled the relationship as a direct effect of deviant peers on later deviant behavior.

In like manner, deviant peers was modeled as the direct consequence of disposition to deviance, self-rejection, and early involvement in deviance. Thus, deviant peers was said to intervene between these variables and later deviant behavior. Again, while we have hypothesized constructs that intervene, we did not estimate these hypothetical intervening constructs in the present analysis. Rather, we modeled disposition to deviance, self-rejection, and early deviance as having direct effects on deviant peer associations. It remains for future analyses to determine if the hypothetical constructs do in fact intervene.

## Conclusion

We have estimated a model that elaborates a previously reported explanatory model of deviant behavior. The earlier model is elaborated by specifying a direct effect of deviant peer association on later deviant behavior and direct effects of earlier deviant behavior and disposition to deviance on deviant peer association. The results support the hypothesized model and are consistent with other empirical reports. The panel study permits a clearer specification of the temporal ordering among latent constructs across waves than is possible in many cross-sectional studies, and allows for the testing of alternative specifications of within-wave effects.

The results suggest that any of several competing theories that hypothesize a final common pathway to deviant behavior are inadequate to account for deviant behavior. Rather, the observation of independent direct effects suggests that diverse theoretical perspectives contribute to a more inclusive explanation of deviant behavior. The general theory that guides these analyses reflects a synthesis of several theoretical orientations. The compatibility of the results of the analyses with the increasingly elaborated theoretically informed models suggests the viability of this more inclusive guiding theoretical system.

## Model IV: Negative Social Sanctions from the Labeling Perspective

In the preceding analyses, deviant behavior was modeled as the outcome of association with deviant peers, disposition to deviance (reflecting attitudes toward conventional and deviant adaptations), self-rejecting attitudes associated with failure and rejection in conventional associations, and the direct and indirect effects of earlier deviant behavior (Kaplan et al., 1987). The model was informed by a general theory of deviant behavior (Kaplan, 1972, 1975b, 1980, 1982, 1984) that incorporates propositions from a number of less inclusive theories. The labeling perspective is particularly represented by inclusion of the propositions that assert relationships between negative social sanctions in response to deviant behavior and continuity or escalation of deviant behavior. In the present analyses, we estimate a model that is elaborated in accordance with, and thereby addresses the viability of, these propositions. The earlier hypothesized and observed model is elaborated by specifying that negative social sanctions mediate the direct and indirect effects of earlier deviant behavior on later deviant behavior.

Social sanctions are reactions by others to the real or imagined behavior of an individual. The sanctions serve as rewards or punishments for the behavior either by the intentions of the others or by the perception of the individual. The concept has been presented in sociological contexts as potentially powerful for understanding the processes underlying the continuation or escalation of deviant behavior. Two competing bodies of literature have developed that relate to the effect of punishment on behavior (Sherman & Berk, 1984). The deterrence literature hypothesizes that the pain of punishment deters people from repeating crimes for which they are punished. Labeling theory, on the other hand, fosters "the ironic view that punishment often makes individuals more likely to commit crimes because of altered interactional structure, foreclosed legal opportunities and secondary deviance" (Sherman & Beck, 1984, p. 261). The present analysis estimates a model that is elaborated in accordance with the implications of labeling theory.

The empirical support and theoretical basis of the labeling hypothesis (that individuals will engage in further deviance as a result of punitive response) have been evaluated extensively over the years.

# Empirical Support

Punitive social responses influence subsequent acquisition of deviant identities and conformity to deviant roles. Farrington (1977) concluded that publicly labeled youths had higher self-reported delinquency scores than the nonlabeled youths. More recently, Palamara, Cullen, and Gersten (1986) observed that police and mental health intervention had both independent and interactive effects on increasing juvenile delinquency. They also noted that the effects varied according to the form of juvenile deviance (delinquency, anxiety, and general psychological impairment) under consideration. Apprehended youths tended to commit more offenses subsequently than the unapprehended controls (Gold, 1970; Gold & Williams, 1969). Compatible findings were reported by Ageton and Elliott (1974), Klein (1974), Klemke (1978), O'Connor (1970), and Wheeler (1978).

However, other investigators have concluded that formal negative sanctions do not influence commitment to deviant careers (Gove, 1975; Hawkins, 1976; Hepburn, 1977; Wellford, 1975), do not influence variables that are hypothesized to mediate the relationship between sanctions and deviance (Foster, Dinitz, & Reckless, 1972), or do, indeed, deter rather than amplify deviance (Sherman & Berk, 1984). Thus, Foster et al. (1972) failed to observe that apprehended boys perceived interpersonal difficulties associated with being apprehended. Sherman and Berk (1984), in a field experiment on domestic violence, found that arrested subjects showed significantly less subsequent violence than those not arrested.

Reasons for such apparent inconsistencies may include "poor matching of control subjects, inadequate adjustment or control for pre-intervention levels of delinquency or behavioral impairment and the operationalization of 'secondary deviance' into criteria of questionable validity such as delinquency recidivism and school performance" (Palamara et al., 1986, p. 91). Certain of the problems may lead to the unwarranted conclusion that a labeling effect does not exist. For example, the lack of self-reports of difficulties among apprehended boys (Foster et al., 1972) may reflect defensive distortions rather than veridical responses. Other problems may spuriously enhance the relationship between societal reaction and deviant behavior. Thus, the delinquency measure specifically reflects labeling by teachers and mothers in the study by Palamara et al. (1986). The observed relationship between social reaction and later deviance may reflect only the relationship between one form of labeling and another form of labeling (that reflected in the measure of deviance).

In any case, the numerous studies that report positive associations between negative social sanctions and amplified deviance suggest that at least under certain conditions negative sanctions influence subsequent performance of deviant behavior. These findings are sufficiently encouraging to stimulate further research on the mechanisms that are said to mediate the relationship between social sanctions and deviance.

## Theoretical Issues

Theoretical statements concerning negative social sanctions and continuity of deviant behavior frequently lack clarity, detail, and systematic organization. Consequently, labeling research has been "characterized as relativistic, amorphous and subject to a serious lack of specification" (Howard & Levinson, 1985, p. 191).

Numerous conceptually overlapping and putatively mutually influential explanatory constructs have been cited as intervening between negative social sanctions and continuity of deviant behavior. Certain of these constructs refer to the responses of others to the "deviant" acts. As a consequence of negative social sanctions, the responses of others may include publicly labeling the person as a deviant, being sensitive to disvalued aspects of the deviant while ignoring worthier aspects of the person, isolating the deviant from conventional society, imputing negative characteristics to the person that are independent of the initial deviant act, and reinterpreting past and present behaviors by the subject in negative terms. As Farrell (1987, pp. 2–3) summarizes the major premises of labeling theory, original or primary deviations,

> would remain transient and often subside without the reinforcing effects of the social response. Through the designation of deviance as a master status, application of a negative stereotype, and retrospective and concurrent reinterpretation, however, the individual tends to become engulfed in the deviant role and to organize life and identity around the facts of the deviation.

Other constructs are conceptualized in terms of self-responses by the deviant. Such social consequences of negative sanctions include changes in the deviant's beliefs, values, feelings, and behaviors. These responses by the deviant, then, are assumed to influence acquisition of deviant identity and increased involvement with deviant roles and behavior. Within the labeling framework the most significant responses have the self as the object of the feelings, although the objects of the deviant's responses may be individual or collective others. Thus, Wells (1978, p. 192), commenting on the labeling hypothesis, observes that

> this proposition asserted that social control events serve to systematize and prolong deviance by altering (via stigmatization) the self-concept and the social identity of the person labeled. In this respect, self-concept is at once both a cause and an effect of the deviation, self-concept change (a) being an effect of an initial deviation as mediated by social control events, and (b) being also an important precondition of secondary deviation.

In an attempt to increase the degree of clarity, detail, and systematization, we organize the mutually influential social and personal responses that are thought to mediate the effects of negative social sanctions on continuity of deviance around three explanatory constructs. The personal and social responses that are influenced by negative social sanctions are interpreted as reflecting or influencing the deviant actor's: (1) loss of motivation to conform to, and acquisition of motivation to deviate from, conventional norms, (2) association with deviant peers, and (3) reevaluation of deviant identities and behaviors. These three outcomes in turn have direct or indirect influences on the continuity or escalation of deviant behavior. We consider the consequences of negative sanctions for each of these three constructs in turn.

## *Loss of Motivation to Conform*

Negative sanctions have consequences for the deviant person's motivation to conform to or deviate from conventional norms. The negative sanctions and the social consequences of negative sanctions influence the person's self-perceptions, self-evaluations, and self-feelings. These self-referent responses in turn influence the person's motivations with regard to conforming to conventional expectations.

Negative social sanctions in response to initial deviant responses increase the likelihood that the deviant actor will be publicly identified as a deviant. The public identification of the person as a deviant, according to the labeling hypothesis, in turn has adverse social consequences for the deviant actor. The labeling hypothesis maintains that being publicly identified as deviant results in a "spoiled" public identity. It contends that being labeled "deviant" results in a degree of social liability (i.e., exclusion from participation in certain conventional groups or activities) that would not occur if the deviance were not made a matter of public knowledge (Foster et al., 1972).

These consequences, secondary to the earlier punitive responses, also serve as negative social sanctions that signify and excite public identification of the person as deviant. The person who committed the deviant act can become a target of collective moral outrage in any number of ways. The outrage may be enunciated by one individual toward a group with which the subject now identifies. As such, the subject feels the outrage as a consequence of being labeled. Further, others, who now recognize the deviant label as an appropriate identity for the subject, respond with outrage directed at that particular person.

Negative social sanctions and social ostracism, which are secondary to stigmatization, are intrinsically disvalued. In addition, they reflect the deprivation of resources, which are instrumental to the achievement of personal goals. Further, the associated deprivation of educational and employment opportunities, and of social cooperation in general (Link, 1982; Mankoff, 1971; Schwartz & Skolnick, 1962), impedes the successful approximation of other social values. The deprivations that result from social exclusion are exacerbated by the voluntary social withdrawal of the deviant actor out of a fear of rejection and other maladaptive defensive maneuvers (Link, 1987).

Both the actual experiences of negative social sanctions and of secondary adverse social responses affect the person's self-perceptions. The deviant actor perceives himself as the object of punitive responses and of stigmatization, social exclusion, and deprivation of social resources. The deviant actor further comes to expect that these circumstances will influence adversely the probabilities of gaining satisfaction of his needs. These self-perceptions create negative self-evaluations since: (1) acceptance by others and access to social resources often are salient criteria for self-evaluation and (2) such adverse responses are interpretable by the deviant actor as indicators of one's worth (particularly in ambiguous circumstances and where more objective indicators for self-evaluation are lacking). Since the person is highly motivated to evaluate himself positively, a negative self-evaluation elicits highly distressful self-rejecting feelings (Kaplan, 1986).

The person's self-referent responses (self-perceptions, self-evaluation, self-feelings) to negative social sanctions influence the person's affective investment in the conventional order. The individual loses motivation to conform to conventional expectations because: (1) the negative self-feelings, evoked by the self-devaluing experiences of being publicly identified and punished as a deviant, come to be associated with the conventional order, and (2) the deviant actor anticipates that stigmatization as a deviant and concomitant exclusion from conventional society pose possibly insurmountable barriers to reentry into conventional society and access to the resources (including social acceptance itself) that reflect or are instrumental to the achievement of personal needs. The person not only loses motivation to conform to conventional expectations, but also acquires motivation to deviate from conventional norms. Deviation from conventional standards represents repudiation of the evaluative standards that the deviant actor associates with being stigmatized and deprived of future rewards.

The motivation to deviate from conventional expectations increases the probability that the deviant actor in fact will become aware of and adopt deviant patterns of behavior (including affiliation with deviant peers) not only because the deviant behavior represents a rejection of conventional patterns of behavior but also because the person continues to require fulfillment of personal needs through alternative mechanisms than the now-rejected conventional patterns. Deviant behavior is facilitated by the loss of motivation to conform to conventional expectations that would ordinarily inhibit deviant behavior because of emotional investment in the conventional patterns, and the salience of the recognition that conformity to conventional expectations is associated with access to social resources that are necessary for the satisfaction of personal needs.

### Association with Deviant Peers

Negative social sanctions increase association with deviant peers. The effect of negative social sanctions on increased association with deviant peers is anticipated on the basis of a number of considerations (Akers, 1985; Farrell, 1987; Kaplan, 1984). First, the stigma that is secondary to negative social sanctions limits the opportunities for the deviant actor to interact with conventional others in conventional contexts. Members of conventional groups are less willing to interact with those who are publicly identified as deviant by virtue of their being the (presumably appropriate) object of social rejection. Thus, the likelihood of association with deviant peers is increased because alternative conventional modes of interaction with conventional others are closed off due to the reluctance of conventional others to (re)admit the deviant actor into conventional society. The self-labeling as the object of formal and informal sanctions influences concurrently the deviant actor to recognize the difficulty of reentry into conventional society. As a result, the deviant actor decreases interaction in conventional spheres and, thus, increases interaction in deviant peer associations.

Second, certain social sanctions impose structural imperatives that require association with deviant peers. Most apparent is the decision to incarcerate, which involves forced interaction with deviant peers while it precludes frequent interaction with members of conventional groups. To a lesser degree, expulsion or suspension from school also constrains interaction with others to those who are the objects of similar sanctions and who also are precluded from engaging in normal social interaction.

Third, negative social sanctions and their correlates influence the deviant actor's motivation to seek out deviant peer associations and to be receptive to such interactional opportunities. As stated earlier, the individual is unable to satisfy his need for social acceptance and has restricted access to resources available in conventional contexts. Among the self-protective/self-enhancing responses that the person adopts is the seeking of membership in groups of deviant peers in order to adopt a set of values that: (1) the person may alternately approximate after failure to approximate conventional values (including those that devalue the earlier deviant behavior) and (2) symbolizes rejection of the conventional standards according to which the person devalues himself and is devalued by others. The achievement of the values of, and consequent acceptance by, deviant peers, as well as the symbolic rejection of the conventional values, offer promise of enhanced self-attitudes.

Fourth, public negative sanctions identify the person to deviant peers. Insofar as the deviant peers (like the deviant actor) are motivated to seek satisfaction of their needs in deviant peer networks, the publicly identified deviant actor is attractive to the deviant peers who attempt to recruit him as part of their network. The recruitment is facilitated by the accessibility of the deviant actor secondary to his exclusion from conventional society, and by the amenability of the deviant actor to overtures from deviant peers that results from the actor's motivation to forestall rejection by conventional others and enhance self-attitudes.

The increased association with deviant peers, a consequence of negative social sanctions, has a direct impact on the future performance of deviant behavior. Association with deviant peers: (1) facilitates the performance of deviant acts when the person is motivated to perform such acts, (2) provides the person with a source of gratification (i.e., offers personal and interpersonal rewards) for engaging in deviant behavior, and (3) decreases the effectiveness of personal and social control mechanisms that might inhibit the acting out of deviant dispositions (Kaplan et al., 1987).

## Reevaluation of Deviant Identities and Behaviors

Negative social sanctions cause the deviant actor to positively value deviant behaviors and identities. The person becomes attracted to deviant behavior for reasons related to the reduction of self-rejecting feelings and the affirmation of self-worth.

First, the deviant actor comes to evaluate deviant behavior and identities positively in order to assuage the distressful self-feelings that are the direct or indirect consequences of negative social sanctions. Coleman (1986), citing studies of the aged and those with stigmatizing physical conditions, observes that many stigmatized individuals come to question the bases for defining normality and "regain their identity through redefining normality and realizing that it is acceptable to be who they are" (p. 225). Similar processes are hypothesized to occur with individuals whose behaviors are judged to be delinquent or otherwise abnormal. Negative social sanctions lead the individual to conceive of himself as one who is the object of negative social sanctions and as one who experiences intrinsically and instrumentally disvalued outcomes such as loss of income and exclusion from conventional groups. Since the ability to evoke positive responses from others and to secure resources are among the evaluative standards by which the person judges his own worth, negative social sanctions lead the individual to judge himself negatively. Negative self-evaluation causes the person to experience highly distressful self-rejecting feelings and further leads the person to an evaluation of being essentially bad. Such a self-conception is inherently unacceptable and exacerbates the self-esteem motive. Given the need to maintain one's self-esteem (Kaplan, 1986), the individual behaves in ways that will forestall or assuage the continued experience of self-rejecting feelings. These include the reevaluation of the self-ascribed and other-ascribed deviant identities and behavior so that these become valued. The stigmatized social identity and the associated deviant acts are defined as having positive value and become the basis for self-accepting rather than self-rejecting responses. The new emotional commitment to the deviant identity obviates the distressful feelings that are experienced by an individual on recognition of being the object of negative social sanctions. The commitment to the deviant identity and norms redefine the deviant acts as appropriate and the conventional sanctions as inappropriate or irrelevant within the perspective of the newly adopted (deviant) value system.

Second, the person comes to value deviant patterns of behavior and identities because they reflect achievable standards according to which the deviant actor may evaluate himself as a person of worth, and, consequently, experience positive self-feelings. Since negative social sanctions exclude the deviant actor from conventional circles and restrict access to resources that are necessary to achieve conventionally defined goals, the deviant actor has increased difficulty in approximating conventional standards. Among the adaptive responses made by the person is the attraction to an alternative set of deviant standards that, as a result of perceived or real increased opportunity, are more easily approximated than the conventional ones. By approximating the now positively valued standards, the person may justifiably evaluate himself positively and experience positive self-feelings.

Third, a commitment to deviant behavior and identities excuses and forestalls future instances of failure to approximate conventional standards. As a result of the social exclusion and deprivation of resources that are reflected in or result from negative social sanctions, the person is unable to meet the demands (independent of those proscribing the initial deviant behavior) that are made on him by representatives of the conventional order. The stigmatizing consequences of the negative social sanctions exacerbate the previous failures to conform to social expectations that have been implicated in the onset of the deviant behavior (Kaplan, 1980; Kaplan, Martin, & Johnson, 1986). The distressful negative self-feelings that accompany these failures are mitigated by using the deviant behavior to excuse the failures. By continuing to behave in a deviant fashion and, thereby, continuing to evoke a labeling response, the individual is enabled to blame the continuing failure to meet social expectations on the label itself. In this way, the individual excuses himself by attributing failure to being socially stigmatized (whether or not the stigma is justified is irrelevant, although the implication, from the stigmatized person's perspective, is that it is not justified). The positive evaluation of deviant identities and behaviors also forestalls the experience of failure by lowering the relevance of conventional expectations that the person has of himself. The emotional commitment to a deviant identity precludes the need to attempt to conform to conventional expectations, attempts that in the past have proved to be futile or unrewarding and that frequently motivated the initial deviant acts. By precluding attempts to conform to conventional expectations the individual forestalls further self-rejecting experiences. As Pyszczynski and Greenberg (1987, pp. 118–119) observe:

> a negative self-image may be maintained because it minimizes demands on the individual for successful and competent behavior in the future and minimizes the potential for disappointment.... By viewing oneself as a loser one can avoid endeavors where additional failures are likely to occur. In addition, when negative outcomes do occur, they may have less impact because they are expected.

The excuse of past failures mitigates distress and thus reinforces the positive evaluation of deviant behaviors and identities.

Fourth, the deviant actor frequently comes to value deviant activities and identities because they reflect or are instrumental in the achievement of conventionally valued ends. Stigmatization exacerbates the need for self-approval. Since social stigmatization frequently deprives the person of the resources that are necessary to achieve conventionally defined goals, the deviant actor may come to value deviant patterns of behavior that are instrumental to the achievement of these goals. For example, unable to achieve material rewards by legitimate means, the person uses techniques of theft or fraud to gain these ends. Further, the deviant acts themselves may reflect conventionally valued ends, as when the successful performance of deviant acts provides the person with a sense of self-efficacy or when the performance of a particularly hazardous deviant act is interpretable as reflecting another valued end such as bravery.

Having transformed the value of deviant behaviors and identities from negative to positive, the deviant actor is motivated to behave in ways that validate the deviant identities. The deviant identity is now accepted as a basis for self-evaluation. To continue to perform the deviant behavior is to validate the deviant identity. Once he comes to value the identity, he is motivated to conform to the normative expectations that he sees as defining that identity. Insofar as he successfully conforms to those normative expectations and validates the identity, he is enabled to evaluate himself positively. In this sense, the deviant behavior or roles in response to the sanctions are "secondary deviation" since they become "means of defense, attack, or adaptation to the overt and covert problems created by the societal reaction to the primary deviation" (Lemert, 1967, p. 17). Thus, negative social sanctions (and their correlates) influence the continuity or escalation of deviant behavior by motivating the positive evaluation of deviant behavior and identities.

The effects of reevaluation of deviant identities and behaviors are independent of the consequence of loss of motivation to conform and acquisition of motivation to deviate from conventional norms. In the latter case, negative social sanctions (and their correlates) cause a change in attitudes toward conventional activities (withdrawal of positive affect and investment of negative affect). In the former case, negative social sanctions cause a change in attitudes toward deviant activities (increased positive affective investment).

The reevaluation of deviant activities and identities is also to be distinguished from the mediating effects of association with deviant peers. The reevaluation of the deviant role may be accomplished with or without group support. Although it is clear that deviant peer associations may provide social support for the reevaluation, it is equally clear that such reevaluative definitions may occur through internal symbolic transformations.

Loss of motivation to conform to, and acquisition of motivation to deviate from, normative expectations, as well as association with deviant peers, have direct effects on facilitating the positive valuation of deviant behavior. The individual's rejection of social conventions and the loss of motivation to conform to normative expectations reduces the costs of identifying with deviant roles. Insofar as conformity to social conventions and attracting positive responses from representatives of conventional society are no longer bases for positive self-evaluation, and, indeed, insofar as conventional others now constitute a negative reference group, the positive evaluation of deviant behaviors and identities does not pose a threat to one's self-esteem or the possession of valued resources.

Association with deviant peers facilitates acquisition of deviant identities and conformity with deviant roles by providing social support for this role and insulating the person from the experience and perception of conventional sanctions for such role performance. Association in deviant groups provides the social and cultural support necessary for the individual to become committed to his position and to redefine his role in more positive terms. Not unlike the situation in any other group, the normative system of the deviant group serves to validate the behavior of group members (Farrell, 1987).

The validation of deviant behavior by deviant groups permits the deviant actor to positively evaluate the norms. The person, by accepting the deviant norms, provides a basis for deviant self-enhancing experiences. First, the norms of the deviant group provide justification for the earlier deviant behavior. Second, acceptance of the norms, expressed through conforming behavior, evokes approving responses from other members of the deviant group. The frequent self-enhancing effects of becoming part of such societies or communities are evidenced in a very rich literature (for a summary, see, e.g., Pfuhl, 1986, pp. 169–171). Reference may be made, for example, to the aristocratizing effect on the membership of belonging to secret societies of deviants (Simmel, 1950). In such a group the members feel a positive sense of the honor and special nature of membership. Aristocratization redefines stigmatized traits or behaviors such that they become honorific. Thus, membership in such groups facilitates the reevaluation process and confirms this process. The association with deviant peers also insulates the deviants from countervailing stigmatizing responses emanating from the more conventional community. The process of identification with, and positive affirmation of, the deviant role is not unlike the processes involved in social movement whereby an individual publicly affirms and takes pride in himself and expresses solidarity with similarly stigmatized individuals (Kaplan & Liu, 2000).

## Elaborating a Model of Deviant Behavior

The viability of the labeling hypothesis depends on the specification and testing of hypotheses regarding the mechanisms that mediate the relationship between societal reaction to deviance and subsequent performance of deviant behavior. We have offered a statement of these hypothetical mechanisms, in some instances specifying earlier stated views in a more systematic manner. In other instances, we have specified effects that offer new explanations of the processes, which diminish existing lacunae. We have argued that negative social sanctions in response to earlier deviant behavior influence the later performance of deviant behavior. This influence is mediated by the effects of negative social sanctions on: (1) loss of motivation to engage in and acquisition of motivation to deviate from conventional activities and roles, (2) association with deviant peers, and (3) positive evaluation of deviant identities and behaviors. These phenomena in turn directly or indirectly influence the continuity, or increased intensity, frequency, and range of deviant behavior.

This formulation has implications for the elaboration of a previously estimated theoretically informed model of deviant behavior (hereafter designated the baseline model). We describe in turn the baseline and elaborated models. We then estimate the elaborated model.

### Baseline Model

In an earlier study (Kaplan et al., 1987), we estimated an explanatory model that accounts for deviance at a later point in time in terms of four explanatory constructs: deviance at an earlier point in time, self-rejecting experiences, disposition to deviance, and association with deviant peers. The theoretical basis of the baseline model is presented in earlier papers (Kaplan, Johnson, & Bailey, 1986, 1987; Kaplan, Martin, & Johnson, 1986). The model, represented by the broken-line path diagram, is summarized in Figure 3.6.

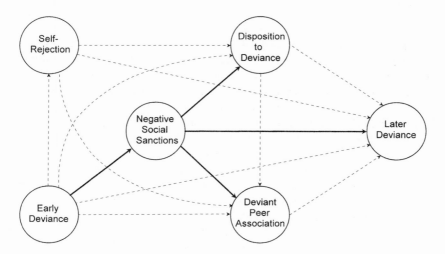

**Figure 3.6.** Third elaboration (solid lines) of the model of deviant behavior: the role of negative social sanctions.

As a framework for examining certain implications of the labeling perspective in the elaborated model, the most significant features of the baseline model relate to the direct and indirect effects of early involvement in deviance on later deviance. In the earlier analysis (Kaplan et al., 1987) prior involvement in deviance was hypothesized and observed to exercise direct effects on disposition to deviance and deviant peer associations and, via these effects, to exercise indirect effects on later deviant behavior. Further, it was hypothesized and observed that, net of these effects, prior involvement in deviance would have a direct effect on later deviance.

### Elaborated Model

The baseline model now is elaborated based on the hypothesis that negative social sanctions mediate the effects of prior deviance on later deviance. Negative social sanctions is hypothesized to mediate both the direct effects of prior deviance on later deviance and the effects of prior deviance on disposition to deviance and deviant peer associations (both of which directly or indirectly influence later deviance). That is, negative social sanctions is modeled as the outcome of early deviance and as having direct effects on disposition to deviance, deviant peer associations, and later deviance. The elaboration is represented by the solid lines in the figure. By mediating the effects of early deviance on disposition to deviance and deviant peer associations, negative social sanctions exercises indirect influence on later deviance. Formal negative social sanctions exercises a direct effect on later deviance and mediates the influence of early deviance on later deviance. That is, engaging in early deviant behavior increases the occurrence of sanctions, and those sanctions in turn increase later deviant behavior.

The performance of deviant acts tends to provoke negative social sanctions. The strength of this relationship is influenced by a number of social contingencies (including characteristics of the deviant actor, the deviant act, and the characteristics of those who administer the sanctions) that affect the social perception and evaluation of the deviant actor and deviant behavior (Bernstein, Kelley, & Doyle, 1977; Howard & Levinson, 1985; Scheff, 1966). For present purposes of estimating the mediating effect of negative social sanctions, however, only deviant behavior is modeled as influencing negative social sanctions.

The construct of negative social sanctions is modeled as having a direct effect on disposition to deviance, deviant peer associations, and later deviance. The direct effect on disposition to deviance reflects the theoretically indicated influence of negative social sanctions on the loss of motivation to conform to, and the acquisition of motivation to deviate from, conventional expectations. This effect is predicated on the theoretical premises (described above in greater detail and not directly measured in these analyses) that negative social sanctions influence self-perceptions as the object of punitive responses and stigmatization, social exclusion, and deprivation of social resources. These self-perceptions and consequent negative self-evaluations and distressful self-feelings lead to the loss of motivation to conform to, and motivation to deviate from, conventional expectations because: (1) distressful self-rejecting feelings stemming from the social sanctions are associated with the conventional order, (2) the deviant actor anticipates barriers to reentry into conventional society, and (3) the deviation from conventional standards symbolizes repudiation of the standards according to which the person has been rejected in the past and may be expected to be negatively sanctioned in the future.

The modeling of a direct effect of negative social sanctions on deviant peer associations reflects theoretical considerations that negative social sanctions: (1) constrain interacting with conventional others, (2) forces interaction with deviant peers, (3) motivates the deviant actor to seek out deviant peers in an attempt to satisfy the need for self-approval, and (4) identifies the person as a deviant to other deviant actors who are similarly motivated to engage in deviant peer associations. Again, however, these theoretical constructs are not modeled in the present analysis.

The modeling of a direct effect of negative social sanctions on later deviance is predicated on the expectation that negative social sanctions leads the deviant actor to reevaluate deviant behavior and identities more positively. The positive evaluation of the behavior motivates the person to perform deviant acts that are compatible with the more positively valued deviant identities. The person comes to value deviant behavior and identities as a result of being the object of negative social sanctions for a number of reasons, all of which relate to the reduction of distressful self-rejecting feelings and to the affirmation of self-worth. As an object of negative social sanctions, the deviant actor is disposed to positively value deviant behavior and identities in order to: (1) obviate self-rejecting feelings by redefining the initial deviant acts as appropriate and conventional social sanctions as inappropriate or irrelevant within the perspective of the newly adopted deviant value system, (2) provide a set of standards for self-evaluation that are more easily approximated than conventional standards given that the deviant actor is now deprived of resources that reflect or are prerequisite to the achievement of conventional goals, (3) justify continuing failure to approximate conventional standards by blaming the circumstance of being the object of negative social sanctions, and (4) approximate conventional standards that are sometimes reflected in, or achieved through, deviant means. However, the mediating role of processes leading to reevaluation of deviant behavior and identities in the relationship between early deviance and later deviance is not explicitly modeled in the analysis presently under consideration.

In sum, reflecting theoretical deviations from the labeling perspective, negative social sanctions are modeled as mediating the influence of early deviance on disposition to deviance and deviant peer associations. Negative social sanctions are modeled also as mediating the independent direct effect of early deviance on later deviance.

Empirical confirmation of the elaborated model would provide support for the theoretical premises on which the elaboration was based (Kaplan, 1972, 1975b, 1980, 1982, 1984) and for the general proposition from the labeling perspective that "societal reaction, official or unofficial, to behavior which is that defined as unlawful or deviant may have an impact on the self-concept and subsequent behavior of the person labeled" (Williams, 1976, p. 2). However, we also recognize that alternative theoretical formulations could be compatible with the elaborated model.

## Method

The elaborated model is estimated using the LISREL VI program for analysis of linear structural relationships among latent constructs in a three-wave panel data set.

### Sample

The subjects are the same sample of junior high students in the Houston Independent School District in 1971. The survey is a three-wave panel study beginning in 1971 (Time 1) and repeated in 1972 (Time 2) and 1973 (Time 3). The questionnaires generally were completed in class. Usable questionnaires were returned by 7618 students (82%) at Time 1. A total of 3148 students were present for all three administrations, constituting 41% of the usable sample interviewed at Time 1. Of these, 2561 subjects provided data for all measures used in the analyses presented here.

### Latent Constructs and Measurement Variables

The elaborated model specifies relationships among six latent constructs (self-rejection, deviance at Time 1, negative social sanctions, disposition to deviance, deviant peer associations, and deviance at Time 3) and 14 measurement variables (multiple-item-additive scales). Five of the six latent constructs are measured exactly as specified in Model III. The new latent construct is negative social sanctions, and it has a unique measurement style. The construct also has implications for the decision to model deviance in the way we have conceptualized it in earlier models. First we present the measurement characteristics for negative social sanctions.

Negative social sanctions is measured by a single-indicator, three-item scale drawn from the second wave of the panel, Time 2. Since the items refer to experiences that occurred between the first two waves, the construct is modeled as occurring between Time 1 and Time 2 (as the consequence of Time 1 deviance and the precursor of other Time 2 variables). The three items refer to self-reports of the following experiences during the period between the first and second test administrations: suspended or expelled from school; had anything to do with police, sheriff, or juvenile officers; taken to the office for punishment. Negative social sanctions is conceptualized as responses by others to the behavior of the subject that, by the intention of the others or perception by the subject, serves as a punishment for the subject's behavior.

The measurement parameters for this construct are underidentified within the context of this model. That is, unless certain assumptions are explicitly made, both the error term and factor loading cannot be estimated. Usually the assumptions made are that the single indicator is measured without error (i.e., the error term is zero). Such a variable is commonly said to be given a perfect indicator of the construct. Given three repeated measures, the alternative assumption can be made that each time the variable is measured, a fixed proportion of the score is "true" and the remaining nonzero variance is error. Using the technique described by Kessler and Greenberg (1981, p. 148), we estimated this proportion of true score and fixed the error term to its estimated value according to the equation

$$e^2 = (1 - r^2)\, s^2 \tag{3.1}$$

where $e^2$ is the error variance, $r$ is the estimated reliability (proportion of true score), and $s^2$ is the total observed variation in the variable. The construct was measured as a scale with fixed reliability rather than as a multiple indicator latent construct because the separate indicators were dichotomous variables reflecting the occurrence of rare events. The potential skew of these variables in a covariance matrix introduces special estimation problems (Kim & Rabjohn, 1980) that are avoided by this approach.

Including negative social sanctions in the model has implications for the measurement of deviance. Among the most important of these is the general theoretical orientation that attempts to address the question of why an individual adopts any mode of deviance from among a range of possible deviant patterns rather than the question of why a person adopts some specific pattern. With particular reference to the relationship between deviance in general and negative social sanctions, part of the explanation for the inconsistent conclusions in the literature regarding the influence of societal reaction on later deviant behavior may be traced to the measure of deviance. The consequences of societal reaction may take any of numerous deviant forms. The specific mode of deviance is a function of a variety of situational contingencies. Perhaps, in order to estimate the effect of societal reaction on later deviance, deviance has to be modeled in a more general fashion as a performance of any of a range of deviant patterns of behavior.

Palamara et al. (1986) observed (we believe, correctly) that many researchers involved in labeling research appear to accept the assumption of etiological specificity whereby the individual who is labeled as one who engages in a specific form of deviance will continue to behave according to that specific deviant pattern. However, in so doing, researchers may be precluded from observing important labeling effects on other modes of deviance. By studying how a sanction impinges on the level of only one form of crime or deviance, they have ignored the probability that the sanction may precipitate more intensified involvement in other deviant adaptations (Palamara et al., 1986).

While Palamara et al. (1986) take as an implication of this that the impact of formal interventions on deviant behavior should be tested by examining the relationship for different forms of deviance, we take this observation to require more general indices of deviant behavior. Use of a general measure of deviance is warranted here since there is nothing in the labeling literature that requires that the stabilization of a deviant career be isomorphic with the initial deviance. Societal reactions to initial deviance may lead to the expression of alternative deviant forms depending on a number of situational contingencies. The defining criterion for the deviant response is only that it represents alternatives to conventional responses that have failed to offer gratifications of a person's needs that existed prior to the punitive responses or as a consequence of punitive responses.

### Data Analysis

Both the baseline model (Kaplan et al., 1988) and the elaborated model were estimated using correlation and standard deviation matrices of self-reported variables as input to LISREL-VI (Jöreskog & Sörbom, 1984).

This computer program provides maximum-likelihood estimates (MLE) of model parameters that are specified as "free." The estimation process is an iterating procedure that minimizes a function of the differences between observed covariance patterns and the covariances estimated by the model. The "free" parameters in the model are actually unknown values in linear equations that are used to construct the model.

Each model consists of measurement (observed) variables and latent constructs (unobserved variables). The latent constructs are theoretical variables among which there is a hypothesized causal structure. This is the latent structural equation model and the parameter estimates in these equations are presumed to represent causal effects of one theoretical construct on another. The measurement variables are those for which the observed covariance matrix is used as analytic input to the program. These variables are specified as indicators of the latent constructs and therefore are hypothesized to share a common theoretical basis. The measurement model thus provides estimates of how reliable and valid these observed variables are, and relative to their common theoretical basis, how much error is associated with each measure. The estimation of MLE models is made so that the factor loadings and error terms along with the structural parameters form equations that can be used to predict each of the observed covariations among all variables. The adequacy of this simultaneous prediction of all effects can be used as a criterion for evaluating the model. A chi-square test of the difference between observed and predicted covariances can be made for any given causal model and pattern of measurement parameters. In addition to this overall indicator, other methods for assessing the fit of individual parts of the model are also available. These will be discussed below where we evaluate the elaborated model.

The elaborated model is estimated in conformity to the hypothesized structural effects. That is, it is assumed that all of the reliable variation between observed variables can be accounted for in terms of the theoretical variables. Any unique variation in any measurement variable is thus assumed to be uncorrelated, net of the sources of common variance, with any other measurement variable. This assumption is useful in an elaboration of a theoretical model because it allows the researcher to assess the impact of hypothesized causal structure with the introduction of new theoretical constructs. However, as they are introduced in the elaboration strategy, additional measurement variables increase the likelihood of "correlated errors." We, therefore, examine the possibility that some of the unique measurement residuals have statistically significant covariance beyond the variation accounted for by the structural model. The significant "correlated error terms" are discussed in terms of the implications they have for hypothesized causal structural effects.

The elaborated model is based on the postulate that the relationship observed between theoretical constructs that do not share both temporal and theoretical synchronicity actually represents a causal process that can be explained partially by the introduction of intervening variables. These intervening causal processes, which lack temporal synchronicity, are distinctly obvious in the estimation of multivariate models drawn from panel studies in which variables from earlier panel waves indirectly affect variables from later panel waves via variables drawn from panels subsequent to the earlier variables and antecedent to the later variables. Specifically in the present study, negative social sanctions is hypothesized to intervene in the causal relationships between Time 1 deviance, on the one hand, and Time 2 disposition to deviance, Time 2 deviant peer associations, and Time 3 deviance, on the other hand.

# Results

The means, standard deviations, and intercorrelations of the 14 measurement variables used in the estimation of the causal models are presented in Table 3.1. The labels in the table refer to the variables discussed in the measurement model immediately below. The results are presented in three sections: (1) the specification of the measurement model, (2) the estimation of effects between latent constructs in the elaborated model and a comparison of this structural model with the baseline structural model, and (3) an assessment of fit, both for the theoretical elaborated model and for the elaborated model after it is adjusted for correlated error terms to account for unique measurement effects.

## *Measurement Model*

The parameter estimates for the measurement model, the "factor loadings," are presented in Table 3.6. Again, as noted earlier, the measurement characteristics of constructs will change as they are specified in the context of newly elaborated models. The important features, however, should not change. The ability of latent variables to consistently exhibit the same measurement properties in the

Table 3.6.   Measurement Model Parameters for Model IV – Standardized (Unstandardized)

|  | Model IV | | |
|---|---|---|---|
|  | U | S | T |
| Early deviance |  |  |  |
| PREV | 1.00 | 0.59 |  |
| MOD | 1.30 | 0.66 | 20.46 |
| RARE | 0.94 | 0.57 | 19.36 |
| Self-rejection |  |  |  |
| SRJT | 1.00 | 0.53 |  |
| RJTT | 0.21 | 0.68 | 17.62 |
| RJTP | 0.50 | 0.51 | 16.30 |
| Negative social sanctions |  |  |  |
| ATAUTH | 1.00 | 0.78 |  |
| Disposition to deviance |  |  |  |
| DSCO | 1.00 | 0.70 |  |
| ASD | 0.80 | 0.57 | 19.26 |
| Deviant peer associations |  |  |  |
| KASDEV | 1.67 | 0.51 | 18.94 |
| FRNDEV | 1.00 | 0.74 |  |
| Later deviance |  |  |  |
| PREV | 1.00 | 0.71 |  |
| MOD | 1.03 | 0.73 | 27.87 |
| RARE | 0.70 | 0.56 | 23.35 |
| Chi-square, *df* | 83, 50 |  |  |
| GFI | 1.00 |  |  |
| AGFI | 0.99 |  |  |
| RMSEA | 0.02 |  |  |

context of different models is a good indication of their validity. If measurement characteristics change dramatically, the construct likely lacks an important dimension of validity. This is an important advantage of the elaboration strategy. After elaboration, we find that all measures can be considered as reliable and valid indicators of the underlying latent construct, all loadings are large, and the freely estimated parameters are highly significant. We next consider the new measurement parameters for the latent construct of negative social sanctions.

The latent construct, Time 2 negative social sanctions, is estimated with a fixed error variance determined by Equation (3.1). The resultant reliability produces a fixed "factor loading" for negative social sanctions (NSS) of 0.780. This measure is intended to reflect the increased risk of receiving sanctions from agents of social control (police, school authorities) in response to deviant behavior.

### Structural Relations Model

The elaborated structural relations model is summarized in Figure 3.7. The results for the elaborated model may be compared with those for the baseline model presented above. Presentation of both models is based on parameter estimates obtained for the theoretical models, with correlated error terms and autocorrelation between repeated measures of deviance. The elaborated model specifies Time 2 negative social sanctions as mediating the effects of Time 1 deviance on Time 2 disposition to deviance, Time 2 deviant peer associations, and Time 3 deviance; that is, as partially decomposing the direct effects of Time 1

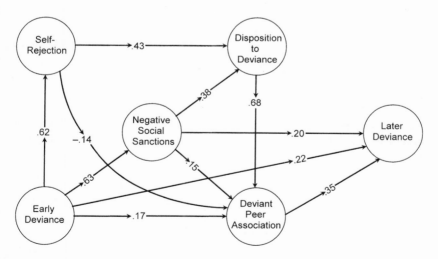

**Figure 3.7.** The standardized structural effects for the third elaboration of the model of deviant behavior: the role of negative social sanctions.

deviance on the second and third wave constructs that were observed in the baseline model. Further, negative social sanctions was expected, as a common causal antecedent, to increase the explained variance in second and third panel constructs over that observed in the baseline model.

*Negative Social Sanctions as an Intervening Explanatory Variable.* The hypothesis that negative social sanctions would mediate and partially decompose the effects (observed in the baseline model) of Time 1 deviance on Time 2 disposition to deviance, Time 3 deviant peer associations, and Time 3 deviance received strong support. Time 1 deviance had a strong effect (0.63) on Time 2 negative social sanctions (that occurred between Time 1 and Time 2); and Time 2 negative social sanctions had appreciable effects on Time 2 disposition to deviance (0.38), Time 2 deviant peer associations (0.15), and Time 3 deviance (0.20). All of these hypothesized effects were significant beyond the level of $p = 0.001$.

As expected, the influence of Time 1 deviance on Time 2 disposition to deviance is mediated by negative social sanctions, reducing the baseline influence of deviance on later disposition to deviance. Virtually all of the effect of early deviance on later disposition to deviance is mediated by societal reaction to the early deviance. The Time 1 deviance direct effect of 0.30 on later disposition to deviance was reduced to 0.11. Indeed even this modest effect is obviated when certain correlated errors are specified. The specification of positive correlated error between RJTT and NSS and between MOST1 and SDRG enhances the effect of Time 1 deviance on negative social sanctions. This enhanced effect renders the net residual direct effect of Time 1 deviance on Time 2 disposition to deviance nonsignificant. Specification of positive correlated error between RARE1 and ASD1 reduces, further, the direct effect of Time 1 deviance on Time 2 disposition to deviance. In short, after the model is adjusted for certain correlated error terms, to account for unique measurement effects, the direct effect of Time 1 deviance on Time 2 disposition to deviance observed is completely mediated by intervening negative social sanctions. Apparently, the effect of deviance on disposition to deviance is accounted for by correlates of adverse social reactions to the initial deviance or by the intrinsically distressful adverse social reactions. Among the correlates of adverse social reaction is the recognition by the deviant actor of a decreased likelihood of achieving gratification of one's needs within the social network that stigmatized the deviant actor.

In like manner, as expected, much of the direct effect observed in the baseline model of Time 1 deviance on Time 2 deviant peer associations is accounted for by the mediation of Time 2 negative social sanctions. Presumably in part as a result of adverse social reaction, the person becomes attractive to deviant peers and becomes attracted to deviant peers by virtue of being excluded from conventional interactions. As an intervening variable, negative social sanctions attenuates, but does not completely decompose, the direct effect of Time 1 deviance on Time 2 deviant peer associations. The direct effect of Time 1 deviance on Time 2 deviant peer associations is 0.17 in the baseline model and in the elaborated model.

Finally, the influence of Time 1 deviance on Time 3 deviance observed in the second elaboration (0.33) is attenuated appreciably by the mediating effects of negative social sanctions. The effect is reduced to 0.22. Negative social sanctions accounts for a significant proportion of the observed stability of deviant behavior, as expected. Presumably, the adverse social reaction leads to forced acceptance of a "spoiled" deviant identity, the subsequent positive evaluation of the deviant identity, and conforming to the defining role characteristics (that is, deviant behavior) of the deviant identity.

*Negative Social Sanctions as a Causal Antecedent.* Negative social sanctions in the elaborated models modestly increases the explained variance in second and third panel constructs over that observed in the baseline model. The $R^2$ for disposition to deviance is 0.49 in the elaborated model compared with 0.38 in the earlier model. The $R^2$ for deviant peer associations is 0.65 compared with 0.63 in the earlier model. Finally, the overall explained variance in Time 3 deviance increases to 0.52 in the elaborated model from 0.51 in the earlier model.

The addition of negative social sanctions as a causal variable in the elaborated model resulted in the attenuation of relationships hypothesized and observed in the baseline model due to the common causal impact of negative social sanctions. The within-wave effect of disposition to deviance at Time 2 on deviant peer association at Time 2 observed in the baseline model is attenuated by virtue of the common influence of negative social sanctions on both disposition to deviance at Time 2 and deviant peer associations at Time 2. The within-wave effect is reduced from 0.76 in the baseline model to 0.68 in the elaborated model. However, disposition to deviance still exerts a strong effect on deviant peer associations. Similarly, the influence of deviant peer associations at Time 2 on deviance at Time 3 that was noted in the baseline model is attenuated in the elaborated model due to the common effects of earlier negative social sanctions on both of these variables. Nevertheless, deviant peer associations continues to exercise an appreciable and significant direct effect on later deviance. The effect is reduced from 0.44 in the baseline model to 0.35 in the elaborated model.

Finally, the effect of disposition to deviance at Time 2 on later deviance at Time 3 that was observed in the baseline model is attenuated modestly due to the common antecedent effects of negative social sanctions. Again, an effect of disposition to deviance on later deviance remains noteworthy and significant. However, as will be observed below, this effect is further reduced to nonsignificance when certain correlated errors are specified in the model.

In any case, negative social sanctions, as hypothesized, was observed to: (1) be a consequence of deviance at Time 1 and (2) mediate the effects of deviance at Time 1 on Time 2 disposition to deviance, Time 2 deviant peer associations, and Time 3 deviance.

## *Assessment of Fit*

One method for assessing the fit of the models to the observed data is the ratio of chi-square to its degrees of freedom. In the elaborated model with correlated errors, the chi-square value is 83 with 50 *df*, providing a ratio of 1.66. Considering the large sample size ($N = 2561$), we judge this value to be adequate (see Wheaton et al., 1977). In addition, the GFI is at its maximum value of 1.0. This overall measure is independent of sample size (Jöreskog & Sörbom, 1984).

These values refer to the overall fit of the models. However, a more detailed assessment can be made by examining the normalized residuals (Jöreskog & Sörbom, 1984). On closer inspection of these residuals, we note that of the 105 variances and covariances estimated by the elaborated model, only 10 were significantly different from their observed values. The correlations between RARE1 deviance and SDRG and FRNDEV were both significant with a standardized value of $-0.05$. Other values for the following pairs of variables are: MOST1 and SDRG (0.05); MOST1 and NSS (0.05); ASD and FRNDEV ($-0.10$); FRNDEV and RARE3 ($-0.05$); MOST1 and FRNDEV (0.05); RARE1 and ASD (0.06); RJTT and NSS (0.07); and ASD and RARE3 (0.07). When these relationships were tested, by specifying correlated error terms between pairs of measurement models, none obviated the hypothesized structural parameters relating to the antecedents and consequence of negative social sanctions.

# Discussion of Model IV

## *Confirmation of Theory*

As part of a more general theory of deviant behavior (Kaplan, 1972, 1975b, 1980, 1983, 1984), we have attempted to articulate the variables and the relationships among them that are presumed to intervene between social sanctions for prior deviance and continuation or escalation of deviance. We have specified social consequences of negative social sanctions. We have drawn distinctions between, and delineated relationships among, self-conceptions of being the object of negative sanctions and of performing illicit behaviors, self-evaluation as deviating from or conforming to personal or group values, negative or positive self-feelings that accompany the self-evaluative responses, and the self-enhancing/self-protective mechanisms (including deviant responses) that are motivated by negative self-feelings (Kaplan, 1986).

We also described constructs that reflect alienation from conventional society (disposition to deviance) and association with deviant peers (deviant peer association) and specified their effects on later deviance. The direct and indirect effects of these constructs are said to describe the processes that are evoked by social sanctions for prior deviance and in turn influence the continuity or escalation of deviant behavior. Many of these theoretical linkages are implicit, if not explicit, in statements expressing the labeling perspective.

We estimated a model that specifies a number of the theoretically indicated linkages. The results of the analysis are compatible with theoretical expectations regarding the processes by which punitive societal reaction to deviant behavior influences subsequent performance of deviant behavior. The process was specified particularly with regard to: (1) the mediating role of disposition to deviance and deviant peer associations and (2) the independent direct effect of negative social sanctions on later deviance. Theoretically, the experience of being the object of negative social sanctions in response to earlier deviance carries with it social and personal consequences that have the ultimate effect of reinforcing the deviance. We argue here that the reinforcement occurs via: (1) increasing alienation from the conventional world, (2) increasing interaction with deviant peers, and (3) motivating the person to positively value and identify with the deviant status and to positively value himself to the extent that he conforms to the normative expectations (including those requiring the performance of deviant acts) that define appropriate behavior for individuals who occupy that status. If the person is unable to neutralize the adverse consequences (including distressful self-rejecting feelings) of negative social consequences through conventional means, the deviant actor will attempt to mitigate the consequences in any of a number of ways that facilitate stabilization or increased intensity, frequency, and range of deviant behavior. Among these are the rejection of the conventional normative system by which the person was punished, association with deviant peers by the standards of which one may prove himself, and redefining the evaluative significance of the deviant identity so that what is rejected by conventional society becomes admirable by the revised personal system of values. All of these techniques would result in continued or increased involvement with deviant activities.

The present model postulates that all of these processes are operative. Therefore, the model specifies that early involvement in deviance is positively associated with negative social sanctions. Negative social sanctions, in turn, indirectly influences deviant behavior via increased alienation from the conventional system (disposition to deviance), indirectly influences an increase or continuity of deviant behavior via affiliation with deviant peers (deviant peer association), and has a direct effect on later deviance (presumably by influencing the person to identify with and positively value the deviant identity as a basis for overall positive self-evaluation).

The results of the analysis are congruent with the theoretically informed model. Being the object of negative social sanctions clearly does have an effect on Time 3 deviance independent of the effect of Time 1 deviance that evoked the negative social sanctions. The effect of the social sanctions is, as expected, complex. It operates by its effects on disposition to deviance and deviant peer associations, as well as by other effects that presumably underlie the observed direct effect of negative social sanctions on Time 3 deviance. These effects are observed without taking into account such contingencies as the type of social reaction and the type of deviance in question (Palamara et al., 1986). The significant effects of social reactions to earlier deviance on later deviance might be even more marked as such contingencies are added in future analyses.

The results of the analyses herein reported are compatible with the general theory of deviant behavior that informs the model (Kaplan, 1972, 1975b, 1980, 1982, 1984). Certain of the results, but not all, also are compatible with other sociological models that similarly integrate the assumptions of such approaches including the strain, social and cultural support, and labeling theories or focus on one or another perspective. Thus, Farrell summarizes his general argument by asserting that

> society defines deviance as a salient and discrediting position prescribed in terms of a stereotype. Such a definition and the reactions that ensue restrict alternative roles that the individual may assume, thereby limiting the nature and boundaries of subsequent interaction. The effect is to become engulfed in the deviant role and to define oneself in terms of its expectations. Operating as a stigma, the social response and self-definition then produce stress and the subsequent need for adaptation. A frequent adaptive outcome is to shift one's reference associations, often to a group whose members have experienced similar difficulties and wherein one is capable of conformity and the attainment of a more positive status. As the individual receives input from the new associations and attaches meaning to them, he redefines his situation. The result is a form of behavior dependent upon his and group member's conceptions of the deviant role. Because those who form these associations are likely to come to view themselves in terms of the stereotype, it is this role conception which serves as the basis for such secondary deviance. In that the group norms validate the role, a more positive self-definition is likely to evolve from the interaction. (Farrell, 1987, p. 7)

The hypothetical effects of social sanctions on attitudes toward conventional and deviant activities and on associations with conventional or deviant peers are interpreted more specifically in terms of the social learning perspective. Akers argues that

> to the extent that labeling people deviant and treating them differently sometimes makes them more deviant it may be viewed as a social learning process. First, the apprehension and official labeling of some people may reduce their chances to pursue conventional alternatives to achieve the same rewards they have obtained by deviant means. This in turn may increase the chance that they will become more deeply involved in groups which add reinforcement to and rationalizations for their deviant behavior. Second, being publicly branded deviants may support the disapproval of persons by their neighbors, relatives, and others in the community, who then fail to respond in a rewarding way to their efforts to 'reform' .... Third, the conditions under which persons are

> punished or 'treated' as a result of their legal or official assignment to deviant status may be conducive to learning new or maintaining old patterns of deviant behavior. Incarceration in prison may enable criminals to learn additional criminal behavior. The structure of rewards and punishment in the mental hospital ward often reinforces 'sick' behavior. (Akers, 1985, p. 69)

The findings in the present study relating to the indirect effects of negative social sanctions on deviance via deviant peer associations are clearly compatible with these theoretical positions. However, it is not as clear that these positions imply the observed independent direct effects of negative social sanctions, and the indirect effects of negative social sanctions via disposition to deviance, on later deviance. Nor are the relationships precluded by these treatments. But these observed relationships are predicted according to the general theory that guides the present analysis.

It should be emphasized that, although the intervening roles of certain of the theoretically indicated variables have been demonstrated, the mediating roles of other of the theoretically indicated explanatory constructs are yet to be tested. Thus, the results do not provide direct evidence for (although it is compatible with) the putative role of changes in self-concept and self-feeling that result from negative social sanctions on disposition to deviance and (directly or indirectly) on deviant peer associations. Nor does it provide direct support for the postulated mediating role of the exacerbation of the self-esteem motive on continuity of deviant behavior (via reevaluation of the deviant identity and associated behaviors). Again, however, the observed direct effect of negative social sanctions on deviant behavior, net of the indirect effects via disposition to deviance and deviant peer associations, is compatible with this association. Nevertheless, the theoretical statement regarding the mechanisms that mediate the influence of punitive societal reactions to initial deviance on later deviant behavior provides a basis for further elaboration and reestimation of the theoretically informed model.

## The Deterrence Hypothesis

A frequently proposed explanation for deviant behavior is the deterrence hypothesis "whereby individuals are coerced, threatened, and sanctioned into conformity" (Piliavin, Thornton, Gartner, & Matsueda, 1986, p. 101). Within a rational choice model, a person would be deterred from engaging in deviant acts if the person perceived high probability of consequent punishment, the expectation of severe punishment, and little likelihood of reward as a result of the deviant behavior. Since negative social sanctions to initial deviance would serve to influence the perceptions of high probability of future punishment and low likelihood for rewards for future deviant behavior, from the deterrence perspective, the experience of negative social sanctions would be hypothesized to have an inhibiting effect on subsequent performance of deviant behavior.

The expectation persists in the literature despite the absence of firm and consistent empirical support. First, if deviant acts were positively related to negative social sanctions, the deterrence hypothesis would lead to the expectation that early deviance would inhibit later deviant behavior because of the increased perception of risk resulting from negative social sanctions. However, the literature is not consistent with this expectation. Findings from longitudinal studies indicate that persons who reported committing crimes between waves had lower subsequent perceptions of risk than those who did not report committing crimes, persons' early perceptions of risks were unrelated to these reports of crime, and persons' earlier and later perceptions of risk were not stable (Piliavin et al., 1986). Second, no consistent deterrent effect of perceived severity has been observed (Piliavin et al., 1986). Third,

> while most studies find a consistent but modest effect of perceived certainty of formal sanctions ... others find that this effect is conditional holding only for persons who are uncommitted to conventional morality ... or highly motivated to deviate. (Piliavin et al., 1986, pp. 102–103)

However, Piliavin et al. (1986, p. 114) found that in contrast to other research, which concludes that deterrence should be more effective in less conventional samples, in their samples containing criminally motivated and morally uncommitted persons, perceptions of the risk of sanctions did not account for criminal behavior.

On the other hand, these same investigators concluded that persons who perceive greater opportunities to earn money illegally and who hold more respect for illegitimate occupations relative to legitimate jobs have more to gain and less to lose by violating the law and therefore are significantly more likely to do so. This result is consistent with the reasoning in the present study that led us to predict a direct effect of negative social sanctions on deviance. We reasoned that individuals who are the objects of negative social sanctions for earlier deviant behavior respond to ensuing self-rejecting feelings by coming to positively value and identify with the deviant behavior and roles, and so increase the likelihood of performing deviant acts in the future.

Like these findings the results of the present analysis are inconsistent with expectations based on the deterrence hypothesis, but rather are congruent with the labeling hypothesis. From the deterrence perspective it is reasonable to anticipate that negative social reactions to deviance would constitute an adverse circumstance that the individual would subjectively associate with the deviance. Consequently, the individual would associate deviant behavior with noxious consequences and therefore would decrease or cease deviant behavior. However, in our data, this is clearly not the case. All direct and indirect consequences of social reaction to deviance are positive rather than inverse (as would be expected if societal reaction inhibited deviant behavior).

Apparently, adverse social reactions (rather than the deviant behavior that evoked the adverse social reaction) are associated in the person's own mind with the stressful circumstances. Thus, the individual's responses appear directed to defend against the adverse social reactions rather than to defend against performance of deviant behavior. Insofar as the individual experiences social rejection, he becomes disposed to adopt deviant patterns of behavior as sources of gratification and to eschew conventional patterns since these patterns are associated with the experience of distress for the individual. Further, social rejection and response to deviant behavior makes it difficult for the person to be accepted by and interact with representatives of conventional society on an ongoing basis. Since the person is unable to gain gratifications from the conventional others who exclude the person from their society, the person seeks and finds alternative sources of gratification—notably deviant peers. At the same time, the attenuation of affective ties with conventional society brings the deviant actor beyond the range of affective influence of negative social sanctions. Under the conditions of our study, if negative social sanctions have a deterrent effect on later deviant behavior, this effect must operate via other mediating variables (such as expectations of further punishment) that perhaps may mitigate, but do not obviate the net positive effect of negative sanctions on amplification or continuity of deviance.

It is also possible that the circumstances of the present study do not reflect fully the circumstances in which a deterrent effect of negative social sanctions might be observed. Negative social sanctions might have a deterrent rather than a stabilizing or amplifying effect on future deviant behavior, for example, for certain types of deviant acts. The variables affecting the deterrability of juvenile delinquency, white-collar crime, armed robbery, and domestic violence may be quite different. Careful accumulation of findings from different settings will help us differentiate the variables that are crime- or situation-specific and those that apply across settings (Sherman & Berk, 1984, p. 262).

Finally, it is possible that negative social sanctions exercises a deterrent effect for the specific deviant act that elicits negative social sanctions. That is, if we had measured deviance in terms of a single indicator at Times 1 and 2, it is possible that negative social labeling would have been inversely related to the measure of deviance at Time 2. However, with a more general measure of deviance, negative social sanctions appears to facilitate the performance of deviant acts. In short, negative social sanctions may deter the specific act that evoked the punitive response but still lead to identification with a more general deviant role and the performance of other deviant acts as a defensive response to the self-devaluing experiences that are associated with being the object of negative social sanctions.

In any case, in the circumstances reflected in this study, the results are compatible with the expectation most explicitly developed in writings from the labeling or societal reaction perspective since negative social sanctions are observed to have direct and indirect positive effects on later deviance. These are contrary to expectations from the deterrence perspective, which would have led to the prediction of an inverse relationship between negative social sanctions and later deviance.

## A Research Agenda for Negative Social Sanctions

Future research concerning the relationship between negative social sanctions and deviance should focus on: (1) the further decomposition of the direct and indirect paths between negative social sanctions and later deviance, (2) the conditions under which these relationships are observed, and (3) the explanatory value of negative social sanctions relative to other explanatory constructs in accounting for changes in deviant behavior.

*Intervening Variables.* The results of the analysis are compatible with the theoretical premises regarding the variables that intervene in these relationships, but they do not demonstrate that all of these variables intervene. The operationalization and estimation of the mediating variables remain tasks for future research. Cases in point are the putative roles of exclusion from conventional society and changes in self-referent response.

From the labeling perspective, as this perspective is integrated within the general theory that guides these analyses, deviant actors become entrenched in deviant roles because they have been the objects of negative social sanctions that influence or are reflected in exclusion from continuity in or resumption of social roles in the conventional community. Theoretically, social exclusion has diverse ramifications for subsequent performance of deviant behavior. For example, exclusion from normal social roles alienates an individual from the conventional structure. The individual loses motivation to try to conform to conventional norms because he recognizes that it is unlikely he will be accepted regardless of how hard he tries to conform. Indeed, he becomes motivated to deviate from conventional norms because he recognizes the conventional world as the source of actions that exclude him from conventional means to satisfy his range of needs. As a result, the individual must seek alternatives to conventional norms, deviant patterns of behavior that offer promise of satisfaction of his needs.

Exclusion from normal interaction also makes the individual more attractive and visible to other deviant individuals who are seeking satisfaction of a range of their needs including interaction with and gaining approval from others. Hence, the individual may be invited to join with other deviant individuals from whom they may learn and be supported for deviant activities. This outcome is particularly likely since the individual himself is seeking deviant alternatives to the conventional means of which he is deprived in order to satisfy his needs.

Finally, exclusion from conventional society in which the individual is socialized leads to negative self-evaluations and distressful self-feelings and motivation to forestall such negative self-feelings or, at least, to assuage them. To this end, the individual may revalue the behaviors and identities that were associated with the distressful outcomes such that they are more positively valued. By emotionally committing himself to the value of the behaviors that elicited negative responses, the individual provides a basis for positive self-evaluation and consequent positive self-feelings. The continued performance of deviant acts testifies to the individual's conformity to norms that define a newly valued social identity. These theoretical linkages that assert mediating roles of social exclusion in accounting for the influence of negative social sanctions on later deviance should be near the top of a research agenda that seeks further elaboration of a general theory of deviant behavior.

Similarly, differentiated self-referent responses theoretically mediate the effects of negative social sanctions (and their social correlates) on the stabilization or increase of later deviance. Negative social sanctions have direct or indirect effects on self-conception, self-evaluation, and self-feelings that, in turn, have direct or indirect (via disposition to deviance and deviant peer associations) effects on later deviance as a more or less functional adaptive response to prior self-referent responses. These earlier responses include self-conceptions of being the object of negative social sanctions and/or of having performed personally and socially disvalued acts, consequent negative self-evaluations, and concomitant distressful self-rejecting feelings that motivate the person to alter his self-values and, thereby, to permit identification with now-valued deviant roles and the performance of now-valued deviant behavior toward the goal of increasing positive self-evaluation and self-feelings. The three paths from negative social sanctions to later deviance that were hypothesized and observed are interpretable as reflecting three different routes to self-acceptance. The effect of negative social sanctions on disposition to deviance may reflect the rejection of the sources of self-devaluation, the conventional moral order. The deviant behavior that indirectly results from negative social sanctions reflects symbolic rejection of the normative standards according to which one must judge oneself to fail. The indirect effect of societal reaction on later deviant behavior via deviant peer associations may reflect the function of deviant behavior as earning the respect of deviant others and self-respect by conforming to behavioral standards that are endorsed by deviant peers. The conformity to conduct norms of deviant peers permits one to approximate standards that might earn one positive self-evaluation.

Finally, the direct effects of negative social sanctions on deviant behavior may reflect the person's commitment to the deviant identity along with the acceptance of appropriate role behaviors as standards for positive self-evaluation. Deviant behavior represents a conformity to the standards for self-evaluation associated with a now-valued deviant identity. The rejection by others as reflected in the societal reaction to initial deviance to a degree precludes any virtue in rejecting the deviant self-image. In this condition, then, the positive evaluation of a heretofore-disreputable image represents a viable adaptation to the need for positive self-evaluation. Were it not for the exclusion of the person from conventional life that is implied by the societal reaction to initial deviance, the person might be more motivated to reject the deviant self-image as incompatible with a more stable (conforming) self-conception. The theoretical statement that underlies the estimated model specifies in greater detail than usual the processes that mediate the influence of negative social sanctions on later deviance. Statements from the labeling perspective do point out that a key part of the labeling process

> pertains to the way in which deviance labeling produces changes in the actors' own self-identifications and self-evaluations. The basic proposition is simply that the social act of tagging or labeling a person a deviant tends to alter the self-conception of the labeled person toward incorporating this identification. Labeling events, both public and private, will precipitate a transformation from identification as "the person who did X" into a self-identification as "me", the kind of person who does X. (Wells, 1978, p. 200)

It is not always clear in the literature how self-perception as the object of negative sanctions is transformed into acceptance of a deviant identity. The deviance amplification literature sometimes provides for a relationship between negative social sanctions and self-rejecting attitudes and the self-recognition of having a deviant identity, but does not always provide explicitly for the motivation to play the deviant role. That is, the literature does not provide a clear statement of the motivational advantages of not only perceiving oneself as having a deviant identity but also realizing that identity by providing confirming deviant behavior. However, the present theoretical statement provides for the motivational processes and supportive social arrangements that mediate the transformation. The theoretical basis for predicting effects of negative social labeling on deviance rests on the expectation that negative social labeling exacerbates the self-esteem motive and evokes a need to justify the earlier performance of deviant acts and the personal worth of the actors in general by positively valuing the deviant role and associated deviant behaviors. In short, the subjective association of being rejected by conventional groups is viewed as a consequence of negative social labeling and the motivation for continuity or escalation of the deviant behavior. In any case, it remains for future research to operationalize and estimate these mediating processes.

*Conditional Relationships.* In addition to specifying further intervening variables, it may be necessary to further specify the conditions under which the model will hold. The inconsistent conclusions from other research referred to above, as well as any relationships that are far weaker than unity that might derive from research based on the theoretical model under consideration, might be accounted for by specifiable contingencies. Thus, we have argued that the effects of social sanctions on continuity of deviant behavior are mediated by the direct and indirect effects of self-labeling. It is possible that in some of the studies (those that do not observe significant effects of social sanctions on continuity of deviance) the link between social sanctions and self-labeling or the links between self-labeling and disposition to deviance, deviant peer associations, and the need to affirm the validity of past behavior are relatively weak because of any of a number of contingencies, while in the studies that report significant effects between social sanctions and continuity of deviance, other situational contingencies favor the strength of the theoretically indicated effects. The research agenda must then include approaches that would permit specification of the conditions under which the relationship between sanctions and deviant patterns of behavior is observed.

Such contingencies might include insulation from devaluing responses by others in response to formal sanctions, social identity-related phenomena such as those based on gender, age, and race/ethnicity differentiation, factors related to the power of the perpetrator, the existence of social supports serving to maintain social integration, and similarly, social contingencies that are yet imperfectly understood. The results of our analyses may apply to the kinds of behaviors, the kinds of social responses, and the population of adolescents that comprise our cohort. Any or all of these factors may define contingencies under which the hypothesized and observed processes operate. The consideration of the mechanisms that are reflected in such conditional variables should provide the opportunity for a more detailed specification of the theoretical models that explain the relationship between deviant behavior, social responses to deviant behavior, and continuation or escalation of deviant behavior, while resolving the apparent contradictions in previously reported findings.

*Negative Social Sanctions as an Explanatory Variable.*   Critics of the labeling perspective have taken proponents of this point of view to task for seeming to argue that societal reaction to deviance is a necessary or sufficient condition for career deviance. Thus, Mankoff (1971) cites the research of Becker (1963), Cressey (1953), and Lemert (1972) in questioning whether societal reaction to rule breaking is a necessary condition for career deviance. Lemert's (1967) study of check forgers, for example, shows how career deviance and deviant self-conceptions can develop before societal reaction. Similarly, Cressey shows that trust violators often accept a deviant self-concept prior to formal sanctions by employers or agents of social control. For Becker, regular use of marijuana depends on such variables as finding the subjective effects of the drugs to be pleasurable and having adequate supply. Labeling is not necessary for the individual to continue use of marijuana. Due to an underestimation of the importance of social and psychological factors other than labeling in generating deviant careers, labeling theorists ignore the possibility of, for example, true commitment of the rule-breaker to career deviance.

Nor, it is argued, is societal reaction a sufficient condition for career deviance. Mankoff (1971) cites the work of Cameron (1964) and Glaser (1964) in arguing that frequently individuals respond to formal sanctions by ceasing to engage in the deviant behavior. In short, rule-breakers may engage in career deviance without the presence of formal or informal sanctions and may end rule-breaking even where or because sanctions are applied.

Whether labeling is a necessary or sufficient condition for, or even a primary determinant of, career deviance rather than one determinant among many is problematic from the perspective of labeling theorists. Generally, observers ascribe to labeling theorists the premise that labeling is the primary determinant of career deviance (Mankoff, 1971). In any case, the theoretical basis for the model under consideration presumes that social reactions to deviance (negative social sanctions) are among, and not necessarily the most important of, the explanatory factors that are necessary to account for variation in deviant outcomes. That is, any controversy over whether or not the labeling perspective implies that the labeling process is a necessary and/or sufficient condition for career deviance is irrelevant for the present analysis. In the context of the theory that operates the present analysis, negative social sanctions is one among several explanatory factors that account for deviant behavior. This factor is expected to mediate, but not to completely decompose the effect of early deviance on later deviance.

The results of the analysis are congruent with the expectation that negative social sanctions is one among many of the explanatory factors of deviance. While negative social sanctions, of course, do not fully account for variation in deviant behavior, these social reactions to early deviance do exercise indirect and direct (yet undisaggregated) effects on later performance of deviant behavior. Yet it remains to determine what other factors such as the persistence of motives for, or an evaluative commitment to, initial deviant behavior, might increase our understanding of why individuals adopt deviant response patterns. Further, it is clear that negative social sanctions (as we have measured them) are not sufficient to account for the stability of deviant behavior between Times 1 and 3 or even for that portion of the stability coefficient that remains after taking into account the mediating effects of self-rejection and deviant peer associations. After taking into account the mediating effects of negative social sanctions in response to early deviance on later deviance, direct and other indirect effects of early deviance on later deviance continue to be observed.

However, the results do suggest that societal reactions to deviant behavior constitute a meaningful part of the explanation of the stability of deviant behavior since social reactions to labeling when included in the explanatory model further attenuate the relationship between early deviance and later deviance. Future research will determine what other variables (such as attenuation of social controls or any gratifying consequences of early deviance, other than those that may be associated with societal reaction and the other variables that were observed to mediate the relationship between Time 1 and Time 3 deviance) account for the stability of deviant behavior.

# Appendix

*Time 1 Measures of Self-Rejection*

**Rejection by Teachers** (alpha = 0.68)

My teachers are not usually interested in what I say or do.

By my teachers' standards, I am a failure.

My teachers do not like me very much.

My teachers usually put me down.

**Self-Derogation** (alpha = 0.69)

I don't like myself as much as I used to.

I used to be a better person than I am now.

I wish I could have more respect for myself.

I feel I do not have much to be proud of.

All in all, I am inclined to feel that I am a failure.

At times, I think I am no good at all.

I certainly feel useless at times.

Do you often feel downcast and dejected?

On the whole, I am satisfied with myself. (no)

I take a positive attitude toward myself. (no)

My life is a lot more satisfying now than it used to be. (no)

I like myself a lot better now than I used to. (no)

I am a better person now than I used to be. (no)

**Rejection by Parents** (alpha = −0.55)

As long as I can remember, my parents have put me down.

My parents are usually not very interested in what I say.

My parents do not like me very much.

*Time 2 Measures of Disposition to Deviance*

**Antisocial Defenses** (alpha = −0.53)

If you want people to like you, you have to tell them what they want to hear, even if it isn't the truth.

If someone insulted me, I would probably think about ways I could get even.

If someone insulted me, I would probably avoid talking to him in the future.

I don't care much about other people's feelings.

**Disaffection with the Conventional Community** (alpha = 0.57)

Would you like to quit school as soon as possible?

I would like to leave home.

If you stick to law and order, you will never fix what is wrong with this
country.

The law is always against the ordinary guy.

I have a better chance of doing well if I cut corners than if I play it straight.

The kids who mess up with the law seem to be better off than those who play
it straight.

### Time 2 Measures of Deviant Peer Association

**Kids at School Are Deviant** (alpha = 0.77)

Do many of the kids at school take an active part in social protest either at
school or outside of school?

Do many of the kids at school take narcotic drugs?

Do many of the kids at school damage or destroy public or private property
that doesn't belong to them?

Do many of the kids at school break into and enter a home, store, or
building?

Do many of the kids at school carry razors, switchblades, or guns as
weapons?

Do many of the kids at school take little things (worth less than $2) that
don't belong to them?

Do many of the kids at school smoke marijuana (grass)?

**Friends Are Deviant** (alpha = 0.74)

Do many of your good friends smoke marijuana?

Do many of your good friends take narcotic drugs to get high?

Most of my close friends are the kinds of kids who get in trouble a lot.

### Time 1 Measures of Deviance

**Most Prevalent** (alpha = 0.52)

Within the last month did you:

take less than $2?

get angry and break things?

receive failing grades?

use wine, beer, or liquor two times (within the last week)?

skip school without an excuse?

smoke marijuana (grass)?

**Moderate Prevalence** (alpha = 0.55)

Within the last month did you:

take between $2 and $50?

carry a weapon?

start a fistfight?

take narcotic drugs?
take things from someone else's desk or locker at school?
Do you usually obey your teachers? (no)
**Least Prevalent** (alpha = 0.55)
Within the last month did you:
take part in gang fights?
use force to get money or valuables from another person?
break into and enter a home, store, or building?
damage or destroy public or private property on purpose that didn't
belong to you?
take a car for a ride without the owner's knowledge?
take things worth more than $50?
beat up someone without cause?

## *Time 3 Measures of Deviance*

**Most Prevalent** (alpha = 0.64)
Within the last year did you:
take less than $2?
get angry and break things?
receive failing grades?
use wine, beer, or liquor two times (within the last week)?
skip school without an excuse?
smoke marijuana (grass)?
**Moderate Prevalence** (alpha = 0.66)
Within the last year did you:
take between $2 and $50?
carry a weapon?
start a fistfight?
take narcotic drugs?
take things from someone else's desk or locker at school?
Do you usually obey your teachers? (no)
**Least Prevalent** (alpha = 0.74)
Within the last year did you:
take part in gang fights?
use force to get money or valuables from another person?
break into and enter a home, store, or building?
damage or destroy public or private property on purpose that didn't
belong to you?
take a car for a ride without the owner's knowledge?
take things worth more than $50?
beat up someone without cause?

# 4

## Gender as a Moderator in Explanations of Adolescent Deviance

Almost without exception, studies that address adolescent delinquency or young adult deviance conclude that males commit more acts of deviance than females. This finding is very likely true, particularly when we consider traditional notions of delinquency and deviance to include such acts as theft, interpersonal aggression, other acts of violence, use of weapons, drugs, alcohol, and so on. Therefore, because males do commit more acts that are contranormative within this traditional concept of deviance and delinquency, questions can be raised as to whether or not the processes that lead to deviance are the same for both males and females, or whether there are other factors that suppress or counteract the processes that influence deviance. Differential effects of the deviance-causing process can be attributed to several dimensions of traditional deviance models.

First, one may question whether or not the notion of deviance can be invariably ascribed across gender. Are the traditional notions of acts of deviance and delinquency meaningful for males in the same way they are meaningful for females? This question asks if there is factorial invariance across measurement items for males and females. A differential factorial structure across gender would indicate and supply support for the argument made by Macoby and Jacklin (1974) who suggest that males and females do not actually differ in the amount of contranormative behavior. Rather, they engage in different types of contranormative behavior. Since traditional notions of contranormative behavior include the presumed male gendered acts of delinquency, violence, and other conduct disorders, then "naturally" males score higher. But if one were to consider alternative forms of deviance that include internalized acts of aggression, self-directed violence, or other kinds of responses to stress, then females might manifest roughly the same (or higher) rates of contranormative behavior as males.

A second issue involving differential effects of the deviance-provoking process is that of whether or not the process itself is differentially applicable to males and females. That is, if one were to consider elements of social control or labeling processes, social control agents may not respond to females in the same way that they respond to males for any given particular act of deviance, and so the labeling of behaviors may be differentially applied to males and females for similar acts of deviance. Further, if the distressful feelings associated with the frustration of the self-esteem motive are motivating factors that differentially involve male and female subjects, then males and females may be more or less likely to adapt to such distressful feelings through external acting out or through internalized maladaptations. Thus, independent of factorial invariance across groups, it is possible that differential structural relations between the underlying factors would be observed. Each of these issues can be addressed through sub-group comparisons to detect factorial invariance and invariance of the covariance structure.

Recently, some researchers have begun to argue that the differences in items reflecting deviance by males or females have been decreasing (Figueira-McDonough, Barton, & Sarri, 1981). These authors argue that earlier research that focused on delinquency and adolescent deviance, particularly those studies that occurred prior to 1970, were conceived on the basis of sex role socialization and gender stereotypes that most often confirmed differences between male and female offenders. These gender-specific stereotypes included the assumption that attenuation of bonds to parents was the major causal factor among female delinquents, providing them with frustration of, or lack of, motivation to achieve traditional "feminine" goals. Recently, others have argued, given the historical trend toward greater homogeneity for gender roles and less stereotyped role socialization, that differences between males and females in other areas, including delinquency, should dissipate (Mason, Czajka, & Arber, 1976; Thornton & Freedman, 1979).

## Gender and Deviance: A Critique of the Literature

Some of the foregoing literature and articles and some chapters in the volume by Warren (1981) address the issue of male and female gender differences in deviance, delinquency, and other nonnormative behaviors without the studies having the benefit of some or all of the following characteristics: (1) a guiding theoretical perspective that allows specification of causal processes, (2) longitudinal data that would permit the proper estimation of this causal process, (3) comparison of factor structures by multiple indicators or estimates of reliability of indicators, (4) the ability to accomplish the three foregoing characteristics simultaneously and to compare males and females on these characteristics within the same model, (5) the avoidance of reliance on static comparisons of means, percentages, or proportions in order to assess gender differences, and (6) data collected over time and at different ages during a critical historical period.

Nevertheless, each of the articles did attempt to make some contribution or elaboration of the differences between males and females. For example, Figueira-McDonough et al. (1981) did attempt to compare gender similarities on the basis of a prespecified theoretical statement. Unfortunately, their causal analysis did not benefit from longitudinal data. These authors argue that comparisons between males and females with regard to delinquency ought not to be based on the relative frequency or severity of the delinquent acts but rather ought to be based on whether or not each individual subject would likely violate some conventional standard. In this sense, they argue for a dichotomous comparison between delinquents and nondelinquents as well as between males and females. In such an analysis, drawn from a 1980 survey conducted in public and parochial schools of four Midwestern communities, the researchers found that approval of subcultural deviance and participation in social activities with peers had the strongest direct effects on subcultural deviance and the magnitudes of the effects were similar for males and females. Further, in a test of the stereotypical hypotheses that female deviance is more likely to occur in response to an attenuation of ties to the subject's parents, the researchers found that parental attachment is equal for males and females. Finally, the researchers observed that the number of significant direct and indirect influences on deviance from variables in their model that include background sociodemographics, attachments to parents and school, normative orientations (both conventional and subcultural), achievement, and self-concept was greater among females than males. This led them to conclude that the effects of the variables in their causal model needed to act in greater concert in order to produce the delinquent outcome than was required among the male subgroup.

Three articles in the Warren (1981) volume address the expected differential impact and response of agents of social control based on gender differentials. The primary position for differential impact is made by those who argue the position of the "chivalry hypothesis." The chivalry hypothesis states that all individuals involved in the deviance- or delinquency-provoking process will tend to be less likely to: report deviant acts, respond to deviant acts in an official manner, to process that deviant subject once an official response to a deviant act has taken place, to punish that subject, and to punish severely if punished at all, based on the simple characteristic of female gender. Either the victims of the crime do not perceive it to be as serious if the actor is female, or the authorities are less likely to perceive the act as serious if committed by a female. In the event that the act is perceived as serious, it may seem that the female is a less appropriate target for the application of negative social sanctions.

This chivalry hypothesis is put forth by Tjaden and Tjaden (1981). Their hypothesis is based on an analysis of the differential treatment of adult female offenders from a western state in 1976. The Tjadens concluded that men are more likely to be arrested and adjudicated even when controlling on type of offense, and women are more likely to receive probation or a deferred sentence even after controlling for variables known to be associated with sentencing decisions. However, the researchers admitted that the male subjects were more likely to be put under surveillance (i.e., on parole or probation) than were their female counterparts. Thus, it seems very likely that without having controlled for the number or range of offenses among nondetected male and female deviant actors, all of the differences may be due to a prior selection factor that is directly related to the probability of increased surveillance.

In fact, in the same volume, Shelden (1981) argues that, at least when considering one form of deviant behavior (acts of immorality), the chivalry hypothesis is quite dead. With regard to immoral acts, Shelden found that women were more likely to be severely treated by officials whereas men, having committed similar acts, were more likely to be ignored. This position then really argues for differential meanings of deviant acts and for an inherent differential tolerance based on normative expectations. The differential tolerance hypothesis would suggest that females, who are expected to act morally, are sanctioned when they do act immorally. Males, who are not expected to act morally or in some cases are expected to act immorally, will not likely be sanctioned for such behaviors.

Finally, in an analysis from the same volume, Feyerherm (1981) compared the chivalry hypothesis to an alternative hypothesis, the methods hypothesis, for accounting for differences between male and female delinquency rates. The argument that Feyerherm made was that any differences between males and females would be more likely to be found in the measurement parameters of delinquency rather than in the causal or structural associations among such causal models.

In order to do this, Feyerherm conducted a series of analyses in which five specific areas of delinquency and one overall area of delinquency were compared for mean and expected deviations from the mean in males and females. These five areas of deviance or delinquency were termed, malicious delinquency, theft, serious delinquency, soft drug use, and hard drug use. In the final analysis, in which Feyerherm selected among those males and females who had reported at least one act of deviance, he found no significant differences in the expected deviation from the mean between males and females for malicious acts, serious delinquency, soft drug use, or hard drug use, or on the total overall scale. Only for theft was a marginally significant difference noted.

The analysis of covariation included a bivariate covariate of sex with police contact scores. The significance for these bivariate covariates were as reported above, thus suggesting that after controlling on methodological characteristics associated with measurement of deviance, and after controlling on at least membership in a "delinquent act group," there is no chivalry effect discernible that favors nonpolice contact for females. In effect, Feyerherm is arguing for a measurement variable model that differs across genders but for a similar or equivalent structural model between reports of deviance and greater authoritative intervention.

# Theoretical Model

In the analysis presented in Chapter 3, deviant behavior was modeled as the outcome of association with deviant peers, disposition to deviance (reflecting attitudes toward conventional and deviant adaptations), negative social sanctions by authoritative representatives of the conventional order, self-rejecting attitudes associated with failure and rejection in conventional associations, and the direct and indirect effects of earlier deviant behavior. The model was informed by a general theory of deviant behavior (Kaplan, 1972, 1975b, 1980, 1982, 1984) that incorporates propositions from a number of less inclusive theories. In this chapter, we will examine each of the major latent constructs in this model with a view toward developing an understanding of the common and gender-specific ways that deviance develops among male and female adolescents.

## *Association with Deviant Peers*

The increased association with deviant peers, a consequence of negative social sanctions, has a direct impact on the future performance of deviant behavior. Association with deviant peers: (1) facilitates the performance of deviant acts, (2) provides the person with a source of gratification (i.e., offers personal and interpersonal rewards for engaging in deviant behavior), and (3) decreases the effectiveness of personal and social control mechanisms that might inhibit the acting out of deviant dispositions (Kaplan et al., 1987). In a sense, association with deviant peers provides an atmosphere in which deviant subcultures can emerge. These subcultures may be informal and unstructured, as in the case of adolescents who associate solely to engage in a deviant act in which they have a common interest or for which they show a common preference (e.g., drinking parties, "getting high," shoplifting, weekend vandalism). For the most part, these adolescents return to their families and a normative environment following these acts of deviant behavior. The subcultures may also be very structured, long-term social groups or gangs. Once individuals enter such a group, they may become enmeshed in a range of deviant behaviors over extended periods. They may also have limited and decreasing contact with a normative environment once they enter such groups.

Some theories suggest there "is a relative absence of a deviant subculture for female delinquents, and absence of subcultural as well as cultural support for female delinquency" (Morris, 1965, p. 251). This view is based on several assumptions about adolescent female roles. Naffine (1987, p. 32) claims that this view of differential association theory concludes that the "greater uniformity and conventionality of the female is a logical outcome of a cloistered existence in which any activity not directly related to the domestic role is discouraged." Thus, this view uses the apparent evidence that there are lower rates of female delinquency to support the premise that there is no deviant subculture for women. The conclusion, therefore, is used to support the premise of the argument. But it is the premise itself that is in need of proof, and the argument is false—*petitio principii*. No evidence exists to suggest that the functions of awareness of and participation in deviant subcultures are any different for males than females. Naffine has argued, quite to the contrary, that in "fact one could well reason that, given the greater conformity of girls in general, they need a greater 'push' into delinquency, via delinquent peers, than boys" (1987, p. 35).

It is difficult to compare the findings of Figueira-McDonough et al. (1981) with the present analysis because these authors did not provide the definitions of the items in their scales. However, from a description of their scales, it appears that rough comparisons can be made to our model. For example, the involvement with peers seems to be a rough indicator of the availability of opportunities, support, instruction, and value orientation necessary to engage in deviant acts. Thus, if their scale is stable across genders (that is, it has roughly the same scale properties, something the authors did not test), then, since the effects were roughly similar for males and females, we would expect in our model that association with and knowledge of deviant peers might be roughly equally influential in the causal process leading to deviance for males and females.

### *Disposition to Deviance*

The motivation to deviate from conventional expectations increases the awareness and adoption of deviant alternatives because the deviant behavior represents a rejection of conventional patterns and allows fulfillment of personal needs through alternative mechanisms. The loss of motivation to conform and the acquisition of motivation to deviate have been conceptualized as key links in the process leading toward deviant behavior. The bias in existing theory is that this link has been implied as a missing or less relevant one for females (Naffine, 1987). For example, if nonconformity and individuality are conceptualized as desired qualities of the masculine identity, and conversely, conformity and dependence (commitment, attachment to conventional others) are conceptualized as stereotypically feminine, then the loss of motivation to conform and the acquisition of motivation to deviate provide promise as an alternative to the failure and strain associated with conventional standards for males only. Nonconformity is motivationally relevant for sex-typed masculine identities. For sex-typed feminine identities, such motivations would prove only to exacerbate the strain associated with self-rejection.

Thus, males are invested with a traditional sense of agency, the ability to respond to self-devaluing circumstances through acquired initiative and motivation. Females are not invested with such agency, lacking the ability to be motivated to respond to self-devaluing circumstances in any way except to remain passive and continue to be conformist.

However, in contradistinction to these positions, the same arguments made above with reference to deviant peers would lead to the prediction that disposition to deviance would have equivalent effects on later deviance for males and females.

## Self-Rejection

The traditional theories of structured strain or anomie (Cloward & Ohlin, 1960) have been criticized for their failure to properly account for female deviance (Leonard, 1982; Naffine, 1987). Simply stated, failure to achieve according to conventional standards provokes deviant responses. The reason critics give for the failure of strain theory to account for female deviance is that strain theory stereotypes conventional standards in terms of traditional male roles and primarily in terms of financial success. Strain theory could be revised to include frustration of gender-specific goals as causes of subsequent deviant responses. To be sure, historical trends, such as the shift of women toward achieving independent financial success, may yet partially vindicate this narrow conceptualization of structured strain. Nevertheless, currently the conceptualization does remain narrow and the assumption of universally accepted goals and values does seem unwarranted. As Lemert (1972) suggests, such a position would predict too little deviance among the upper class. The real contribution of strain theory, it seems to us, is the suggestion that frustration of conventional goals causes initial loss of motivation to conform and the concomitant motivation to begin to deviate. Thus, strain, measured in terms of results of failure such as self-rejection rather than in terms of specific, and possibly class- or gender-biased causes of strain, seems to be a more efficacious and universal reflection of the causal process allowing for effects on deviant attitudes for females as well as males.

## Early Deviance

Some suggest that there is a greater tolerance for male misbehavior and greater control of females. This argument follows the sex-typed theory of adolescent development that suggests male "misbehavior" is an expression of desired male attributes and serves to provide proof of masculinity. Thus, ironically, the behavior is socially valued and "deviant." The result is that males are less likely to be targeted for official sanctions. On the other hand, because female deviance is stereotypically role incongruent it is perceived as more reprehensible. The result is that females are more likely to be targeted for official sanctions.

Conversely, some suggest that females are less likely to be targeted for official sanctions. This position maintains that females are treated with paternalism and chivalry by legal authorities as well as by the female's victim. In addition, the lower response rate of legal authorities toward females is regarded by some as an indication of official tendencies to view females' misbehavior as illness rather than crime. But we have shown in a separate analysis that female adolescents who were aggressive or violent were not more likely than males to be treated by mental health professionals (Johnson & Kaplan, 1988). The question remains, however, as to whether or not they are less likely to be sanctioned by legal authorities.

A portion of our model deals with the causal influence that early deviance has on the reaction of school and law enforcement officials who report such deviant acts. The labeling perspective is particularly represented by inclusion of the propositions that assert relationships between negative social sanctions in response to deviant behavior and continuity or escalation of deviant behavior. The result of the negative social sanction by representatives of the conventional order, in our earlier models, was also specified to be a causative factor in later deviance. The positive causal influences of early deviance on negative social sanctions and of negative social sanctions on subsequent deviance were described in the "labeling" portion of the theoretically integrated model.

Although our data do not include acts of immorality, the differential tolerance hypothesis can be examined by looking at the obverse of this hypothesis: that is, females are not expected to violate norms of dependency and passivity, therefore aggressive acts among females will more likely be sanctioned than they will be among males. Indications for this effect may appear in two portions of the model. First, the relatively rare acts of deviant behavior that are more aggressive may not load as strongly on the deviance construct for females as they do for males if this is a less relevant behavior for female delinquency or if general deviance among females excludes the possibility that this measurement variable would have the same rate of official response. If the structural parameter for general deviance is to be stable, then the effect would be overestimated for rare deviance if rare deviance were to have a greater response rate than general deviance. Perhaps, a positive unique association may also exist between rare deviance and authoritative responses. The second possibility, given the unique effects between rare deviance and authoritative responses, may simply be the enhanced effect of official responses to the traditional general acts of deviance that, in some likelihood, may be male gender biased.

### Negative Social Sanctions

The literature on negative social sanctions and labeling effects of these sanctions as they apply to gender differentials is decidedly mixed. Negative social sanctions and social ostracism, which is secondary to stigmatization, are intrinsically disvalued. In addition, they reflect the deprivation of resources that are instrumental to the achievement of personal goals. Further, the associated deprivation of educational and employment opportunities, and of social cooperation in general (Link, 1982; Mankoff, 1971; Schwartz & Skolnick, 1962), impedes the successful approximation of other social values. The deprivations that result from social exclusion are exacerbated by the voluntary social withdrawal of the deviant actor out of a fear of rejection and other maladaptive defensive maneuvers (Link, 1987).

The individual loses motivation to conform to conventional expectations because: (1) being publicly identified and punished as a deviant is associated with the conventional order and (2) the deviant actor anticipates that stigmatization and exclusion from conventional society pose barriers to reentry and access to the resources that are instrumental to achievement. The person not only loses motivation to conform to conventional expectations, but also acquires motivation to deviate from conventional norms. Deviation represents repudiation of the standards associated with being stigmatized and deprived of future rewards.

Negative social sanctions increase association with deviant peers. The effects of negative social sanctions on increased association with deviant peers are anticipated on the basis of a number of considerations (Akers, 1985; Farrell, 1987; Kaplan, 1984). First, the stigma that is secondary to negative social sanctions limits the opportunities for the deviant actor to interact with conventional others in conventional contexts. Members of conventional groups are less willing to interact with those who are publicly identified as deviant by virtue of their being the (presumably appropriate) object of social rejection. Thus, the likelihood of association with deviant peers is increased because alternative conventional modes of interaction with conventional others are closed off due to the reluctance of conventional others to readmit the deviant actor into conventional society. As a result, the deviant actor decreases interaction in conventional spheres and, thus, increases interaction in deviant peer associations.

Second, certain social sanctions impose structural imperatives that require association with deviant peers. Most apparent is the decision to incarcerate, which involves forced interaction with deviant peers while it precludes frequent interaction with members of conventional groups. To a lesser degree, expulsion or suspension from school also constrains interaction with others to those who are the objects of similar sanctions and who also are precluded from engaging in normal social interaction.

Third, negative social sanctions and their correlates influence the deviant actor's motivation to seek out and to be receptive to deviant peer associations. Acceptance by deviant peers, adoption of deviant values, as well as the symbolic rejection of the conventional values are responses that mitigate the negative impact of such social sanctions.

Fourth, public negative sanctions identify the person to deviant peers. The publicly identified deviant actor is attractive to the deviant peers who attempt to recruit him as part of their network. The recruitment is facilitated by the accessibility of the deviant actor secondary to his exclusion from conventional society, and by the amenability of the deviant actor to overtures from deviant peers.

Negative social sanctions cause the deviant actor to positively value deviant behaviors and identities. First, the deviant actor comes to evaluate deviant behavior and identities positively in order to assuage the distressful self-feelings that are the direct or indirect consequences of negative social sanctions. The reevaluation of the self-ascribed and other-ascribed deviant identities and behavior as positively valued reduces the emotional impact of the negative social sanctions. The commitment to the deviant identity and norms redefines the deviant acts as appropriate and the conventional sanctions as inappropriate or irrelevant within the perspective of the newly adopted (deviant) value system.

Second, the person comes to value deviant patterns and identities because they reflect achievable standards. Since negative social sanctions exclude the deviant actor from conventional circles and restrict access to resources that are necessary to achieve conventionally defined goals, the deviant actor has increased difficulty in approximating conventional standards. Among the adaptive responses made by the person is the attraction to a set of deviant standards that, as a result of perceived or real increased opportunity, are more easily approximated than the conventional ones.

Third, the deviant behavior and subsequent sanctions are used to excuse the failures to conform. By continuing to behave in a deviant fashion and to evoke a labeling response, the individual can excuse himself by attributing failure to being socially stigmatized. Excusing past failures mitigates distress and thus reinforces the positive evaluation of deviant behaviors and identities.

Fourth, the deviant actor frequently comes to value deviant activities and identities because they reflect or are instrumental in the achievement of conventionally valued ends. The deviant actor may come to value deviant patterns that are instrumental to the achievement of these goals. For example, unable to achieve material rewards by legitimate means, the person uses techniques of theft or fraud to gain these ends. Further, the deviant acts themselves may reflect conventionally valued ends, as when the successful performance of deviant acts provides the person with a sense of self-efficacy or when the performance of a particularly hazardous deviant act is interpretable as reflecting another valued end such as bravery.

Having transformed the value of deviant behaviors and identities from negative to positive, the deviant actor is motivated to behave in ways that validate the deviant identities. The deviant identity is now accepted as a basis for self-evaluation. Once he comes to value the identity, he is motivated to conform to the normative expectations that he sees as defining that identity. The deviant behavior or roles in response to the sanctions are "secondary deviation" since they become "means of defense, attack, or adaptation to the overt and covert problems created by the societal reaction to the primary deviation" (Lemert, 1967, p. 17). Thus, negative social sanctions (and their correlates) influence the continuity or escalation of deviant behavior by motivating the positive evaluation of deviant behavior and identities.

The effects of reevaluation of deviant identities and behaviors are independent of the consequences of loss of motivation to conform to and acquisition of motivation to deviate from conventional norms. In the latter case, negative social sanctions (and their correlates) cause a change in attitudes toward conventional activities (withdrawal of positive affect and investment of negative affect). In the former case, negative social sanctions cause a change in attitudes toward deviant activities (increased positive affective investment).

The reevaluation of deviant activities and identities is also to be distinguished from the mediating effects of association with deviant peers. The reevaluation of the deviant role may be accomplished with or without group support. Although it is clear that deviant peer associations may provide social support for the reevaluation, it is equally clear that such reevaluative definitions may occur through internal symbolic transformations.

The argument has been made that, once sanctioned, the females are less pressured to conform to the deviant label and can more readily return to acceptable social roles. Females may be able to reject the deviant label by conventional standards rather than being forced to adopt deviant standards in order to reevaluate the deviant identity. For example, they may be able to continue to view themselves positively because they see themselves as essentially nonviolent, passive, and conforming and thus less deserving of a deviant label.

The construct of negative social sanctions is modeled as having a direct effect on disposition to deviance, deviant peer associations, and later deviance. The direct effect on disposition to deviance reflects the theoretically indicated influence of negative social sanctions on the loss of motivation to conform to, and the acquisition of motivation to deviate from, conventional expectations. The loss of motivation to conform to, and motivation to deviate from, conventional expectations result because: (1) distressful self-rejecting feelings stemming from the social sanctions are associated with the conventional order, (2) the deviant actor anticipates barriers to reentry into conventional society, and (3) the deviation from conventional standards symbolizes repudiation of the standards according to which the person has been rejected in the past and may be expected to be negatively sanctioned in the future.

The modeling of a direct effect of negative social sanctions on deviant peer associations reflects theoretical considerations that negative social sanctions: (1) constrain interacting with conventional others, (2) force interaction with deviant peers, (3) motivate the deviant actor to seek out deviant peers in an attempt to satisfy the need for self-approval, and (4) identify the person as a deviant to other deviant actors who are similarly motivated to engage in deviant peer associations. However, these theoretical constructs are not modeled in the present analysis.

The modeling of a direct effect of negative social sanctions on later deviance is predicated on the expectation that negative social sanctions lead the deviant actor to reevaluate deviant behavior and identities more positively. As an object of negative social sanctions, the deviant actor is disposed to positively value deviant behavior and identities in order to: (1) obviate self-rejecting feelings by redefining the initial deviant acts as appropriate and conventional social sanctions as inappropriate or irrelevant within the perspective of the newly adopted deviant value system, (2) provide a set of standards for self-evaluation that are more easily approximated, (3) justify continuing failure to approximate conventional standards by blaming the stigma of negative social sanctions, and (4) approximate conventional standards that are sometimes reflected in, or achieved through, deviant means. However, the mediating role of processes leading to reevaluation of deviant behavior and identities in the relationship between early deviance and later deviance is not explicitly modeled in the analysis presently under consideration.

The approach taken in the present analysis is one that will allow the estimation of causal processes that contain the conditioning effect of the gender variable. We will be estimating the same model across gender groups allowing some of the coefficients to be equal in both groups and allowing some of the coefficients to be different. The possibility that gender may condition several of these effects and the possibility that the conditioning of the effects will impact on the measurement variable portion of the model or on several processes described in the causal model suggest that the most expedient way to proceed is again to specify the general causal process based on temporal priority and assume factorial structures among the observed variables, and then to sequentially elaborate this model by a series of nested hypotheses. The following assumptions are made. First, it is assumed that a theoretical structure exists that accounts for the observed relationship among the several specified variables. This theoretical structure is derived from the general statement presented in earlier chapters. Similarly, we assume that the latent constructs of self-rejection, negative social sanctions, disposition to deviance, deviant peer associations, later deviance, and earlier deviance all exhibit the same theoretical properties and are part of the causal process that is ordered in the same way across genders based on, first, temporal priority and, second, theoretical specification.

Next, we expect to find certain unique associations among the observed variables that are independent of the causal structure between latent constructs and these unique associations will not necessarily be reflected in all of the subgroups. In effect, this expectation is based on the presumption of finding certain methodological artifacts that may (1) account for unique associations among measurement variables and (2) account for differential measurement properties of these variables conditioned by gender. The decision to model these unique associations is based on the same criteria as presented earlier: first, that the estimation of the unique effect is necessary to account for the observed relationships between two measurement variables, and second, that the estimation of the unique effect either contributes to the enhancement of the quality between measurement portions of the model, or independently, contributes to the stabilization of the structural effects across groups. Again, if the unique effect does not fulfill either of the criteria, it will be dealt with on an ad hoc basis and indications and caveats will be issued by the researcher.

The first priority will be to maintain stable measurement estimates of the model, and then estimate equivalent measurement portions of the model, testing through nested models whether or not the same variables in both male and female gender groups have the same measurement properties (i.e., have the same scale of measurement and relative reliabilities) and the same or similar pattern of measurement properties can be detected. Next, structural parameters that are theoretically expected to be zero, that appear to be zero in both groups, or that fail to reach levels of significance will be tested by trimming of the recursive model. Following this, nontheoretical parameters that appear to be zero in one group but not the other will be tested similarly by trimming from the model. Finally, the remaining structural parameters among latent constructs will be examined and those that appear to be identical will be fixed to be equal in both groups and the nested model with the associated degree of freedom will provide a test for the equivalence of the parameter that represents a specified causal process.

This method and model go significantly beyond the earlier cited research. Causal processes are estimated in a longitudinal panel design rather than in cross-sectional analysis. The hypothesized causal sequence is based on a theory-driven approach to model building. The method enjoys the inherent values and benefits of linear structural modeling that include the multiple indicator approach with the possible estimation of "true" causal effects among theoretically indicated constructs, based on assumptions of other than zero error variance, and based on the ability to estimate simultaneously both measurement and structural parameters.

## Method

### Data

The data are derived from the same panel cohort examined in the earlier models, except that the data used for estimating the causal models are derived from the input of covariance and standard deviation matrices separately for males ($N = 1115$) and females ($N = 1498$).

*Sample and Data Collection.*   The subject sample represents the same junior high students in the 36 junior high schools of the Houston Independent School District in 1971 who were examined in Chapter 3.

### Analysis

The null hypothesis is that the measurement variables have a covariance structure that is invariant across groups, indicating that they are to some extent perfectly measured variables that measure a unidimensional structure across males and females. The alternative is that with some measurement error, the measurement variables are generally considered to be indicators of a presumed underlying theoretical structure that with an associated gain in degrees of freedom and thus a more parsimonious approach to the data can be adequately represented by that theoretical model. The subsequent hypotheses are all nested in the hypotheses of invariant covariance structure. In order to test the null hypothesis, the models for each gender were estimated using correlation and standard deviation matrices of self-reported variables as input to LISREL-VI (Jöreskog & Sörbom, 1984).

This computer program provides maximum-likelihood estimates (MLE) of model parameters that are specified as "free." The estimation process is an iterating procedure that minimizes a function of the differences between observed covariance patterns and the covariances estimated by the model. The "free" parameters in the model are actually unknown values in linear equations that are used to construct the model.

Each model consists of measurement (observed) variables and latent constructs (unobserved variables). The latent constructs are theoretical variables among which there is a hypothesized causal structure. This is the latent structural equation model and the parameter estimates in these equations are presumed to represent causal effects of one theoretical construct on another. The measurement variables are those for which the observed covariance matrix is used as analytic input to the program. These variables are specified as indicators of the latent constructs and therefore are hypothesized to share a common theoretical basis. The measurement model thus provides estimates of how reliable and valid these observed variables are and, relative to their common theoretical basis, how much error is associated with each measure. The estimation of MLE models is made so that the factor loadings and error terms along with the structural parameters form equations that can be used to predict each of the observed covariations among all variables. The adequacy of this simultaneous prediction of all effects can be used as a criterion for evaluating the model. A chi-square test of the difference between observed and predicted covariances can be made for any given causal model and pattern of measurement parameters. In addition to this overall indicator, other methods for assessing the fit of individual parts of the model are also available. These will be discussed below where we evaluate the elaborated model.

The model specifies relationships among six latent constructs (self-rejection, deviance at Time 1, negative social sanctions, disposition to deviance, deviant peer associations at Time 2, and deviance at Time 3) and 14 measurement variables (multiple-item-additive scales). These are the same items that appear in the models presented in Chapter 3.

## Results

Results indicate that a model in which the variances and covariances of the 14 observed variables are assumed equal across the two gender subgroups can be rejected. This model, known as the null hypothesis, has a chi-square value of 544.57 with 105 associated degrees of freedom. The chi-square value is significant and greater than the decision criterion of a five-to-one ratio of chi-square to degrees of freedom, but only marginally. The next crucial question involves whether or not these measurement variables can be significantly and more adequately represented by a presumed underlying theoretical structure. The test of this hypothesis, Hypothesis 1 (H1), is that the measurement portion of the model is similar across both subgroups. The chi-square value for this hypothesis is 330.50 with 126 associated degrees of freedom. Thus, the delta statistic, which is distributed as a chi-square value and provides a test for significant improvement in fit based on the difference in chi-square values distributed across the difference in degrees of freedom, provides a value of 214.07 with 21 associated degrees of freedom. This is highly significant and lends a great deal of support to the assertion of similar factor structures among male and female subgroups for these 14 measurement variables. The next hypothesis, H2, is nested in H1 and assumes that the factor structure is not only similar but is equivalent in both groups. The results of this test provide a chi-square value of 391.07 distributed with 134 degrees of freedom. The delta statistic associated with this result is 60.57 with 12 degrees of freedom. Thus, there is a significant decrement in fit of the overall model when one assumes that all of the measurement parameters are equivalent in both groups. By examination of several of the criterion of goodness-of-fit statistics, including modification indices, normalized residuals, first-order derivatives, and the overall chi-square goodness of fit, it was determined that a suitable representation of the measurement model could not be attained without relaxing the assumption of equivalent measurement variable parameters for 3 of the 14 measurement coefficients. Relaxing the assumption that the measure of rare deviance (RARE1) is not equivalent at Time 1 for both males and females, that the measure of rare deviance (RARE3) at Time 3 is not equivalent for both males and females, and assuming that the measure of antisocial defenses (ASD) measured at Time 2 is not set to the same equivalent scale for both males and females as an indicator of disposition to deviance, returns an overall goodness of fit model with a chi-square of 338.84 and 131 associated degrees of freedom. This model is not significantly different from the less restricted measurement model (H1) in which merely a similar pattern of measurement variables could have been assumed. Thus, based on this delta statistic (chi-square = 8.34, 5 $df$), we can assume that the measurement parameters and properties of the remaining 11 variables are identical for both males and females. Allowing for a number of unique associations, some of which are common to both subgroups and some of which are unique to both subgroups, the model appeared to reach a plateau of stable measurement properties.

The apparent stabilization of the model with regard to the measurement parameters allows us to follow the next step in the planned sequence of analyses in which structural parameters that appear to equal zero in both groups and that were not theoretically indicated could be trimmed from the model. The structural parameters between early self-rejection and later Time 3 deviance and the structural parameter between self-rejection and subsequent negative social sanction were trimmed from the model for both males and females by setting their value equal to zero. The more parsimonious model with an associated gain of four degrees of freedom had a delta statistic of 2.01 which was nonsignificant, indicating that a significant loss in ability to account for the observed variables was not realized by theoretically trimming these effects.

The next stage of model trimming involved the specification of no effects between latent constructs for one group but not the other where they appeared to be zero. Thus, the stability of deviance represented by the structural coefficient between Time 1 deviance and Time 3 deviance was trimmed from the model for females and the structural parameter between Time 2 disposition to deviance and Time 3 deviance was trimmed from the model for females. Similarly, the structural parameter between early deviance and later disposition to deviance among females and the structural parameter between negative social sanctions and later association with deviant peer association were trimmed from the model for females. The effect of early self-rejection on later deviant peer association among males was trimmed from the model. These effects were not necessary to adequately account for the observed measurement variables and can be hypothesized as nondirect causal processes. Through these processes, a stable structural portion of the theoretical model was being achieved with, at Hypothesis 18, a chi-square value of 187.90 and 124 associated degrees of freedom. Therefore, we decided at this stage to begin assessing equivalent invariant structural processes across gender groups. It was determined, based on visual examination of the MLE of unstandardized structural parameters, that the effects of negative social sanctions on later deviance, the effect of early deviance on later negative social sanctions, and the effect of disposition to deviance on later deviant peer associations were equivalent for both males and females. The respective delta statistics for each of these hypotheses, each distributed with one degree of freedom, were 0.36, 0.25, and 3.18, all of which were nonsignificant. The next most nearly equivalent parameter across genders was the effect of negative social sanctions on later dispositions to deviance. A test of the hypothesis that these structural processes were equivalent for both males and females was rejected by the delta statistic which provided a chi-square value of 5.59 with one degree of freedom. However, the difference in magnitude was so small that we specified them as equivalent with the male value as the reference point. This specification did not appreciably affect the remaining significant differences or their effect sizes.

At this point, the model was examined for several unique effects that would serve to provide an improvement in the overall fit of the model. After specification of these unique effects a nonsignificant chi-square overall fit value was obtained equal to a chi-square of 145.91 with 121 degrees of freedom ($p=0.061$). The parameter estimates for the measurement model, correlated errors, and structural model are presented in Table 4.1.

**Table 4.1.   Parameter Estimates: Measurement Model, Correlated Errors, and Structural Model**

| | Males $n = 1115$ $\chi^2 = 78.72$, 85 $df$ $p = 0.671$ | | Females $n = 1498$ $\chi^2 = 93.96$, 85 $df$ $p = 0.237$ | |
|---|---|---|---|---|
| | U | S | U | S |
| Measurement model | | | | |
| Early deviance | | | | |
| MOST1 | 1.000 | 0.633 | 1.000 | 0.590 |
| MOD1 | 1.106 | 0.615 | 1.106 | 0.581 |
| RARE1 | 0.914 | 0.574 | 0.577 | 0.390 |
| Self-rejection | | | | |
| SDRG | 1.000 | 0.540 | 1.000 | 0.482 |
| RJTT | 0.532 | 0.700 | 0.532 | 0.679 |
| RJTP | 0.210 | 0.483 | 0.210 | 0.471 |
| Negative social sanctions | | | | |
| AUTH | 1.000 | 0.755 | 1.000 | 0.762 |
| Disposition to deviance | | | | |
| ASD | 1.000 | 0.588 | 1.000 | 0.605 |
| DSCO | 1.251 | 0.747 | 1.251 | 0.695 |
| Deviant peer associations | | | | |
| KASDEV | 1.000 | 0.490 | 1.000 | 0.498 |
| FRNDEV | 0.627 | 0.730 | 0.627 | 0.734 |
| Later deviance | | | | |
| MOST3 | 1.000 | 0.722 | 1.000 | 0.692 |
| MOD3 | 0.974 | 0.707 | 0.974 | 0.686 |
| RARE3 | 0.788 | 0.599 | 0.519 | 0.449 |
| Correlated errors | | | | |
| MOST1 with MOST3 | 0.009 | | 0.004 | |
| MOD1 with MOD2 | −0.002 | | −0.004 | |
| RARE1 with RARE3 | 0.006 | | 0.006 | |
| MOST1 with SDRG | | | 0.046 | |
| MOD1 with RARE1 | 0.017 | | 0.012 | |
| RARE1 with SDRG | −0.072 | | | |
| RARE1 with RJTP | | | 0.017 | |
| RARE1 with ASD | | | 0.040 | |
| RARE1 with FRNDEV | | | −0.017 | |
| SDRG with ASD | | | 0.248 | |
| SDRG with AUTH | −0.148 | | | |
| RJTP with SDRG | | | 0.135 | |
| RJTP with DSCO | | | 0.038 | |
| RJTT with RARE3 | | | −0.019 | |
| ASD with FRNDEV | −0.070 | | −0.076 | |
| RARE3 with ASD | 0.068 | | | |

**Table 4.1.   (Continued)**

| | Males<br>$n = 1115$<br>$\chi^2 = 78.72$, 85 $df$<br>$p = 0.671$ | | Females<br>$n = 1498$<br>$\chi^2 = 93.96$, 85 $df$<br>$p = 0.237$ | |
|---|---|---|---|---|
| | U | S | U | S |
| MOST3 with ASD | 0.034 | | | |
| FRNDEV with RARE3 | | | −0.022 | |
| MOD3 with RARE3 | | | 0.014 | |
| Structural models | | | | |
| Early deviance on: | | | | |
| Self-rejection | 3.423 | 0.627 | 4.606 | 0.725 |
| Negative social sanctions | 1.404 | 0.635 | 1.404 | 0.626 |
| Deviant peer associations | 0.463 | 0.105 | 2.515 | 0.440 |
| Later deviance | 0.318 | 0.234 | 0.000 | 0.000 |
| Self-rejection on: | | | | |
| Disposition to deviance | 0.206 | 0.371 | 0.268 | 0.480 |
| Deviant peer associations | 0.000 | 0.000 | −0.175 | −0.194 |
| Negative social sanctions on: | | | | |
| Disposition to deviance | 0.511 | 0.372 | 0.511 | 0.324 |
| Deviant peer associations | 0.398 | 0.200 | 0.364 | 0.143 |
| Later deviance | 0.112 | 0.183 | 0.112 | 0.156 |
| Disposition to deviance on: | | | | |
| Deviant peer associations | 0.824 | 0.569 | 0.824 | 0.511 |
| Deviant peer associations on: | | | | |
| Later deviance | 0.118 | 0.382 | 0.184 | 0.654 |

### *Measurement Model*

*Early Deviance.*    The measurement model of early deviance is characterized by the scale of the measurement variable most prevalent deviant behavior (MOST1). The scale is fixed to this measurement variable for both males and females thus providing a common measurement basis for the latent construct. As noted earlier, the measurement variable of rare (RARE1) deviance is not equivalent for both males and females, but the measurement variable of moderate deviance (MOD1) is equivalent for both males and females. The indicator of rare deviance on the general deviant construct is, as compared with the scale of prevalent deviance, significantly larger for males (0.914) than for females (0.577). This is in part due to a greater number of unique associations of rare deviance with other measurement variables in the model for females, and is in part due to the lesser degree of relevance of this variable for female deviance. That is, a greater portion of the variance in this measurement variable is attributable to "error" for the females than is attributable to "error" for the males.

*Self-Rejection.* The scale for the latent construct of self-rejection is fixed to the measurement variable of self-derogation (SDRG) for both males and females and is equivalent for both groups. In fact, considering the other two measurement variables of this latent construct it can be declared invariant for both males and females (see Hoelter, 1983, pp. 834–846).

*Negative Social Sanctions.* The scale for the latent construct of negative social sanctions is fixed according to the researcher-determined values for the three-item index of self-reports of formal sanctions from representatives of the conventional order including school officials and law enforcement officials (AUTH). The scale is declared invariant across the two gender groups but the relative reliability of the scale for males and females is determined by estimates of viability based on three measurement periods. The reliability for males is fixed to the value of 0.821; the reliability for females is fixed to the value of 0.746. Under the assumption of differential reliability of the variable for males and females, the scaling properties can be assumed to be invariant across gender.

*Disposition to Deviance.* The measurement properties of this latent construct were assumed to scale to the value of antisocial defenses (ASD). This assumption that this scale property was equivalent for both males and females proved untenable. Once the assumption was relaxed, however, it became apparent that the relative contribution of the other measurement variable, disaffection with conventional order (DSCO), could be declared invariant across groups. The relative contribution of antisocial defenses to this latent construct is greater for males than females. The difference appears to be solely attributable to a lack of relevance of the antisocial defenses for the latent construct of disposition to deviance among females, since the relatively smaller loading is due almost entirely to greater error variance among this variable. In fact, the contribution of unique associations to the differences in this measurement variable across groups is practically nil since the number of unique associations is greater among males than among females. Thus, although earlier, rare deviance variables for the early deviance construct was less relevant for females because of increased number unique associations, the same conclusion is not apparent for this latent construct.

*Deviant Peer Associations.* The scale of the construct deviant peer associations is fixed and equal across gender to the measurement variable of awareness of deviant behavior among school peers (KASDEV). It is also invariant across gender for both of the measurement variables. This is important for the subsequent conclusions to be drawn from the model, since any differences in structural parameters as a result of the causal influence of this variable cannot be attributed to differential measurement properties.

*Later Deviance.* The construct of later deviance, fixed to the measurement variable of most prevalent deviance (MOST3), has the same scale of measurement for both males and females. In addition, the relative contribution of moderate deviance (MOD3) is invariant across gender. However, as with early deviance, the relative contribution of rare deviance (RARE3) is greater for males than for females (0.788 versus 0.519). The relatively larger loading of this variable on the latent construct of deviance is in part due to a greater reliability of measurement property (i.e., a smaller proportion of "error") for males than for females and also due to a lesser contribution of unique associations to the other measurement variables.

### Correlated Errors

Among the 91 covariances, and independent of the three autocorrelated error terms between repeated measures in the model, there were 12 significant unique associations among measurement variables for females and 6 unique measurement variable associations among males. Two of these unique associations are present in both male and female subgroups. A positive unique correlated error term between Time 1 rare (RARE1) and Time 1 moderate (MOD1) deviance is present for both male and female genders. They are also of roughly the same unstandardized magnitude. In addition, and also of roughly the same unstandardized magnitude, there is a unique negative association between antisocial defenses (ASD) and association with deviant friends (FRNDEV). This effect occurs for both gender groups and is roughly of the same magnitude in each group. Further, this effect is carried through from the general model. The effect represents a correction to the overestimation of the relationship between these two measurement variables by the structural parameter between dispositions to deviance and deviant peer associations. The effect probably represents the continuation or modification of more primitive regressive defense mechanisms' influence on the motivation to seek out or participate in a friendship network of any kind. None of the other correlated error terms are consistent across both gender groups. Therefore, we will discuss them separately by gender.

For the female subjects, the structural parameter between early deviance and self-rejection is not sufficient to account for the observed relationship between the measurement variable of prevalent deviance (MOST1) and the self-derogation scale (SDRG). The significant unique association between these two measurement variables is positive. In addition, as noted earlier, the rare deviant behavior scale (RARE1) has several unique associations; among them are a positive unique association with felt rejection by parents, a positive association with antisocial defenses (ASD), and a negative association with belonging to a deviant friendship network (FRNDEV). These effects may represent a recognition of the potential for disapproval of these relatively more severe, aggressive, and/or violent acts of deviant behavior on the part of the young female adolescents. It also recognizes a consistency between the type of deviant behavior (more severe, more aggressive) and the particular mode of adaptation represented by the more regressive and antisocial defense mechanisms. Further, the fact that the relatively more rare forms of deviance are positively associated with the antisocial defenses (ASD) and negatively associated with belonging to a deviant peer friendship network remains consistent throughout the model.

In addition, the self-derogation scale that is an indicator of self-rejection has two unique associations with other measurement variables in the model. There is a unique association between self-derogation (SDRG) and felt rejection by parents (RJTP), and a unique association between self-derogation and antisocial defenses (ASD). Both of these relations are positive.

The unique association between measurement variables that are indicators of the same latent construct occurs three times among the females. In this case, as in the other two cases, it probably represents a common dependence on an unspecified causal source. It is possible that the unspecified common causal source could be the stereotypical gender role socialization hypothesis that female adolescents are more sensitive to or socialized to be more sensitive to the need for approval of, and maintenance of bonds with parents than are males. Thus, this differential socialization emphasis may create a slightly greater degree of covariation among these two measurement variables than would be expected in terms of their contribution to the underlying latent construct of global self-rejection.

The unique association between self-derogation (SDRG) and antisocial defenses (ASD) is consistent with the notion that female adolescents, as a result of their differential socialization, tend to internalize their distressful self-feelings whereas male adolescents tend to externalize by acting out their distressful feelings. The suggestion has been that this is a behavioral phenomenon, but the positive unique associations between self-derogation and antisocial defenses in this example suggest that the phenomenon may be motivationally relevant as well as behaviorally observed. That is, the particular measurement variable for this latent construct represents a motivation to utilize more regressive defense mechanisms, to some extent internalizing responses to distressful situations, whereas the other measurement variable of disaffection with the conventional order (DSCO) represents a greater tendency to externalize blame. However, the unique association between perceived rejection by parents (RJTP) and disaffection with the conventional order suggests that parental rejection is a major source of alienation for females.

Perceived rejection by teachers (RJTT) has a unique negative association with later rare forms of deviant behavior (RARE3). This may be because female adolescents are less likely to violate norms within the school environment and are less likely therefore to elicit rejecting responses from teachers, decreasing the relevance of this measurement variable for later acts of deviance. It may also represent a tendency for females to be source specific in their reaction to perceived rejection. That is, the more prevalent and most prevalent deviance scales tend to be weighted more heavily to acts of deviant behavior committed in the school environment, and thus perceived rejection by teachers would elicit those responses. On the other hand, the more rare forms of deviant behavior, less weighted toward the school environment, would be less likely to be elicited by such felt rejection.

In addition to the foregoing, association within a deviant peer friendship network has a unique negative association with later rare deviance. Finally, a unique positive association is observed between rare forms of deviant behavior and moderate forms of deviant behavior at Time 3 for females.

Among the males, there are four additional unique associations not discussed earlier. Early relatively rare forms of deviant behavior (RARE1) have a unique negative association with the self-derogation scale (SDRG). This unique negative effect represents a correction to the overestimation of the association between these two measurement variables by the structural parameter between early deviance and self-rejection. In addition, there is a unique negative association between self-derogation and the measurement variable indicating negative social sanctions. This effect had been noticed earlier in the general model, although it appears to be solely a male phenomenon. We speculated at that time that it represented a lack of self-confidence and ego strength that would tend to reduce the visibility of these self-derogating male adolescents, and also reflected a countervailing effect of self-derogation that may perversely increase motivation to conform, thus decreasing likelihood of contact with school or law enforcement officials.

Finally, antisocial defenses (ASD) has two positive unique associations with later measurement variables: the most prevalent forms of deviant behavior (MOST3) and the rare forms of deviant behavior (RARE3). These unique associations may represent a greater degree of concordance between motivationally relevant attitudes and behavioral outcomes present in these two scales.

### Structural Parameters

In a fully recursive model of six latent constructs there is a possibility of 15 structural parameters. Of these 15 structural parameters, 8 are invariant across gender: 4 are structurally equivalent to zero and 4 are nonzero structurally equivalent parameters. Of the remaining 7 parameters, 3 are roughly of the same magnitude even though they are significantly different, representing moderation of the effect in one versus the other group. Two more are of the same sign although they are both significantly and substantively greater in their effect among the female gender group (the structural parameter between early deviance and self-rejection, and the effect between early deviance and deviant peer associations). And finally, 2 of the structural parameters are significantly different, 1 being nonzero in one

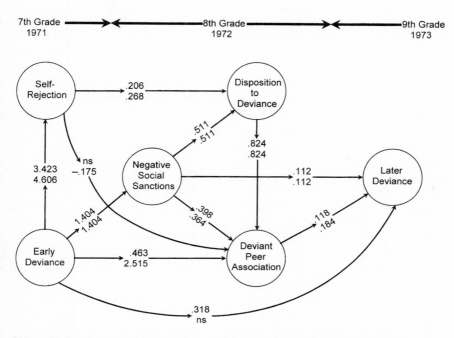

**Figure 4.1.** Multigroup analyses of adolescent deviance: males (above) and females (below).

gender group and zero in the other. These two effects are the stability of deviance across this 3-year period where the stability coefficient is zero for the female gender and a nonzero positive effect for the male gender, and the effect between self-rejection and later deviant peer associations, where the parameter is zero for the male gender and negative nonzero for the female gender. The unstandardized coefficients for both males and females are reported in Figure 4.1.

## Discussion

The process of comparison of the differential processes leading to deviant behavior among males and females reveals more similarities than dissimilarities across genders. The comparison tended to disconfirm nearly all of the previously hypothesized gender-specific causal processes. Where there were differences between the genders, the structural parameters involved were causal processes not heretofore suggested as being gender related. For example, the chivalry hypothesis, which suggests that females are less likely to have contact with authorities, was disconfirmed both in terms of its cause and effect in this model. The structural parameter between early deviance and responses by authorities was positive, significant, and invariant across both gender groups. This effect is consistent with the finding of Feyerherm (1981) and others suggesting that once measurement properties of the deviance scales are controlled, the underlying causal processes of the relations between deviant behavior and contact with authorities are the same for males and females.

In addition, the consequences of contact with authorities as a consequence of deviance (the structural effect of negative social sanctions on later deviance) are identical across gender groups. Although the consequences of intervention usually are examined with regard to the judicial system, in particular the sentencing and disposition of cases, in this model we are examining the consequences of the labeling effects of such responses. The labeling effects appear to be invariant with regard to the direct effect on later deviance. Thus, it appears that female adolescents are not more vulnerable to the forces of conventional social control, that they are not more susceptible to the labeling or stigmatizing effect of contact with authorities, and that they do not have relatively less social power to be able to resist the labeling effects of such contacts. And conversely, females were not able to more readily dismiss the effects of labeling and either resume a more conventional role orientation or avoid further deviance.

Early deviance by females is more likely to lead to the self-attribution of having a spoiled or deviant identity than it is for males, and early deviance by females is more likely to lead to the attribution by peers of being deviant and so make them more likely to be objects of recruitment in deviant peer associations. This is what would be expected if "deviance" reflected inappropriate behavior for females to a greater extent than similar behaviors reflected inappropriate behavior for males.

Among the implications of these findings is that the deviant reputations and the deviant self-attributions of female deviants are the result of peer group definitions rather than definitions by authority figures. Note that engaging in early deviance is no more or less likely to evoke negative social sanctions by school personnel and authorities for males than for females. For adults, any deviant behavior regardless of gender is likely to evoke negative social sanctions (this is assuming that the levels of gender-specific behaviors that evoke negative social sanctions are comparable).

The coefficient between self-rejection and later dispositions to deviance is significantly larger for females than for males, although they are of the same sign and roughly of the same substantive magnitude in this model. We suspect that the significantly greater effect of earlier self-rejection on later disposition to deviance for females may be accounted for by the greater investment of females in the virtues of conformity. To the extent that females play by the rules, that is, conform to the expectations of parents and teachers, they would be expected to have benign experiences and develop self-accepting attitudes. To the extent that they are not able to develop self-accepting attitudes due to the failure to evoke positive responses from teachers and parents, they become disproportionately (because of their greater investment) disappointed and lose motivation to conform to conventional expectations and become motivated to deviate from those expectations. Males are less emotionally invested in conforming to expectations of parents and school personnel; and when they do disappoint the expectations of these others, they have more structured conventional alternatives through which they can maintain their self-esteem in the face of experiences of rejection and failure in the eyes of school personnel and parents. Such alternatives may include opportunities to achieve in terms of peer-related activities or the development of personal skills.

Most interesting, in terms of the role that the frustration of the self-esteem motive plays in the motivation to behave deviantly, is the negative countervailing effect of self-rejection on later deviant peer associations. This negative countervailing effect appeared in the general model and is present among the female gender subgroup. It is absent for male adolescents. We suspect that this negative direct structural effect represents two influences of early self-rejection: (1) the greater internalization of standards that prohibit acting out dispositions to deviate on the part of females and (2) the lesser availability of deviant peer networks for females as opposed to males. That is, the opportunity structure for deviance is not as available to female adolescents. This latter suggestion, however, does not gainsay the importance of a deviant peer network for the provision of opportunities, support, and socialization into deviant behavior-producing environments. In fact, as the model indicates, the availability of a deviant peer network and awareness of opportunities presented by these deviant peers is significantly a greater or more influential process on the production of later deviant behavior among females than it is among males. This latter effect, in large part, accounts for the ability of the model to completely decompose the stability of deviance over time, fully accounting for both the initiation and the continuation of deviant behavior among females, whereas the model is less able to fully account for the continuation of deviant behavior among males.

The somewhat larger effect of negative social sanctions on association with deviant peers for males rather than females may be accounted for by the fact that deviant adolescents select their associates according to their reputation. Among deviant male adolescents, reputation is more likely to be built on being the object of punitive responses by authorities. Hence, males who are the object of negative social sanctions build a reputation on that fact and become more attractive to deviant peers. For females, reputation as being the object of negative social sanctions is less relevant in making one attractive to deviant peers.

The differential effects of deviant peer associations on later deviance suggest that the acceptance of deviant peers as a positive reference group has a stronger and more lasting effect for females than for males. Females who associate with deviant peers are more likely to fall under interpersonal influence (perhaps out of a greater need to affiliate) than males. Further, females are more effective in adapting to the interpersonal expectations of their peers. They have been taught techniques of how to get along.

# 5

## Multigroup Analysis of the General Theory of Deviant Behavior
### *Three-Wave Panel Analysis by Race*

### Race/Ethnicity and Deviance: A Critique of the Literature

Several good theoretical rationales could be offered that suggest moderating effects of race/ethnicity on the parameter estimates in the model. This is the case for both the measurement and structural equation portions of the previously estimated model. For example, Matsueda and Heimer (1987) suggest that when considering control theory it is possible that neighborhood delinquency will produce more delinquency among African-Americans by inhibiting strong formation of conventional attachments and beliefs. To this extent, informal social control would not provide the same inhibiting effects for African-Americans as for white-Anglos. Others have also argued that white-Anglos are more vulnerable to informal sanctions and that African-Americans would be more vulnerable to formal sanctions when considering theories of social control (Tittle, 1980). Similarly, Matsueda and Heimer (1987) have argued that conditioning effects of race may be apparent in considering differential association theories such that determinants of deviant definitions may vary by race. But they maintain this theory would predict that the determinant of deviant behavior by those definitions will not vary by race. Thus, they argue for both conditioning effects by race as well as expected invariance by race. Presumably the determinants of deviant definitions that vary by race are the social structural parameters that determine the experience of racial minorities within the social structure, and within certain social institutions including the family and school, but that once these factors have defined the normative and contranormative environmental definitions, the extent of the definitions that are favorable, in terms of motivating factors, will influence the onset of delinquency equally in both groups.

There has also been a long and varied research agenda designed to detect racial differences across a wide range of deviance-relevant theories. Two early considerations of the labeling perspective suggest that there may be differential patterns of social responses to deviant behavior depending on the characteristics of the deviant. For example, Hollander (1958) presented the notion that an individual has "idiosyncratic credit" that determines the amount of nonconforming behavior that is allowed before formal sanctions are applied. The credit is earned by conforming to the normative structure over a period of time and may differ for each person based on social factors that may include race. One such hypothesis may include a notion that racial minorities have less idiosyncratic credit and therefore will more likely receive social sanctions based on the same level of nonconforming behavior.

Another example of the differential response rate of formal sanctions to deviant behavior and the role this plays in the labeling process, was presented by Edwin Lemert (1951). He suggested that formal social sanctions are applied to individuals and vary according to a formula that produces a "tolerance quotient." The tolerance quotient is determined by the nature of the deviant act and the nature of the social group, in which the act was performed. A decreased tolerance would be expected under conditions that the individual was violating norms of social groups of which he was not a member or perceived to have differential membership status (such as minority status) and under conditions in which the offense was perceived as more or less serious.

Finally, theoretical models that include the specification of the role of self-referent behavioral responses, including the theoretical model presented in the present context, might be expected to vary by race based on earlier studies that consider racial differences including the following findings: African-Americans tend to be more external than white-Anglos in terms of locus of control (Lefcourt, 1972; Phares, 1976) and African-Americans tend to have a lower need to achieve based on lowered self-esteem (McClelland, 1960; Veroff & Peele, 1969). These combined findings have led to speculation that the lower need to achieve and the external locus of control among African-Americans influence a sense of fatalism and passive acceptance of the social environment, and that they lead to less active attempts to master or change that environment, which leads to blaming others or the environment for their own behavior.

The foregoing studies and conclusions are based on several questionable conceptual and methodological decisions that do not allow an unconditional acceptance of their findings. First, many of these studies have been performed over a wide range of historical periods that have included dramatic changes in the way that several minorities have been perceived in this society. Second, all of the aforementioned studies were cross-sectional in nature thus permitting only static comparisons across groups. Often, static comparisons can show differences between groups (such as differences in the mean) whereas process-oriented methodologies indicate that relations between theoretical concepts are substantially identical. And even in situations where the relations among the theoretical constructs are examined rather than the static differences, the findings that there are process-related differences or even process-related equalities may be hampered by the nature or specification of the process. For example, if the relationship between two theoretical constructs is specified based on the constraints inherent in cross-sectional design, the invariance between groups may be due to the methodological artifact of the cross-sectional nature of the design. A good case in point is the specifications of the effect between the theoretical construct of definitions favorable to deviance and peer attachments in the analysis presented by Matsueda and Heimer (1987). As Matsueda himself noted earlier (1982, p. 500), if the causal direction of the effects in the analysis were reversed so that definitions favorable to deviance had a direct effect on peer influence, then the later variable would have the direct effect on delinquency rather than the earlier variable. It is also equally likely in this cross-sectional design that although this change in causal direction of the effects between these two constructs would favor one over the other's influence on later delinquency, the nature of the effect between the two constructs would be substantially indistinguishable. If one is not readily able to distinguish the difference between two models based on different causal models specified, it remains equally evident that it is difficult to detect differences in the process between the groups.

The solutions to all of these problems include the estimation of causal models in which the processes among variables are compared across groups (such as racial minorities) and the models span wider periods of time, neither of which solutions is available in cross-sectional designs. The approach taken in the present analysis is one that will allow the estimation of causal processes models that contain the multiple conditioning effects of group variables such as race. In effect, we will be estimating the same model across groups allowing some of the coefficients to be equal in both groups and allowing some of the coefficients to be different. The possibility that race may condition several of these effects and the possibility that the conditioning of the effects will affect several processes described in the model suggest that the most expedient way to proceed is to specify a general causal process based on temporal priority and assumed factorial structures among observed variables, and then to sequentially elaborate this model by a series of nested hypotheses.

In order to guide this process several assumptions need to be made. First, it is assumed that a theoretical structure exists that can account for the observed relationship among several variables. This theoretical structure is derived from the model presented in earlier chapters of this volume. In effect, we are specifying that early deviance is a latent construct measured by the same three observed variables and that this construct has validity for all racial groups. Similarly, we assume that the latent constructs of self-rejection, negative social sanctions, dispositions to deviance, deviant peer associations, and later deviance all exhibit the same theoretical properties and are part of a causal process that is ordered in the same way across all three groups based on, first, temporal priority and, second, theoretical specification.

The estimation of the theoretical model predicting to ninth-grade deviance for males and females required that we time order some latent variables when the measurement indicators were collected at the same point in time. We justified the time ordering on the grounds that the items reflecting negative social sanctions referred to a point in time earlier than the point at which the data were collected. However, we assume that the items reflecting disposition to deviance and deviant peer association refer to contemporary states.

Next, the assumption is made that there are certain unique associations among the observed variables that are independent of the causal structure between latent constructs and that these unique associations will not necessarily be reflected in all of the subgroups. The decision to model these unique associations is based on two criteria: first, that the estimation of the unique effect is necessary to account for the observed relations between the two measurement variables, and second, that the estimation of the unique effect either contributes to the enhancement of equality between the measurement portions of the model or independently contributes to the stabilization of the structural parameter effects across groups. If only the first criterion is operative, and the second criterion is not met, then it is likely that the unique association actually represents differential causal processes that are occurring in the subgroup or represents a differential theoretical construct that is not equally valid for all subgroups in the model. If such a situation arises, it will be dealt with on an ad hoc basis, and indications and caveats will be issued by the researcher.

Once we are satisfied that we have a stable measurement portion of the model and that the unique associations among variables can be adequately accounted for, we will proceed to an examination of the structural model. The criterion to test invariance across the structural portion of the model proceeded in a hierarchical fashion. First, all structural parameters that are presumed to be zero, appear to be zero, or are zero in all three groups will be trimmed from the recursive model. Next, structural parameters that appear to be zero in one or more groups but that do not appear to be zero in one or more of the other groups will be trimmed from the model. The impact of this specification will be examined to determine whether or not it serves to equilibrate other structural parameters in the model or whether it serves to disturb the previously estimated measurement model. If certain unique portions of the measurement model can be freed to provide the structural invariance across models, an attempt will be made to do so.

Finally, the model will be examined for structural invariance across groups. In these instances, unstandardized likelihood estimates of the structural parameters will be compared, and those that appear to be of roughly the same magnitude will be set equal across groups. If the assumption that the parameters are equal in groups does not provide a significant increase in the overall fit of the model to the observed covariance structure it will be assumed that the causal processes represented by these parameters influence pari passu the respective consequences of the causal construct.

This model goes beyond the earlier cited research to the extent that: (1) it estimates causal processes over longer periods of time that are represented by cross-sectional analyses, (2) it has the ability to appropriately specify the proper causal sequence of the theoretical constructs, (3) it is able to consider other than static relationships, and (4) it has the inherent benefits of linear latent structural models with multiple indicators (possible estimation of true causal effects among theoretically indicated constructs measured by multiple indicators based on assumptions other than zero error variances). Of course, an additional advantage of the overall model is comparison across three racial groups (white-Anglo, African-American, and Mexican-American).

## Method

The data are derived from the same panel cohort examined in the earlier models, except that the data used for estimating the causal models are derived from the input of covariance matrices separately for white-Anglos ($N = 1531$), African-Americans ($N = 760$), and Mexican-Americans ($N = 251$). The first step in the process is to determine whether or not these covariance matrices are equivalent for all three groups. In the likely event that they are not equivalent, we will then proceed to the assumption that a theoretical model that assumes roughly the same pattern of relationship among these constructs will provide a significant improvement in the ability of the model to account for the observed relationships. Once this is confirmed, and we are satisfied that the theoretical model is a model of the proper scope, we will proceed with the steps to determine measurement and structural invariance across groups. First, a theoretical model of the proper scope should have suitable measurement and estimation processes for the population as a whole. If one does not have a theoretical model that seems relevant for the causal processes among the specified constructs, it is not readily apparent that consideration of subgroup or racial differences would solve this problem. Second, the model should not only provide a significant increment in fit as compared with the model in which covariance invariance is assumed across all groups, but the fit of the theoretical model should be in a range that would suggest that the researcher is making appropriate steps toward improvement. Thus, initial estimation of these models that have the same theoretical patterns across groups should approximate the standard of fit for the entire sample. If they provide a significant increase in fit but do not approximate this standard, it is again likely that there are several problems in the model that would not likely be solved by subgroup estimation methods. The researcher should make a determination at this point whether or not it seems beneficial to proceed with this method or to abandon the theoretical model in favor of an alternative specification.

# Results

The final model was derived in the following stages. The results indicated that a model in which the variances and covariances of 14 observed variables are assumed equal in the three subgroups (white-Anglo, African-American, and Mexican-American), could be rejected. This model, known as the null hypothesis, has a chi-square value of 1932 and 210 associated degrees of freedom. The probability value is highly significant suggesting that an assumption of equivalence is inappropriate for these variables. The next hypothesis nested in the null hypothesis is that there is a similar factor structure among these 14 variables across the three groups. It is assumed that the lambda-$y$ matrix in the LISREL model that represents the factor loadings is roughly of the same magnitude in all three groups and has the same pattern that identifies the theoretical constructs in all three groups. This hypothesis provides a chi-square goodness-of-fit statistic of 356 with 180 degrees of freedom. It provides a model that is roughly of an acceptable magnitude and order according to the Wheaton et al. (1977) criterion.

The next assumption to be tested is that the factor loadings in all three groups are equivalent. This hypothesis provides a chi-square goodness-of-fit statistic equal to 397 with 196 degrees of freedom. The previous hypothesis is nested in this hypothesis and thus a difference in chi-square parameter can be estimated that is distributed as a chi-square statistic with the degrees of freedom equal to the difference in the degrees of freedom of the two models. The delta statistic as it is called (Bentler & Bonett, 1980) provides a chi-square value of 41 with 16 degrees of freedom. This is a significant decrement in the fit of the model and therefore it is highly likely that one or more of the measurement parameters across the three groups are not equal.

Several indicators of lack of fit (including the normalized residuals, first-order derivatives, and modification indices) are examined to determine which parameters do not provide an invariant valid indicator across the three groups. Based on an examination of these values, it was hypothesized that the indicator of the theoretical construct self-rejection in Group 1 (white-Anglos) was not equal to its value in Group 2 (African-Americans). This indicator was the "felt rejection by parents" (RJTP). By relaxing the assumption that these factor loadings are equivalent for both African-Americans and white-Anglos, the model achieves an increase in goodness of fit with a chi-square value of 11 distributed over one degree of freedom. This is a highly significant increase in the overall fit of the model to the data. The loading of rejection by parents is substantially higher on the construct of self-rejection for African-Americans than it is for either Mexican-Americans or white-Anglos.

Several other adjustments of the model were made subsequently, including the relaxation of the assumption that the factor loadings for moderate deviance (MOD1) were equivalent in both the white-Anglo and Mexican-American groups and the assumption that rare deviance loadings were equivalent in both the white-Anglo and Mexican-American groups. In addition, it appeared as if a unique association existed among the two measurement variables of antisocial defenses (ASD) and association with deviant peers in a friendship structure (FRNDEV).

The results of relaxing these assumptions all provided substantial increases in the overall fit of the model. In particular, the relaxation of the assumption that there were only structural relationships between the measurement variables of antisocial defenses (ASD) and having deviant friends (FRNDEV) provided a significant improvement in the fit. This later unique effect was apparent and significant only for the white-Anglo subgroup, however. It indicates that the required motivation to deviate from conventional standards indicated by disposition to deviance overestimates the influence on awareness of and affiliation with deviant peer associations, unless a significant negative unique effect is allowed between the two measurement parameters.

Two other unique associations among measurement variables appeared to exist among the white-Anglo subgroup that did not exist for either the African-American or Mexican-American groups: (1) unique association between responses from conventional authorities, the indicator of negative social sanctions, and the measure of self-derogation and (2) the unique association between disaffection with the conventional order (DSCO) and felt rejection by parents (RJTP). The estimation of the unique effects between these two pairs of measurement variables only for white-Anglos provided a significant increase in the overall fit of the model. The model now has a chi-square value of 289 with 190 degrees of freedom. The model was reestimated at this point with researcher-determined estimates of reliability for the single measurement variable of attention of the authorities. Since a unique association between this measurement variable and another measurement variable was detected, it became necessary to estimate separately the error variance involved in the unique association and the reliable portion of the variance in this variable, previously set to zero. In the reestimated model, the error variance for this variable is assumed to be 0.157 among the white-Anglo subgroup, 0.236 among the African-American subgroup, and 0.223 among the Mexican-American subgroup. These error variance estimates represent respectively 32.3, 52.9, and 43.4% of the total variance.

The next series of three hypotheses indicated that the measurement parameters for African-Americans and white-Anglos were not equivalent for three measurement variable loadings on their constructs: awareness of deviant behavior among school peers (KASDEV) on the latent construct of deviant peer associations; rare deviance on Time 3 construct; and moderate deviance on Time 3 construct of deviance. Only the first of these three hypotheses was supported.

Four additional unique associations among the white-Anglo group were indicated, one among the African-American group, and an additional four among the Mexican-American group. These unique associations included for the first group: a unique association between antisocial defenses (ASD) and Time 1 prevalent deviance (MOST), disaffection with the conventional order (DSCO) and affiliation with deviant friends (FRNDEV), Time 3 rare deviance (RARE3) and Time 2 antisocial defenses (ASD), and Time 3 rare deviance (RARE3) and affiliation with deviant friends (FRNDEV); among African-Americans there appears to be an additional unique association between Time 3 moderate deviance (MOD3) and the single indicator of negative social sanctions; and among Mexican-Americans unique associations between antisocial defenses (ASD) and felt rejection by parents (RJTP), disaffection with the conventional order (DSCO) and Time 1 prevalent deviance (MOST1), Time 3 rare deviance (RARE3) and Time 1 moderate deviance (MOD1), and Time 3 rare deviance (RARE3) and Time 2 antisocial defenses (ASD).

All nine of these unique associations were determined to be significant and also to provide a significant increase in the goodness of fit of the model to the data. The model under consideration at this point, with a chi-square value of 200.6 and 179 associated degrees of freedom, provides an adequate fit to the data with a probability level equal to 0.129. Thus, once we achieved a stable measurement portion of the model under the assumption of several invariant factor loadings across subgroups with several other unique associations, we could make some decisions regarding the structural parameters.

The next hypothesis was the first hypothesis to address structural invariance across all three groups. It remained apparent throughout the previous hypothesis that the effect of early self-derogation on later negative social sanctions was negligible. In fact, the hypothesis that this structural parameter was equal to zero across all three groups was supported.

The next series of hypotheses also represented a lack of a structural effect of self-rejection on later deviant peer associations. The series of hypotheses that sequentially set this structural parameter equal to zero in all three groups is represented by Hypotheses 13 through 15. None of the three hypotheses that posited these structural parameters to be equal to zero were rejected.

At this time it was determined that two of the three subgroups were sufficiently similar in MLE of the unstandardized parameters in the structural models to allow the hypothesis that two structural parameters were invariant across the two subgroups only. The parameters were apparently equal to zero in both subgroups, and were thus trimmed from the model. These parameters include the stability coefficient between Time 1 and Time 3 deviance and the effect of self-derogation on Time 3 deviance for African-American and Mexican-American subgroups.

The stability coefficient among the white-Anglo group and the negative countervailing effect of self-rejection on later deviance remained freely estimated among the white-Anglo subgroup. The specification of these two parameters being equal to zero provided support for the hypothesis. Additionally, a third parameter was apparently zero in the African-American and Mexican-American subgroups. The hypothesis that the effect of negative social sanctions on association with deviant peers was zero was not rejected.

The structural parameter of the effect of disposition to deviance on later deviance was trimmed from the model for the African-American group and the structural parameters for the effects of Time 1 deviance on later deviant peer association were trimmed from the model and set equal to each other among the white-Anglo and Mexican-American groups. The hypotheses that supported these specifications were not rejected.

At this time, the model represented by the sequential nesting hypothesis 20 provides a goodness-of-fit statistic equal to 217.88 with 194 degrees of freedom and has an associated probability level of 0.115. Thus, the trimming of structural effects from the model still allows the adequate representation of observed covariances in the data. However, the model trimming did necessitate a specification of a unique association between awareness of deviant kids in the school environment (KASDEV) and felt rejection from parents (RJTP) among the African-American subgroup.

An examination of the structural parameters allowed us finally to make the decision to set some nonzero structural parameters equivalent across subgroups. The effect of early deviance on later negative social sanctions and the effect of negative social sanctions on subsequent later deviance were set to be structurally invariant across the subgroups of minorities (African-Americans and Mexican-Americans). Neither hypothesis was rejected.

Surprisingly, a theoretically indicated structural effect, the effect of deviant peer associations on later deviance, did not appear to be significant among the Mexican-American subgroup. The need for this structural parameter was tested by the hypothesis that it was equal to zero. We were unable to reject this hypothesis; therefore, in this instance a theoretically indicated structural parameter was trimmed from the model. This trimming was performed because neither differences in measurement parameters nor any specific unique associations among measurement variables appeared to be affecting this relationship. It did not appear that either the specification of possibly negative unique associations across measurement variables indicating these theoretical constructs (for example, FRNDEV with RARE3) nor the deletion of positive unique associations across measurement variables would seem to affect the decision that this parameter was indeed zero. It is set equal to zero in the model. This finding has important theoretical implications that will be addressed in the discussion section.

It appeared at this point that a measurement parameter for felt rejection by teachers (RJTT) on self-rejection was not equivalent across all three groups. The

Mexican-American subgroup parameter estimate was declared free so as to not be equal to the values for African-American and white-Anglo subgroups. This hypothesis was not rejected.

In addition, four other unique associations were considered between association with deviant friends (FRNDEV) and prevalent deviance at Time 1 (MOST1), between antisocial defenses at Time 2 (ASD) and Time 1 rare deviance (RARE1), between disaffection with conventional order (DSCO) and prevalent deviance at Time 1 (MOST1), and between moderate Time 3 deviance (MOD3) and disaffection with conventional order (DSCO). The freeing of the first of these unique associations among the white-Anglo subgroup and the last three of these unique associations among the African-American subgroup provided a substantial increase in the fit of the data to the model.

The final model was estimated when it became apparent that the effect of negative social sanctions on disposition to deviance was zero among the African-American group. Several alternative specifications of this model were examined. However, it was apparent that the enhancement of dispositions to deviance (loss of motivation to conform and acquisition of motivation to deviate) in response to negative social sanctions, was unique to white-Anglo and Mexican-American ethnic groups. The tensions between these processes were noted in the general model but were thought to be the result of several unique associations occurring between antisocial defenses (ASD) and more rare aggressive forms of deviance. However, now it becomes more clear that the tension between the processes actually reflects differences in subgroup experiences. The final model, represented by Hypothesis 28-A, is presented in Figure 5.1. Of the 42 measurement parameters, 21 are invariant across all three groups, 6 are invariant for white-Anglos and African-Americans, 6 are invariant for white-Anglos and Mexican-Americans, and 6 are unique to either the African-American or Mexican-American subgroups (3 parameters have fixed error variances across the groups: AUTH). The measurement model, correlated errors, and structural parameters are summarized in turn.

## Measurement Model

The MLE measurement parameters by race/ethnicity are presented in Table 5.1. The measurement model of Time 1 deviance is characterized by the scale of the most prevalent deviant behavior, that is, the scale of the construct is fixed to the scale of the measurement variable MOST1. This scale is fixed across all three groups and is invariant for the latent construct. Given the scale and the assumption of its invariance, it becomes apparent that the deviance construct is identical in terms of its measurement parameters for white-Anglos and African-Americans. However, the construct is slightly different for the Mexican-American model in which the indicators of moderate and prevalent deviance items have significantly larger relative contributions.

Table 5.1.   MLE Measurement Parameters (Factor Loadings) by Race/Ethnicity

| | White-Anglo | African-American | Mexican-American |
|---|---|---|---|
| Early deviance | | | |
| Prevalent | 1.00 | 1.00 | 1.00 |
| Moderate | 1.121 | 1.121 | 1.539 |
| Rare | 0.917 | 0.917 | 1.085 |
| Self-rejection | | | |
| Self-derogation | 1.00 | 1.00 | 1.00 |
| Teachers | 0.501 | 0.501 | 0.547 |
| Parents | 0.187 | 0.280 | 0.187 |
| Negative social sanctions | 1.00 | 1.00 | 1.00 |
| Disposition to deviance | | | |
| Antisocial defenses | 0.803 | 0.803 | 0.803 |
| Disaffection | 1.00 | 1.00 | 1.00 |
| Deviant peer association | | | |
| Kids at school | 1.00 | 1.00 | 1.00 |
| Friends | 0.631 | 0.421 | 0.631 |
| Later deviance | | | |
| Prevalent | 1.00 | 1.00 | 1.00 |
| Moderate | 1.070 | 1.070 | 1.070 |
| Rare | 0.701 | 0.832 | 0.701 |

The scale of the latent construct of self-rejection is fixed to the measurement variable of self-derogation (SDRG) across all three groups and is declared equivalent in all three groups. Relative to this scale, the perceived rejection by teachers (RJTT) is invariant across white-Anglo and African-American ethnic groups but is substantially larger for Mexican-American ethnic groups, whereas perceived rejection by parents (RJTP) is invariant across white-Anglo and Mexican-American reference groups but substantially larger for African-Americans.

The scale for the latent construct of negative social sanctions is fixed according to researcher-determined values for the three-item index of formal social sanctions applied by authorities (AUTH) in all three groups. The scale is declared invariant across all three subgroups, and the relative reliability of the scale for the three subgroups is 0.821 for white-Anglos, 0.806 for African-Americans, and 0.750 for Mexican-Americans. These are judged to be roughly of the same magnitude.

The scale of the construct disposition to deviance is fixed to the measurement scale of disaffection with conventional order (DSCO). The loadings of two measurement variables for this latent construct are invariant across all three subgroups. Thus, a great deal of confidence can be invested in observations of structural differences in terms of this construct.

The scale of the theoretical construct deviant peer association is fixed and equal across the subgroups to the measurement variable of awareness of deviant behavior among peers in the school environment (KASDEV). The scale of the construct allows for the relative loading of affiliation with deviant friends (FRNDEV) to be invariant across white-Anglo and Mexican-American ethnic groups. However, the relative loading of affiliation with deviant peers (FRNDEV) is significantly smaller among the African-American minority group.

Finally the scale for the construct reflecting deviant behavior at Time 3 is fixed to the measurement variable (and is invariant in all three groups) for the prevalent forms of deviant behavior (MOST1). This scale provide relative and equivalent factor loadings of moderate deviance (MOD3) across all three groups and relative equivalence of rare deviance across white-Anglo and Mexican-American ethnic groups. The loading of rare deviance on this construct among the African-American ethnic group is significantly higher than the relative loadings among white-Anglos and Mexican-Americans.

## Correlated Errors

The measurement parameters for correlated errors are presented in Table 5.2. The unique association among the measurement variables provides evidence of significant effects outside of the structural parameters that summarize the causal properties of the model. Very few of these unique effects are identical across all three subgroups. Among the white-Anglo group, there is a negative unique relationship

**Table 5.2.   Measurement Parameters for Unique Effects**

|  | White-Anglo | African-American | Mexican-American |
|---|---|---|---|
| Autocorrelated errors |  |  |  |
| MOST1, MOST3 | 0.005 | 0.008 | 0.007 |
| MOD1, MOD3 | −0.006 | 0.002 | −0.003 |
| RARE1, RARE3 | 0.004 | 0.002 | 0.028 |
| Unique correlated errors |  |  |  |
| MOST1, ASD2 | −0.030 |  |  |
| MOST1, DSCO |  | −0.039 | 0.038 |
| MOST1, FRNDEV2 | 0.018 |  |  |
| MOD1, RARE3 |  |  | 0.029 |
| RARE1, ASD |  | 0.038 |  |
| SRJT, AUTH | −0.164 |  |  |
| RJTP, ADS |  |  | 0.105 |
| RJTP, DSCO | 0.065 |  |  |
| RJTP, KASDEV |  | −0.135 |  |
| ASD, FRNDEV | −0.156 |  |  |
| ASD, RARE3 | 0.034 |  | 0.085 |
| AUTH, MOD3 |  | −0.034 |  |
| DSCO, MOD3 |  | −0.013 |  |
| DSCO, FRNDEV | 0.093 |  |  |
| FRNDEV, RARE3 | −0.023 |  |  |

between early prevalent modes of deviant behavior and subsequent development of antisocial defenses. This negative unique association may represent the more social aspects of prevalent modes of deviant expression that are incongruent with antisocial defense mechanisms. This observation is further supported by a unique positive association between more prevalent forms of deviant behavior and later association with deviant friends in a peer network (the friend measurement variable being highly weighted toward marijuana use, a more sociable experience). There is also a substantively large and highly significant unique association between early self-derogation and later social sanctions by authorities. This strong negative effect probably indicates the tendency of self-derogating individuals, independent of the perceived rejection by teachers and parents, to remain socially isolated and less visible to others including those in positions of authority.

Additionally, there is a strong positive unique association between felt rejection by parents and later disaffection with conventional others. This positive unique effect may represent a methods artifact in which the perceived rejection by parents and the loss of motivation to conform to the standards of conventional others are weighted toward primary group experiences. It may also represent the increased relevance of parents for an acceptance of the conventional order outside of the primary group experiences that is not adequately expressed by the self-rejection construct.

It is interesting to note that a similar unique effect occurs between parents and the development of antisocial defenses among Mexican-Americans. These two similar effects indicate that, after controlling on the structural process represented by the effects of self-rejection on the loss of motivation to conform and acquisition of motivation to deviate, parents have an increased relevance for one or the other of the indicators of this construct. Rejection by parents increases disaffection with the conventional order among white-Anglos, perhaps because white-Anglo children more closely associate their parents with representatives of the conventional order or perhaps white-Anglo children are more likely to externalize blame to the conventional order based on the experience of rejection by their parents. However, Mexican-American children who experienced rejection by parents are more likely to develop antisocial defenses in response to this perceived rejection, independent of the theoretical structural process. This represents perhaps the lack of association of parental figures with the conventional order or a tendency to internalize blame for the perceived rejection by parents among Mexican-Americans. Both effects are large and substantively meaningful in the context of this model, although neither of them attenuates the hypothesized causal structural parameter between these two theoretical constructs to the point of non-significance.

Considering only the white-Anglo group again, there are two more large substantively meaningful unique effects involving the two measurement variables of disposition to deviance and the affiliation with deviant peers in a friendship network. The large and substantively meaningful structural parameter between disposition to deviance and association with deviant peers significantly overestimates the association between antisocial defenses and association with deviant friends while at the same time it underestimates the relationship between disaffection with the conventional order and association with that deviant friend network. These two unique effects serve to counterbalance the actual effect without attenuating it.

There are three other unique associations in the measurement model as applied to the white-Anglo subgroup. These include a significant positive association between early prevalent deviance and later association with deviant friends, a negative unique effect between affiliation with those deviant friends and rare forms of deviance at Time 3, and a unique positive association between antisocial defenses and later rare forms of deviant behavior. It was hypothesized earlier and supported by these findings that the antisocial defenses will be associated with more rare or aggressive forms of deviance that are less compatible with the sociability dimension of the more prevalent forms of deviance, including the heavy weight toward marijuana use in friendship networks.

Among the African-American subgroup there are five unique associations that are significant. These include a significant positive association between Time 1 rare deviance and Time 2 antisocial defenses. This effect is really a corollary of the negative effect between prevalent deviance and antisocial defenses noted among the white-Anglo group. In essence, the parameters indicate that the rare forms of deviant behavior characterized by aggression are more compatible with the antisocial regressive defense mechanisms than would be indicated by the positive structural parameter between early deviance and later disposition to deviance, or alternatively that the more prevalent deviant items are less compatible with the aggressive antisocial defenses. Independent of this positive association, however, there is a unique negative association between the more prevalent deviant items and disaffection with conventional order. The large structural parameter between early deviance and later disposition to deviance (the largest effect in any subgroup) apparently overestimates the relationship between these two measurement parameters and this negative unique association is required as an adjustment.

A moderate negative and statistically significant unique association exists between perceived rejection by parents and awareness of deviant behavior among peers in the school environment. Further, a significant and substantively large unique negative effect exists between the response from authoritative representatives of the conventional order and later moderate forms of deviance. This may represent a lack of relevance for moderate forms of deviant behavior to the conventional order as represented by authorities of that conventional order who would apply negative sanctions. The moderate forms of deviant behavior may represent for this ethnic group a class of behaviors that lie within the tolerance quotient of their particular ethnic group or may lie within the range of behaviors that are not subjectively associated with punitive responses from authoritative others. In any case, this effect is unique to the African-American subgroup and is one of the substantively largest and thus most interesting of the unique associations across these models.

Finally, we observed a unique negative effect of disaffection from the conventional order on moderate deviance. This negative effect indicates that the structural effects of disposition to deviance on later deviance overestimate the relationship between disaffection with the conventional order and moderate forms of later deviance. Among African-American adolescents, the tendency to commit these more moderate forms of deviance is slightly less dependent on a disaffection with the conventional order than the overall structural parameter indicates.

Considering only the Mexican-American model, and in addition to the earlier noted unique association between felt rejection by parents and antisocial defenses, there are three other significant unique associations. One includes the previously observed positive unique association between later rare forms of deviant behavior and early antisocial defenses, probably indicating the antisocial more aggressive nature of both these attitudes and behaviors. In addition, there is a very large and substantively meaningful positive unique association between earlier prevalent forms of deviant behavior and later disaffection with conventional others. Perhaps these early forms of deviant behavior are more expressive of a subculture that views the behaviors to be symbolic representation of rejection of the conventional order or may present the possibility of the existence of a subcultural perception that these behaviors are relevant for the subculture to the extent that they either (1) reject the conventional order or (2) reflect a passive acceptance of the irrelevance of the conventional order for the subcultural existence.

Finally there is a unique and very large positive relationship between earlier moderate forms of deviance and later rare forms of deviance, perhaps suggesting a progression or escalation of deviant behaviors among this subculture that are independent of the causal processes that lead to initiation of deviant behavior. All of these explanations are consistent with a dominant subcultural influence that rejects the conventional order, views it as irrelevant to the subculture, and provides an alternative network for socialization into increasingly more deviant behavioral outcomes.

## Structural Parameters

The MLE structural parameter estimates (unstandardized) for the three race/ethnic categories are summarized in Figure 5.1. A fully recursive model among the six theoretical constructs in the model provides for 15 possible structural effects. Of these 15 possible structural effects, 2 effects in each of the three groups are equal to zero. The effects of early feelings of self-rejection on later

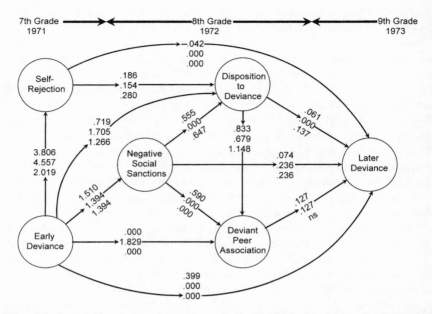

**Figure 5.1.** Structural parameter estimates (unstandardized MLE) for the multigroup analyses of the general theory of deviant behavior: a three-wave panel by race/ethnicity. (Top) White-Anglo; (middle) African-American; (bottom) Mexican-American.

negative social sanctions and the effects of early feelings of self-rejection on later deviant peer associations were zero in each of the three ethnic groups. Three additional effects were zero and equivalent in two of the three ethnic subgroups. The effects of early deviance on later deviance (the stability coefficient of deviance) are equal to zero among both Mexican-Americans and African-Americans. In addition, the effects of early self-rejection on later deviance and the effects of earlier negative social sanctions on later deviant peer associations were zero in both Mexican-American and African-American subgroups.

Additionally, two nonzero structural parameters were equivalent across Mexican-American and African-American subgroups. Effects of Time 1 deviance on later negative social sanctions, and the effect of those negative social sanctions on later Time 3 deviance were equivalent for both minority groups. One nonzero parameter was equivalent across African-American and white-Anglo racial groups but was substantially less among Mexican-Americans, that is, the effect of deviant peer associations on later Time 3 deviance.

The remaining six parameters differed across all three subgroups, namely, the effect of: Time 1 deviance on Time 1 feelings of self-rejection; Time 1 deviance on later disposition to deviance; Time 1 self-rejection on later disposition to deviance;

negative social sanctions on later disposition to deviance; disposition to deviance on deviant peer associations; and disposition to deviance on later Time 3 deviance.

An examination of the structural paths that compose the theoretical model for white-Anglo, African-American, and Mexican American adolescents, respectively, suggests a number of race/ethnic-specific differences. For white-Anglos, all of the hypothesized paths in the theoretical model were observed save one. Early deviance had no significant direct effect on later association with deviant peers. Perhaps white-Anglo subjects who engage in early deviance were protected from self-identification and from identification by peers as being deviant. Being white-Anglo served as a protective factor that precluded self- and other-attributions of deviance. Hence, the white-Anglo adolescent who engaged in deviance was neither attracted to nor attractive to other deviant peers solely by virtue of engaging in early deviance. However, it will be noted that engaging in early deviance by white-Anglo subjects will have an indirect effect on deviant peer associations via becoming the object of negative social sanctions. Once the adolescent's favored position in society has failed to protect him from being the object of negative social sanctions, identification as one who has been stigmatized by society will lead to deviant peer associations, whether due to the reputation that the person has gained as being worthy of deviant peer associations by virtue of having been sanctioned by the authorities, or because the nature of the negative social sanctions introduced facilitating structural circumstances that permitted the individual to participate with deviant peers where no such opportunities had presented themselves before becoming the object of negative social sanctions. At the same time the individual white-Anglo adolescent by becoming stigmatized is prevented from remaining in conventional contexts, free of deviant peer associations. For white-Anglo adolescents being suspended or expelled from school and coming to the attention of the authorities provides opportunities to associate with deviant peers that were not previously present. It will be noted that the model does not effectively decompose the stability effect of early deviance on later deviance.

# Discussion

We discuss the causal contributions of each of the theoretical constructs in turn, reemphasizing again where the structural parameters are declared invariant across groups, and otherwise presenting the differential impact of the constructs on the subsequent portions of the model.

## Early Deviance

The latent construct of early deviance has large and significant effects on felt self-rejection. The effects, however, are not equivalent across groups. The unstandardized MLE of early deviance on self-rejection are significantly greater for African-Americans than for white-Anglos, and the effect is significantly greater for white-Anglos than for Mexican-Americans. And while all effects remain substantively meaningful it appears that the Mexican-American subcultural environment in some way attenuates the relevance of deviant behavior for self-evaluation, and perceived rejection by others.

The social control response related to self-reported levels of earlier deviant behavior are equivalent for both African-Americans and Mexican-Americans. However, the impact of early deviance on subsequent negative social sanctions is significantly greater for the white-Anglo racial group. This is in stark contrast to theories that would predict discriminatory responses based on ethnic minority status by those in positions of authority. Rather, the theoretical position that seems to be supported by these effects is the increased tolerance hypothesis. The apparent logic is that deviant behavior by ethnic minorities is more likely to be tolerated than is deviant behavior by white-Anglo racial groups, primarily because the deviant behavior by white-Anglo subjects appears to be more role incongruent and represents a greater departure from normative expectations than the same deviant act performed by a racial minority member, perhaps who is stereotypically or prejudicially thought to have greater propensities toward these deviant behaviors by those in authority.

Early deviance has significant structural effects on later disposition to deviance among all three racial groups. It was not predicted as a structural effect in the general model, primarily because there were several countervailing effects represented by unique associations that varied across ethnic groups. However, once the subgroup analysis allows the differential unique associations, presented earlier in discussion of the measurement model, to be controlled, it became apparent that a structural parameter does exists between deviance and later disposition to deviance. This represents the role that early deviance serves in maintaining or reinforcing the lack of motivation to conform and the acquired motivation to deviate from conventional standards. This is perhaps due to rewards associated with the deviant behavior that are independent of the consequences of negative social sanctions or deviant peer association. This direct effect of early Time 1 deviance on later disposition to deviance is significantly greater among the African-American minority group, second largest among the Mexican-American ethnic group, and weakest among the white-Anglo racial group.

The effect of early Time 1 deviance on later deviant peer associations is significant, and substantively large, only for the African-American minority group. The effect is zero for both white-Anglo and Mexican-American ethnic groups. Apparently maintenance of friendship networks or involvement in environments in which the deviant actor is a normative element in that environment, is significantly more influential among African-American minority groups. Either the early involvement in deviant behavior is not sufficient to maintain deviant group affiliations or the deviant behavior is not sufficient to make the subject attractive to or desirous of membership in deviant peer-networks in the other groupings. On the other hand, the deviant behavior is a particularly strong predictor of these later deviant peer networks among the African-American minority group.

Early deviance maintains an independent stability coefficient, net of the other structural theoretical constructs in the hypothesized model, for the white-Anglo racial group only. The stability coefficient is entirely decomposed by the intervening explanatory constructs for both Mexican-American and African-American ethnic minorities. The integration and combination of labeling, social control, structural strain, self-esteem, and differential association theories are sufficient to account for the onset and continuity of deviant behavior for the ethnic minorities.

With respect to continuity, the entire continued participation of ethnic minorities in deviant behavior patterns can be accounted for by these explanatory intervening variables. In addition, the onset and continuity for these ethnic minorities is explained at a rate of 63 and 60% for Mexican-American and African-American subgroups, respectively. Thus, the model not only serves as a powerful predictor of onset or initiation of deviant behavior but also explains its continuity. On the other hand, although the explanatory model does adequately account for a substantively equal amount of variance among the white-Anglo racial group (58%), it was not as efficient in decomposing the stability of early deviance over time. The stability coefficient for deviance remains significant among the white-Anglo racial group at a standardized coefficient level of 0.27. The particular combination of these theoretical paradigms is apparently not sufficient to account for the continuity of deviant behavior among the white-Anglo racial group. Apparently there are other yet unspecified influences that serve to maintain this behavior pattern over time.

### Early Self-Rejection

Early self-rejection had a significant positive effect on disposition to deviance among all three racial ethnic groups. The effect was significantly different, however, across all three groups. The effect of self-rejection on the acquired motivation to deviate from conventional standards and the simultaneous loss of motivation to conform to conventional standards was greatest among the Mexican-American ethnic group. This is in spite of the particularly large unique association that exists between perceived rejection by parents and antisocial defenses which are indicators of the two constructs. The role of self-rejecting feelings in increasing the alienation from conventional society seems to be strongest for Mexican-Americans, second strongest for white-Anglos, and weakest among the African-American ethnic minority. If in fact the effect of self-rejection on acquired disposition to deviance reflected a tendency to externalize blame due to a lack of internal locus of control, this finding would contradict the suggestion of earlier research based on static comparisons of African-American and white-Anglo minority groups. In the present context, the inherent distress of self-rejection leads to an attribution of blame to the sources of that self-rejection and such attributions contribute to the enhanced disposition to deviance. Although the effects are significantly different, they are of such substantively relative equal magnitude as to suggest that a similar process is occurring among all three groups, although moderately buffered in the white-Anglo cultural group and more greatly buffered in the African-American ethnic group.

The effects of early self-rejection are significant in only one other instance. Among white-Anglos, they have a significant negative countervailing effect on later Time 3 deviance. This negative countervailing effect, as opposed to the intervening causal constructs proposed in the model, represents a hypothesized internalized social control mechanism, representing a perverse increased motivation to conform, perhaps reflecting hypersocialization among some particular subgroups of white-Anglos. Such explanatory constructs are not specified in the present model and remain to be tested.

### Negative Social Sanctions

The effects of negative social sanctions on later disposition to deviance are significantly different across all three groups and vary from zero among the African-American ethnic group to a high value among the Mexican-American ethnic groups. The effects of official responses by authoritative members of the conventional order serve to significantly enhance the loss of motivation to conform to conventional standards and the acquired motivation to deviate from these standards. However, this alienating effect is observed only among members of white-Anglo and Mexican-American ethnic groups.

This alienation effect is noticeably absent among the African-American minority groups. Negative social sanctions has significant positive effects on association with deviant peers only for the white-Anglo group. The effects of this variable on awareness of deviant peers in the school environment and affiliation with deviant friendship networks are zero for the two ethnic minorities. Negative social sanctions increases the attractiveness of deviant youth to deviant peers by making them more recognizable and acceptable to the deviant peer environment only for the white-Anglo racial group. Apparently the negative social sanctions response is not necessary to label deviant youth to make them acceptable to deviant peer groups or is not necessary to increase their awareness of deviant peer networks among the ethnic minorities. This may be because the deviant peer networks are already sufficiently apparent to ethnic minorities based on socioeconomic-related environmental and structural parameters and because any official responses would not serve to enhance such awareness or prevalence of deviant networks. Further, it appears that the negative social sanctions may not be necessary to make ethnic minority members suitable candidates for memberships in such groups, and that the ethnic affiliation itself may be sufficient for such membership.

However, negative social sanctions, to the extent that they provide a deviant label to the deviant actor and to the extent that the actor is unable to resist that deviant label or to call on self-definitions other than deviant identities, will cause the individual to accept the deviant identity as an integral part of self. Once integrated within the self, the individual is motivated to behave in deviant ways, in order to validate a positively valued deviant identity even independent of any increased alienation or opportunity to engage in deviant behaviors. This process is apparently quite relevant for adolescents, who by their very nature are vulnerable to the labeling effects of adults and particularly adults in authority. The effect also seems to increase along the dimensions of racial minorities such that the two racial minorities manifest equal and significantly greater subsequent deviant behaviors in response to the negative social sanctions. This would be consistent with the interpretation relating to this lack of power to resist the deviant labels associated with their minority status.

## Disposition to Deviance

The effects of disposition to deviance on awareness of deviant peers and affiliation with deviant peers are significantly different across all three groups, greatest among the Mexican-American minorities, next among white-Anglos, and weakest among African-American youths. The effect, however, is very large and very significant in all three groups and is substantively of the same magnitude. The effect is most greatly buffered among the African-American group due largely in part to the joint dependence of these two latent constructs on earlier deviance. Thus, the enhanced motivation to seek out deviant others or become aware of deviant others is in large part mitigated by the rate or prevalence of deviant acts already existent in the early adolescent experience and environment of these African-American youths.

The enhanced effect of this alienating process on the awareness of and affiliation with deviant peers and other deviant opportunities is greatest among the Mexican-American group. This construct serves as the primary mediating explanatory variable in the Mexican-American model. It appears that the Mexican-American culture and the social environmental definitions relevant to the Mexican-American culture are particularly vulnerable to the structured strain and alienating processes represented in this model. For white-Anglo subjects, the effect of disposition to deviance on later deviant peer association is attenuated somewhat due to the unique direct effect of negative social sanctions on deviant peers in this group.

Disposition to deviance has no effect on later deviance for African-Americans. Perhaps this is due to the operation of countervailing processes.

However, it does have a moderate significant effect on later deviance among white-Anglo youths and a substantial direct effect on later deviance among the Mexican-Americans. This is again consistent with the particularly noteworthy experience of the alienating process among Mexican-Americans that is moderated among white-Anglos primarily because of the intervening role of deviant peer associations. Apparently the opportunities for knowledge of, and recruitment into, deviant peer networks are necessary for white-Anglos to become more fully involved in deviant activities. This does not appear to be the case for alienated Mexican-American youths.

### Deviant Peer Associations

Deviant peer associations (1) represent the opportunities for learning deviant behaviors from peers, (2) provide social support and subsequent rewards for engaging in such deviant behaviors, and (3) provide the value definitions and structures that occasion deviant behaviors. The effect of peer associations on deviant behaviors is significantly present and roughly equivalent among white-Anglo and African-American racial groups. The effect, surprisingly, is not significant among Mexican-American minorities. Perhaps, the lack of a significant effect among Mexican-American minorities is due in large part to the common dependence of deviant peer associations and subsequent deviant behavior on the enhanced alienating process represented by disposition to deviance. Additionally, however, there are no unique effects between affiliating with deviant others and antisocial defenses as there are among the white-Anglo youths nor is there any unique effect across disaffection with the conventional order and moderate forms of deviance as there is in the African-American group. Perhaps this reflects a willingness, readiness, or ability of Mexican-American ethnic minority members to respond or act on their own motivations, that is, independent of the need for a group structure to support such behaviors. Such definitions favorable to individual behavioral reactions independent of group support would need to be specified and indicated in the model in order to test this hypothesis. The intended test of the hypothesis would be either to attenuate the direct effect of disposition to deviance on later deviance or to enhance the nonsignificant effect of deviant peer associations on later deviance.

# III

# DEVIANT BEHAVIOR FROM ADOLESCENCE TO YOUNG ADULTHOOD

In Part III the most inclusive theoretical model developed to account for ninth-grade deviance is applied to the explanation of deviant behavior in young adulthood. These analyses permit consideration of what influence, if any, stage in the life course exercises as a moderator of the influence of putative causes of deviant behavior. In Chapter 6 we estimate the most inclusive model as an explanation of young adult deviance for white-Anglo subjects and compare the results with those obtained when estimating the model as an explanation of adolescent deviance for white-Anglo subjects. In general, the same parameters were observed to be positive and significant with two exceptions. Unlike the model for adolescent deviance, no effects of early deviance and deviant peer associations on later deviance were observed on young adult deviance.

In Chapter 7 the general model was estimated separately for male and female subgroupings with regard to its viability as an explanation of young adult deviance. In addition to contrasting the young adult models across gender-differentiated subgroupings, the gender-specific young adult deviance models were compared with the appropriate gender-specific adolescent deviance models. The moderating influence of gender, stage in the life course, and the interaction of these two constructs is apparent.

# 6

# Deviance from Adolescence to Young Adulthood

## The Experience of White-Anglo Adolescents

This chapter examines the development of deviant behavior among adolescents as they mature into young adulthood, applying the same models we developed to explain adolescent deviant behavior.

## Method

### Data

The models estimated in this chapter are derived from data obtained over four panel waves from the same cohort examined in the earlier models, except that the data used for estimating the causal models are derived from the input covariance and standard deviation matrices for white-Anglos only ($N = 1123$).

### Analysis

The initial extension of the model to four waves of the data is accomplished only for white-Anglo subjects because the number of Mexican-American subjects extended over the four waves of the panel ($N = 173$) was not sufficient to enable stable estimates of the approximately 42 parameters in the model. In order to obtain stable estimates the researcher should have ideally at least five times as many subjects as there are parameters to be estimated, and under the best of conditions to have a larger ratio such as ten times as many subjects as there are parameters to be estimated. For the African-American subjects, there appeared to be sufficient subjects available to make estimation of the model feasible. However, the Time 4 indicators of deviance (MOD4 and RARE4) did not seem to form a latent construct for this minority. Thus, because we did not have sufficient numbers to estimate stable models among Mexican-American subjects and because the latent construct of interest was not substantively meaningful for African-American subjects, we report the model based only on the white-Anglo subjects.

The model for white-Anglo subjects was estimated using correlation and standard deviation matrices in self-reported variables as input to LISREL-VI (Jöreskog & Sörbom, 1984). The model specifies relationships among six latent constructs (early deviance, self-rejection, negative social sanctions, disposition to deviance, deviant peer associations, and later deviance) and 13 measurement variables (multiple-item scales). The first two constructs and their six measurement variables were drawn from Time 1 and are identical to the variables in constructs measured in earlier models. The constructs within Time 2 are identical for negative social sanctions and disposition to deviance. The measurement variables for the latent construct of deviant peer associations are drawn from the third wave of the panel. The measurement variables for later deviance are drawn from the fourth wave of the panel. The results for the measurement model, correlated errors, and the structural model are reported separately.

## Results

The parameters for the measurement model and correlated errors are summarized in Table 6.1. The coefficients for the structural model are presented in Figure 6.1.

### Measurement Model

*Early Deviance.* The measurement model of early deviance is represented by fixing the scale of the construct to the measurement variable of most prevalent deviance (MOST1). Moderate deviance and rare deviance both loaded significantly on this construct. The items in these three scales are identical to those appearing in earlier models, drawn from the first wave of the panel.

*Self-Rejection.* As in the earlier models presented in Chapters 3–5, self-rejection is measured with the same items drawn from the first wave of the panel. The scale for the latent construct of self-rejection is fixed to the measurement variable of self-derogation (SDRG). The measurement variables of felt rejection by teachers (RJTT) and felt rejection by parents (RJTP) both loaded significantly and with substantively large loadings on this construct.

Table 6.1.  Measurement Model and Correlated Errors: Adolescent to
            Young Adult Deviance among White-Anglos

|                              | Unstandardized | Standardized |
|------------------------------|:--------------:|:------------:|
| Construct                    |                |              |
| Early deviance               |                |              |
| MOST1                        | 1.00           | 0.62         |
| MOD1                         | 1.07           | 0.59         |
| RARE1                        | 0.79           | 0.51         |
| Self-rejection               |                |              |
| Self-derogation              | 1.00           | 0.49         |
| Rejection by parents         | 0.54           | 0.70         |
| Rejection by teachers        | 0.20           | 0.46         |
| Negative social sanctions    |                |              |
| Attention of authorities     | 1.00           | 0.81         |
| Disposition to deviance      |                |              |
| Disaffection with conventional | 1.00         | 0.70         |
| Antisocial defenses          | 0.75           | 0.55         |
| Deviant peer associations    |                |              |
| Friends deviant              | 1.00           | 0.79         |
| Kids at school are deviant   | 1.30           | 0.48         |
| Later deviance               |                |              |
| MOD4                         | 1.00           | 0.55         |
| RARE4                        | 0.57           | 0.45         |
| Correlated errors            |                |              |
| MOST1, SDRG                  | 0.05           | 0.05         |
| MOST1, ASD                   | −0.04          | −0.08        |
| RARE1, KASDEV                | 0.05           | 0.06         |
| SDRG, AUTH                   | −0.15          | −0.08        |
| RJTP, DSCO                   | 0.06           | 0.08         |
| ASD, KASDEV                  | 0.18           | 0.06         |
| ASD, FRNDEV                  | −0.11          | −0.08        |
| Within-construct error       |                |              |
| MOD1, RARE1                  | 0.02           | 0.11         |

*Negative Social Sanctions.*    The scale for the latent construct of negative
social sanctions is fixed according to the researcher-determined value for the
three-item index of formal sanctions against subjects. The scale has a fixed reliability of 0.821.

*Disposition to Deviance.*    The measurement properties of this latent construct are assumed to scale to the value of disaffection with the conventional order
(DSCO). The measurement variable of antisocial defenses (ASD) loads significantly on this construct. The items in these two scales are identical to those
appearing in earlier models, drawn from the second wave of the panel.

*Deviant Peer Associations.* The scale of the construct of deviant peer associations is fixed to that of the measurement value of association with deviant friends (FRNDEV). The measurement variable of awareness of deviant peers in the school environment (KASDEV) loads significantly on this construct. The measurement variables for the latent construct of deviant peer associations are drawn from the third wave of the panel.

*Later Deviance.* Later deviance, consisting of items obtained from the fourth panel, is modeled as a latent construct indicated by two measures. Each of the measures reflects self-reports of engaging in at least one or more of several deviant behaviors that have prevalence rates falling within a narrow range. The grouping of moderate prevalence at Time 4 (MOD 4) had prevalence rates between 2 and 6%. This grouping consisted of seven self-report items (damage to private or public property, vagrant travel, fighting, betting, stealing, carrying a razor, or attacking someone). The grouping of rare Time 4 (RARE 4) deviance items had prevalence rates ranging from less than 0.3 to 1.7%. This grouping consisted of ten items (breaking and entering, forgery, participating in a riot, taking a car for joyriding, running numbers, participating in a gang fight, robbery, pimping or prostitution, or participating in a radical or revolutionary movement). The two measures were created as dichotomies. In the case of moderate and rare forms of deviance the occurrence of at least one incident of this behavior between the period of 1978 and the time of the interview is taken as indicative of deviant behavior. The construct of later deviance at Time 4 (subsequent to January 1, 1978) is fixed to the measurement properties of moderate Time 4 deviance (MOD4). The measurement variable of rare Time 4 deviance (RARE4) loads significantly on this construct. Later deviance thus differs slightly from earlier deviance (two versus three measurement items), though each of the measures reflects self-reports of engaging in at least one or more of several deviant behaviors in different prevalence categories.

### Correlated Errors

Among the 78 variances and covariances, there were eight unique associations among the measurement variables for these white-Anglo subjects. There is a unique association between rare Time 1 deviance and moderate Time 1 deviance. This means that, independent of the shared covariance as represented in the latent construct of Time 1 deviance, there is an additional positive independent and unique association between these two deviance variables. It is possible that they may represent a more severe form of deviance than one would consider appropriate for a general deviance construct. It may also represent a more specialized form of deviant behavior than one would expect in a general deviance construct, perhaps representing earlier socialization (deviant subcultures) or earlier acquired skills necessary to engage in these relatively less prevalent forms of deviant behavior. In any case, the estimation of this unique association does not substantively diminish the factorial loadings of these measurement variables on the general deviance construct, and the loadings of moderate (MOD1) and rare (RARE1) Time 1 deviance remain large and highly significant, among the most significant of the factor loadings of any of the latent constructs.

In addition, the more prevalent forms of deviant behavior have a unique positive association with the measurement variable of self-derogation, independent of the positive structural parameter between the two latent constructs these measurement variables respectively indicate. The measure of the more prevalent forms of deviant behavior (MOST1) also has a unique strong negative relation to the measurement variable of antisocial defenses (ASD) independent of the direct positive effect of the latent construct of deviance on the latent construct of disposition to deviance. This suggests that the structural relationships between early deviance and later disposition to deviance overstate the extent of the positive association between most prevalent deviance (MOST1) and antisocial defenses (ASD).

Rare Time 1 deviance (RARE1) has a unique positive association with awareness of deviant peers in the school environment (KASDEV). This unique association is positive, and probably represents the extent of the direct structural relationship between early deviance and later deviant peer associations. Thus, among this white-Anglo population, there appears to be no structural effect of early deviance on the entrance into or maintenance of deviant peer associations except to the extent that there is a positive unique association between rare forms of deviance and awareness of deviant peers in the school environment. This exception is independent of the indirect effects of early deviance through other latent constructs in the model.

Self-derogation at Time 1 has a unique negative relationship with the measurement variable of negative social sanctions. There is a lack of any structural effect between self-rejection and negative social sanctions and thus this unique negative effect is independent of the underlying conceptual variables represented in the model. This negative effect may represent the timorousness of the individual in relationship to the presentation of self, leading to the effort to reduce visibility of self and behaviors. The timorousness may also reflect the intervening role of certain behaviors that are designed purposively to reduce the visibility of the individual, especially to significant social others who pose the potential for greater threats to self (e.g., those individuals with the power to assign negative social sanctions).

Additionally, felt rejection by parents (RJTP) has a unique positive association with disaffection with the conventional order (DSCO), independent of the hypothesized increased motivation to deviate or the loss of motivation to conform represented by the positive structural effect between the two respective latent constructs. This positive effect has been interpreted earlier as representing situational specific elements in the disaffection with conventional order (being unhappy at home, wanting to run away from home), and the situational relevance of parents to those motivations.

Finally, antisocial defenses has a unique positive association with awareness of deviance in the school environment (KASDEV) and a unique negative association with association with deviant friends (FRNDEV). This suggests that the structural parameter is a compromise between an overestimation of the relationship between antisocial defenses and association with deviant friendship groups and an underestimation of the relation between antisocial defenses and awareness of deviance in the school environment. This has been interpreted previously in terms of the lack of relevance, or the inability of an individual with antisocial defenses to maintain or become a member of stable friendship groups whether the groups are deviant or conventional in nature.

### Structural Parameters

In a fully recursive model of the six latent constructs there is a possibility of 15 structural parameters. After accounting for the unique associations and trimming the nonsignificant structural parameters from the model, there remained nine significant structural effects, each of which had been previously hypothesized in the process of model elaboration. As Figure 6.1 indicates, early Time 1 deviance has direct positive and significant effects on Time 1 self-rejection, Time 2 negative social sanctions, and Time 2 disposition to deviance. Early self-rejection has a

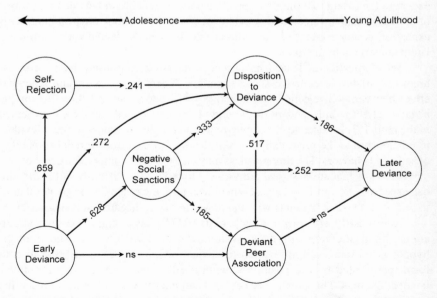

**Figure 6.1.** The standardized structural effects for the model of deviant behavior: adolescence to young adulthood. Chi-square = 51.2, 49 *df*, *p* = 0.388, *n* = 1123.

direct positive effect on later disposition to deviance. Negative social sanctions has direct positive structural effects on later disposition to deviance and deviant peer association and later Time 4 deviance. Time 2 disposition to deviance has direct positive effects on later deviant peer associations and later deviance. Unlike previous models, however, deviant peer association does not have a direct significant effect on later Time 4 deviance.

# Discussion

We examined the theoretical model as it was specified in the earlier three-wave panel. In this model, the model predicting adult deviance, we extend the model over four panel waves. The pattern of structural effects in this model was specified according to the earlier three wave models with the exception that the effects of the earlier constructs drawn from Waves 1 and 2 were extended over three waves predicting deviant peer associations. Thus, the structure of the first three waves of the panel was altered to an additional lag of one panel wave predicting deviant peer associations. In all other respects, with the exception of the extension to the fourth wave, the model remains identical. With these differences in mind, we will examine the patterns of effects that have been revealed in this model of young adult deviance among white-Anglo subjects starting with predictors that are more proximal to the dependent variable.

## *Association with Deviant Peers*

We found that association with deviant peers was not a significant predictor of later Time 4 deviance in this model. Considering that association with deviant peers represents: (1) instrumental and expressive support for engaging in deviant behaviors, (2) a mechanism that attenuates the effectiveness of internalized social control mechanism, and (3) the rewards (or the possible rewards) for engaging in deviant behaviors, the lack of an effect of deviant peer associations on later deviance may indicate the lack of stability of these deviant peer associations over longer periods of time (extending from 1974 through 1978), a 4-year lag at a minimum. Alternately, the lack of an effect of deviant peers on deviant behavior may represent the temporary nature of the effect of reduction of internalized social control experienced during adolescent peer associations. It may also represent the greater restriction or lack of opportunities for the continued instrumental support for engagement in deviant activities as these deviant behaviors move from the realm of adolescent delinquency to young adult crime. Finally, it may represent the greater opportunity to engage in deviant peer associations that exists in the adolescent environment (primarily structured by the school environment) that is lost when the structure of the school environment is lost (i.e., when subjects graduate or drop out of school). The lack of the structure, the lack of the continuity of the attenuation of internalized social control mechanisms, the greater restriction in the variance of the deviant behavior items themselves, and the lack of stability of the deviant peer groups all may contribute to the failure to observe a structural effect between deviant peer associations and later young adult deviant behavior.

### Disposition to Deviance

The effect of disposition to deviance on later deviant peer associations and later young adult deviance is significant. The model suggests that, although greatly attenuated, the effect of disposition to deviance on greater Time 4 deviance reflects the tendency to maintain an influential motivation to deviate from conventional norms and a simultaneous loss of motivation to conform over long periods of time. This acquired motivation to deviate and loss of motivation to conform—which in previous models and under different circumstances, seemed to be mediated by deviant peer associations—in an extended model has effects independent of deviant peer associations. The effect then seems to be independent of any subcultural affiliation or membership group affiliation and alternative primary or secondary groups. At least, the effect remains independent of the type of deviant or primary group memberships that are characterized by adolescence and adolescent delinquency.

In earlier models, the measurement of the dependent variable of deviance was very similar to the items that deviant peers were perceived as engaging in. At Time 4, however, the deviance items represent more serious criminal activities that probably are less coextensive with the behaviors perceived as specified by peers in the school environment. Thus, measurement characteristics may partially explain the lack of a structural effect. However, the lack of relevance of adolescent juvenile peer associations for initiation of later young adult criminal behaviors may be equally relevant. In any case, given the fact that the effect of disposition to deviance on later deviant peer associations remains significant, deviant peer associations may reflect one more indicator of criminal activities, rather than the opportunity or occasion to engage in such activity.

### Negative Social Sanctions

Negative social sanctions have structurally significant effects on all three subsequent constructs in the model. The experience of negative sanctions increases the motivation to deviate and increases the loss of motivation to conform among adolescents. Consistent with earlier models, negative social sanctions increase the tendency for individuals to become aware of deviant peers in the school environment and to increase their association with friendship groups that can be characterized as deviant. Finally, negative social sanctions, independent of their effects on motivation to deviate and association with deviant peers, have a direct positive effect on young adult deviance. This direct effect presumably reflects a self-defensive positive reevaluation of a deviant identity in the service of the self-esteem motive, and a validation of the now positively valued deviant identity through the performance of identity-congruent deviant behaviors.

## Self-Rejection

The effect of this construct on disposition to deviance is again detected in this cohort of young adults. It is slightly weaker than the same effect detected in the adolescent cohort, but nonetheless significant and substantially large enough to support the theoretical expectations of the role this construct plays in explaining deviant behavior. Self-rejection primarily motivates adolescents to reject conventional standards and adopt deviant ones.

## Early Deviance

The major impact of early adolescent deviance on later deviance during young adulthood appears to operate via negative social sanctions. As noted in the adolescent cohort, white-Anglo youths seem to escape the association with deviant peers as a result of early deviance. The route from early deviance to young adult deviance is not direct, it is not sustained by deviant peers, but it does implicate the effect of being labeled when conventional authorities apply stigmatizing negative social sanctions.

# 7

## Deviance and Gender
### *Adolescence to Young Adulthood*

The same general models that were estimated for males and females during adolescence are estimated to examine the moderating influence of gender in explaining young adult deviance.

## Method

### *Data*

The data are derived from the same panel cohort in the earlier models. As in the analyses reported in Chapter 4, the data used for estimating the causal models are derived from the input covariance and standard deviation matrices produced separately for males ($n = 736$) and females ($n = 1139$). The data extend over four panel waves for this analysis.

### *Analysis*

The models for each gender were estimated using correlation and standard deviation matrices for self-reported variables as input to LISREL-VI (Jöreskog & Sörbom, 1984). This computer program provides MLE of model parameters that are specified as "free." The estimation process is an iterative procedure that minimizes the function of the differences between observed covariance patterns and the covariances estimated by the model. The "free" parameters in the model are actually unknown values in linear equations that are used to construct the model.

*Latent Constructs and Measurement Variables.* The model specifies relationships among six latent constructs (early deviance, self-rejection, negative social sanctions, disposition to deviance, deviant peer associations, and later deviance) and 13 measurement variables (multiple-item scales). The variables and constructs within Time 1 are identical to the variables and constructs measured in the earlier analyses. The variables and constructs within Time 2 are identical for negative social sanctions, and disposition to deviance. The measurement variables for the latent construct of deviant peer associations, however, are drawn from the third wave of the panel in the present analyses, rather than from the second wave as in the earlier analyses.

Later deviance is a construct drawn from measurement variables obtained at the fourth wave (young adulthood) of the panel. Deviance at Time 4 is modeled as a latent construct indicated by two measures. Each of the measures reflects self-reports of engaging in one or more of several deviant behaviors that have prevalence rates falling within a narrow range. The grouping of moderate prevalence at Time 4 (MOD4) had prevalence rates between 2 and 6%. This grouping consisted of seven self-report items (damage to private or public property, vagrant travel, fighting, betting, stealing, carrying a razor, or attacking someone). The grouping of rare Time 4 (RARE4) deviance items had prevalence rates ranging from less than 0.3 to 1.7%. This grouping consisted of nine items (breaking and entering, forgery, participating in a riot, taking a car for joyriding, running numbers, participating in a gang fight, robbery, pimping or prostitution, or participating in a radical or revolutionary movement). The two measures were created as dichotomies. In the case of moderate and rare forms of deviance the occurrence of at least one incident of this behavior between the period of 1978 and the time of the interview is taken as indicative of deviant behavior. These procedures created a measurement variable of moderate deviance (MOD4) that has prevalence rates of 19% for males and 9.8% for females and a rare deviance scale (RARE4) that has rates of 5.8% for males and 4.0% for females.

# Results

Results indicate that a model in which the variances and covariances of the 13 observed variables are assumed equal in the two gender subgroups can be rejected. This model, known as the null hypothesis, has a chi-square value of 495.06 with 91 associated degrees of freedom. Therefore, we believe the next crucial questions involve whether or not these measurement variables can be significantly and more adequately represented by the presumed theoretical structure. The test of this hypothesis, Hypothesis 1, is that the measurement portion of a theoretical model is similar across both subgroups. The chi-square value for this hypothesis is 218.17 with 102 associated degrees of freedom. Thus, the delta statistic (Bentler & Bonett, 1980), which is distributed as a chi-square value and provides a test for significant improvement in fit based on the difference in chi-square values distributed across the difference in degrees of freedom, provides a value of 276.89 with 11 degrees of freedom. This is a highly significant improvement in fit and lends a great deal of support to a similar factor structure among male and female subgroups for these 13 measurement variables.

The next hypothesis, H2, is nested in H1, and assumes that the factor structure is not only similar but is equivalent in both groups. The results of this test provide a chi-square value of 241.77 with 109 degrees of freedom. The delta statistic is 23.6 with 7 degrees of freedom, which is significant. Thus, the assumption of the equivalent measurement properties for these 13 variables across male and female gender subgroups is unwarranted. However, it is possible that the significant differences may be attributable to only a few of the 13 variables. By examination of several of the criterion of goodness-of-fit statistics, including modification indices, normalized residuals, and the overall chi-square goodness of fit, it was determined that a suitable representation of the measurement model could not be attained without relaxing the assumption of equivalent measurement parameters for 3 of the 13 measurement coefficients.

Relaxing the assumption that the measurement of rare deviance (RARE1) is not equivalent at Time 1 for both males and females, that the measurement of rare deviance at Time 4 (RARE4) is not equivalent for both males and females, and assuming that the measure of knowledge of deviance among high school peers (KASDEV) measured at Time 3 is not set to the same equivalent scale for both males and females as an indicator of deviant peer associations, returns an overall goodness-of-fit model with a chi-square value of 229.17 with 106 degrees of freedom. Thus, the more restricted model provides a significant improvement in fit of the overall model (chi-square equal to 12.6, 3 $df$) and the delta statistic for comparison of H3 with H1 is significant (chi-square equal to 11.0, 4 $df$).

Allowing for a number of unique associations among measurement variables, which are common to both subgroups and of which some are unique to both subgroups, the model appeared to reach a plateau of stable measurement properties. Therefore, the apparent stabilization of the model with regard to the measurement parameters allows us to follow the next step in the planned sequence of analyses in which structural parameters that appear to equal zero in both groups and that were not theoretically indicated could be trimmed from the model. These steps allow for the comparison of nonzero parameters in both subgroups and allow us to make the determination whether or not they are equivalent in both groups. Prior to the examination of structural invariance across both groups, a theoretical model with stable measurement properties was achieved that had a chi-square value of 196.06 with 105 degrees of freedom.

The next stage of model trimming involves the specification of no effect between latent constructs for which the parameters appeared to be zero. Trimming structural effects from the model and observing the model characteristics to determine whether or not subsequent improvement in the model needed to be made by adjustment of unique effects, produced a stable theoretical model with a nonsignificant chi-square value of 109.23 with 105 degrees of freedom. This model had four structural parameters that were fixed equal to zero across both groups. The direct effect of Time 1 deviance on Time 4 deviance, the stability coefficient, was structurally equivalent for males and females, as were the direct effects of Time 1 self-rejection on Time 2 negative social sanctions, Time 3 deviant peer associations, and later deviance. For males, uniquely, there was no significant structural effect between later Time 4 deviance and Time 2 negative social sanctions.

Once we received a nonsignificant chi-square value and a stable measurement and structural parameter portion of the model, we decided to begin assessing equivalent or invariant structural processes across gender groups. It was determined, based on visual examination of the MLE of unstandardized parameters, that the effects of Time 1 deviance on Time 2 negative sanctions, Time 1 self-rejection on Time 2 disposition to deviance, and Time 2 disposition on Time 3 deviant peer associations were equivalent for males and females. The delta statistic for each of these hypotheses (each distributed with one degree of freedom) were 0.86, 1.27, and 1.47, respectively, all of which were nonsignificant.

### Measurement Model

The measurement models as well as correlated errors for the separate male and female estimations are presented in Table 7.1.

*Early Deviance.*   The measurement model of early deviance is characterized by the scale of the measurement for most prevalent deviant behavior (MOST1). The scale is fixed to this measurement variable for both males and females thus providing a common measurement basis for the latent construct. As noted earlier, the measurement variable of rare deviance (RARE1) is not equivalent for both males and females, but the measurement variable of moderate deviance (MOD1) is equivalent for both males and females. The indicator of rare deviance on the general deviance construct, as compared with the scale of prevalent deviance, is significantly larger for males (0.943) than for females (0.636). This is in part due to a greater number of unique associations of rare deviance with other measurement variables in the model for females, and is due in part to the lesser relevance of this variable for female deviance. That is, a greater proportion of the deviance in this measurement variable is attributable to "error" for the females than is attributable to "error" for the males.

*Self-Rejection.*   The scale for the latent construct of self-rejection is fixed to the measurement variable of self-derogation (SDRG) for both males and females and is equivalent for both groups. In fact, considering the other two measurement variables of this latent construct as well, the measurement model can be declared invariant for both males and females.

**Table 7.1.   Measurement Model and Correlated Errors for Male and Female Adolescence to Young Adult Deviance**

|  | Males | | Females | |
|---|---|---|---|---|
| Construct | | | | |
| Early deviance | | | | |
| MOST1 | 1.00 | | 1.00 | |
| MOD1 | 1.06 | | 1.06 | |
| RARE1 | 0.94 | | 0.64 | |
| Self-rejection | | | | |
| Self-derogation | 1.00 | | 1.00 | |
| Rejection by parents | 0.44 | | 0.44 | |
| Rejection by teachers | 0.19 | | 0.19 | |
| Negative social sanctions | | | | |
| Disaffection with Conventional | 1.00 | | 1.00 | |
| Antisocial defenses | 0.68 | | 0.68 | |
| Deviant peer associations | | | | |
| Friends deviant | 1.00 | | 1.00 | |
| Kids at school are deviant | 1.23 | | 1.46 | |
| Later deviance | | | | |
| MOD4 | 1.00 | | 1.00 | |
| RARE4 | 2.49 | | 1.57 | |
| Correlated errors | | | | |
|  | RARE1, SDRG | −0.08 | MOD1, RJTT | 0.02 |
|  | SDRG, AUTH | −0.18 | RARE1, RJTP | 0.01 |
|  | SDRG, FRNDEV | −0.21 | RARE1, ASD | 0.06 |
|  | | | RARE1, DSCO | 0.02 |
|  | | | SDRG, AUTH | −0.08 |
|  | | | SDRG, ASD | 0.21 |
|  | | | DSCO, KASDEV | 0.18 |
|  | | | ASD, KASDEV | 0.21 |
|  | | | ASD, FRNDEV | −0.09 |
|  | | | ASD, RARE4 | −0.02 |
| Within-construct error | MOD1, RARE1 | 0.02 | MOD1, RARE1 | 0.01 |

*Negative Social Sanctions.*   The scale for the latent construct of negative social sanctions is fixed according to the researcher-determined value for the three-item index of formal sanctions against subjects (reported by subjects) by representatives of the conventional order including school officials and law enforcement officials (AUTH). The scale is declared invariant across the two gender groups but the relative reliability of the scale for males and females is determined by estimates of reliability based on three measurement periods. The reliability for males is fixed at a value of 0.821; the reliability for females is fixed at a value of 0.746. Under the assumption of differential reliability of this variable, the scaling properties can be assumed invariant across gender.

*Disposition to Deviance.* The measurement properties of this latent construct were assumed to scale to the value of disaffection with the conventional order (DSCO). Once the assumption is made that the measurement properties of this variable are assumed invariant across groups, the relative contribution of the other measurement variable of antisocial defenses (ASD) is equivalent across both groups.

*Deviant Peer Associations.* The scale of the construct of deviant peer associations is fixed to the measurement variable of having deviant friends (FRN-DEV). It is invariant across gender groups in terms of the scaling dimensions for this construct. However, assuming equivalent scaling dimensions according to the measurement variable of having deviant friends requires that the assumption of equivalent measurement properties for awareness of deviance among kids at school (KASDEV) is not equal in both groups. The factor loading for KASDEV among males is 1.228 and among females is 1.460.

*Later Deviance.* The construct of later deviance is fixed to the measurement variable of moderate Time 4 deviance (MOD4) and has the same scale of deviance for both males and females. However, as with early deviance, the relative contribution of rare deviance (RARE4) is much greater for males than for females (2.493 versus 1.572). The larger loading of this variable on the latent construct of later deviance is in part due to a greater reliability of measurement for males than for females and also due to a lesser contribution of unique associations to the other measurement variables for males.

### Correlated Errors

As reference to Table 7.1 will indicate, among the 78 covariances, there were 11 unique associations among measurement variables for females and 4 unique associations among measurement variables for males. Two of these unique associations are present in both male and female subgroups. A positive unique correlated error term between Time 1 rare (RARE1) and Time 1 moderate (MOD1) deviance is present for male and for female gender. Each is also of roughly the same unstandardized magnitude. In addition, and also of the same sign but of unequal magnitude, there is a unique negative association between the measurement variable for negative social sanctions (AUTH) and self-derogation (SDRG). The effect occurs for both genders.

None of the other correlated error terms are consistent across both gender groups. Therefore, they will be discussed separately by gender. For females, the structural parameter between the measurement variable of rejection by teachers (RJTT) and Time 1 moderate deviance (MOD1) is positive. And the unique association between Time 1 rare deviance (RARE1) and Time 1 felt rejection by parents

(RJTP) is positive. These two unique correlated error terms are in addition to the already enhanced positive effect of Time 1 deviance on self-rejection. Thus, it appears that both structurally and independent of structural parameters the relationships among early deviance and the measurement variables of early self-rejection are significantly greater for females than for males. In addition, the measurement variables of antisocial defenses and rare deviance (ASD and RARE1) have a unique positive association independent of the structural parameters for females. Early rare deviance also has a positive unique association with disaffection with the conventional order.

The relationship between early self-derogation (SDRG) and later antisocial defenses (ASD) is significant and positive among females. This effect is independent of a strong positive structural parameter between the latent constructs for which these two variables are indicators.

Only the two measurement variables of antisocial defenses (ASD) and disaffection with the conventional order (DSCO) each have strong positive residual effects on awareness of deviance by kids in the school environment (KASDEV). Finally, antisocial defenses (ASD) has significant negative unique associations with deviant peers (FRNDEV) and rare Time 4 deviance (RARE4).

Among the males, there are two additional unique associations not discussed earlier. A negative unique association between early forms of rare deviance and early self-derogation (RARE1 and SDRG) is observed again, carried over from other analyses. In addition, there is a unique negative association between early self-derogation and the measurement variable of having deviant friends (FRNDEV).

## Structural Parameters

The structural parameters for the male (above the line) and female (below the line) models are presented in Figure 7.1. In a fully recursive model of the six latent constructs there is a possibility of 15 structural parameters. Of these 15 structural parameters, 7 are invariant across gender: Four are structurally equivalent to zero, and 3 are nonzero structurally equivalent parameters. The four effects found to be zero for both males and females are the effect of early deviance on later Time 4 deviance, and the effects of self-rejection on negative social sanctions, deviant peer associations, and later Time 4 deviance. The nonzero structurally invariant coefficients are found for the effect of early deviance on negative social sanctions, self-rejection on disposition to deviance, and disposition to deviance on deviant peer associations.

Of the remaining eight parameters, two are of the same sign although they are significantly different from each other. The effect of early deviance on early self-rejection and of negative social sanctions on later dispositions to deviance are significantly greater for females than for males.

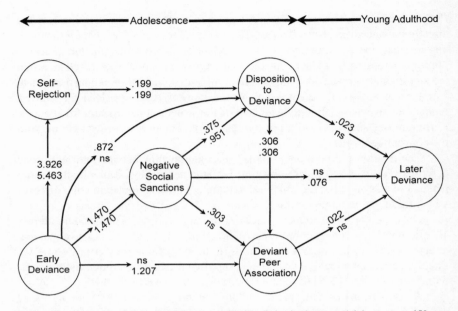

**Figure 7.1.** Moderating Influence of Gender on Deviant Behavior between Adolescence and Young Adulthood. Chi-square = 110.9, 108 *df*, *p* = 0.405. Male *n* = 736; female *n* = 1139.

Of the six remaining parameters, four are positive and significant for males but are zero for females, and two are zero for males but positive and significant for females. The effect of early deviance on disposition to deviance, the effect of disposition to deviance on later deviance, the effect of deviant peer associations on later Time 4 deviance, and the effect of negative social sanctions on deviant peer associations are all positive and significant for males only. The effects of early deviance on later deviant peer associations and of negative social sanctions on later Time 4 deviance are positive and significant for females but are zero structural parameters among males. As in the case of the model predicting ninth-grade deviance, all constructs were predicted more reliably for female than for male adolescents.

## Discussion

We examined the theoretical model as it was estimated for males and females. As in the model predicting adolescent deviance, in the model predicting adult deviance, many more similar effects between gender than dissimilar effects are observed. However, the pattern of structural similarities and dissimilarities by gender when accounting for adolescent delinquency, is not identical to the pattern observed for adult deviance. The adult model predicts self-reports of deviant acts occurring after 1977. In the earlier model, deviance was measured by acts commonly considered to be juvenile delinquency and constituted the self-reports of behaviors that occurred in 1973–1974. In the later instance, the modal age for the subjects was 15 years. In the former instance the modal age would be around 26 years. The latter model accounts for appreciably smaller proportions of the variance in young adult deviance than in ninth-grade deviance. That is, the effects of the predictors are attenuated over time. However, in each case, whether predicting ninth-grade or young adult deviance, the model is more reliable for anticipating female than male deviant behavior.

Further, in the adolescent model, the relationships between negative social sanctions, disposition to deviance, and deviant peer associations were modeled as within-wave effects. However, in the Time 4 adult deviance model the effects of disposition to deviance on deviant peer association, and the effects of negative social sanctions on deviant peer association are modeled as cross-wave effects, lagged by a 1-year period. With these differences in mind, we examine the similarities and dissimilarities both between genders and across models starting with the effects of variables most proximate in time to the dependent variable.

### Associations with Deviant Peers

The effect of deviant peer associations on ninth-grade deviance was observed to be stronger for females than for males. However, in predicting long-term deviance (that is, young adult deviance) males who engaged in deviant peer associations were significantly more likely to engage in young adult deviance while there was no significant relationship for females between deviant peer associations and young adult deviance.

We found, when explaining adolescent delinquency measured by Time 3 deviance, that association with deviant peers was a significant predictor of later deviance for both males and females. In addition, the unstandardized effects of deviant peer associations on later deviance were greater for females than for males. Considering that association with deviant peers represents the instrumental and expressive support for engaging in deviant behavior as well as providing a mechanism that attenuates the effectiveness of internalized social control mechanisms, the larger effect of deviant peer associations on later deviance among adolescents was interpreted in terms of the argument that gender role socialization toward conformity is biased, providing a greater emphasis on conformity for females than for males. Thus, the role of deviant peer socialization is more significant in attenuating the effect of the greater conformity socialization emphasis among females.

Deviant peer associations were much more significant for females in facilitating ninth-grade deviance. However, the effect of deviant peer associations on committing deviant acts during young adulthood became nonsignificant for females while remaining significant for males. We speculate that the changing roles of females between middle adolescence and young adulthood effectively removes them from the influence of deviant peers (perhaps in male-dominated peer relationships). Even if deviant female peer groups sustain themselves over time, entry into other relational contexts (marriage and motherhood, as well as early entry into the job market) precludes a sustained relationship with deviant peers and the associated influence on the commission of deviant acts. What had been deviant peer association now turns to group reinforcing normative pursuits such as those associated with motherhood (e.g., carpooling). Males, on the other hand, being less tied to homebound pursuits, are better able to sustain deviant associations while, perhaps, engaging at the same time in normative pursuits relating to husbandhood, fatherhood, and work force roles. Structural restraints do not permit young adult females to avoid all of their responsibilities (e.g., single motherhood). Young adult males, however, are able to avoid their paternal role responsibilities and permit themselves to be influenced by continuing peer associations into young adulthood.

When looking at the model for Time 4 adult deviance, the effect of deviant peer associations is significant only for males. Thus, whatever enhanced role that association with peers plays for attenuating the conformity emphasis among females, this effect is short-lived. The effect may be short-lived for many reasons: less stability of female deviant peer associations; the temporary nature of attenuation of internal social control mechanisms; the lack of opportunities for continued expressive or instrumental support from gendered deviant peer groups; or the greater prevalence of alternative peer associations that are available for female- than male-gendered subjects. Thus, it may be that as females mature into adulthood, their relationships with deviant peers dissipate and they establish primary group relationships with significant others outside of those early deviant peer associations, primarily, perhaps, the nuclear family relationships. Conversely, it may be that males are likely to continue deviant peer associations even in the event that they establish other primary relationships such as nuclear family membership.

## Disposition to Deviance

A number of differences were noted in the direct effects on male and female deviance when comparing the model explaining ninth-grade deviance with the model explaining young adult deviance. The direct effect of disposition to deviance on ninth-grade deviance was not significant for either male or female subjects. However, the effect of disposition to deviance on young adult deviance was uniquely significant for male subjects. Given the attenuation of ties to the conventional order and the disposition to act out deviant impulses, males were more likely to act out their deviant impulses.

For each gender, the effect of disposition to deviance on deviant peer associations is structurally invariant, both within and across waves. As expected, the effect is greatly attenuated across waves, but still remains highly significant for both models. The model suggests that the motivation to deviate from conventional norms and the simultaneous loss of motivation to conform are key links that are structurally stable in the onset and continuity of deviant behavior. Once individuals, both males and females, lose the motivation to conform to conventional standards and acquire the motivation to deviate, the primary outcome in the process is to seek out or become aware of deviant alternatives, primarily represented by awareness of deviant peers in the school environment and the increased association with deviant peers in a friendship network.

The effect of disposition to deviance on deviant peer associations is, as mentioned earlier, always very strong, and always has a fairly strong zero-order relationship to later deviance. However, as the model indicates, the majority of the zero-order relationship between disposition to deviance and later deviance is mediated by deviant peer associations. This is an effect that holds both within and across waves. However, in the Time 4 adult deviance model the mediating role of deviant peer associations is significant only for males. In addition, it appears that the long-lived effect of disposition to deviance on later deviance remains significant only for males, evidenced by the direct effect in the model. It appears that from a motivational standpoint, the effects for males appear to be powerful predictors of both initiation and continuity of deviant behavior whereas for females the motivational support provided by deviant peer associations and the individually acquired motivation to deviate prior to such support are short-lived phenomena. Again, one could speculate that this is a result of the greater emphasis of conformity for female adolescents, greater success for this socialization emphasis, and the lack of persistent influences that would continue to exacerbate a disposition to deviance or to prolong the stability of deviant peer associations.

## Negative Social Sanctions

In the model predicting adolescent deviance, negative social sanctions have structurally invariant effects across gender on disposition to deviance and later deviance, and had significant positive effects for both genders on later deviant peer associations, although the effect was substantively larger for males than for females. However, none of the effects are structurally invariant in the model predicting later adult deviance.

While no gender-specific effect of negative social sanctions on ninth-grade deviance was observed, a long-range differential effect of negative social sanctions on young adult deviance was observed such that only for females did being the object of negative social sanctions have long-range consequences on the probability of engaging in deviant acts during young adulthood. For females, being the object of negative social sanctions and thus perceiving themselves as having a spoiled social identity is sustained over a longer period of time. Once having accepted a spoiled social identity, females are not easily readmitted into conventional society and must redefine their roles in order to restore self-accepting attitudes. They accomplish this through identifying with the deviant role and defining it as an acceptable if not valued social identity.

The effect of negative social sanctions on later deviant peer associations is significant for males but nonsignificant for females. The stronger effects of negative social sanctions on deviant peer associations observed for males in the model predicting ninth-grade deviance, when both negative social sanctions and deviant peer associations were measured in the eighth grade, remain in effect for the model predicting young adult deviance when negative social sanctions was predicted in the eighth grade and deviant peer associations was predicted in the ninth grade. That the effect was attenuated slightly due to the increased length of time between the predictor and the dependent variable is understandable. The barely significant effect observed for females in the ninth grade model is attenuated to nonsignificance in the model predicting young adult deviance.

Finally, the effect of negative social sanctions on disposition to deviance is substantively larger for females than for males. The loss of structural invariance between genders for the effects of negative social sanctions on adult deviance can perhaps be attributable to the substantive difference in adult deviance as compared with adolescent deviance.

In the model accounting for ninth-grade deviance, no significant difference in the effect of negative social sanctions on disposition to deviance was observed. Both negative social sanctions and disposition to deviance were measured in the eighth grade. In the model predicting deviance during young adulthood, however, negative social sanctions were measured in the eighth grade and disposition to deviance in the ninth grade. In the model predicting ninth-grade deviance no gender-specific effect was observed for the influence of negative social sanctions on disposition to deviance although the effect for both males and females was significant. In the model predicting young adult deviance, however, although both male and female negative social sanctions predicted disposition to deviance at a statistically significant level, the effect was significantly stronger for females.

As suggested earlier in another connection, stigmatization of females, to a much greater extent than for males, precludes reentry into the conventional social order at little or no cost. To be the object of negative social sanctions violates female-specific expectations to a much greater extent than it violates male-specific expectations. Consequently, negative social sanctions for females are more likely to eventuate in feelings of alienation from the conventional order and a disposition to seek alternative modes of deviance. Whether or not they in fact do so (as we discussed above) is contingent on other factors, such as the availability of opportunities for deviance. Why this gender-specific differential should have been observed between the eighth and the ninth grade when it was not observed within the eighth grade may implicate a number of factors. First, the earlier maturing female may become more acutely aware of her unhappy circumstances with regard to adopting conventional adult roles as she nears the point where young adult roles tend to become salient. The differential impact of negative social sanctions on disposition to deviate may require the passage of time before the unsavory reputation of the female adolescent may become known widely throughout the conventional community. Once the stigmatization process has been recognized, the disposition to deviance will be exacerbated, and the labeling effect will be realized.

## Self-Rejection

Considering changes in the antecedents of deviant peer associations for the two models, in the model predicting ninth-grade deviance, we had earlier observed a direct gender-specific effect of self-rejection on deviant peer associations such that, for females only, a significant and inverse effect of self-rejection on deviant peer association measured in the eighth grade was observed. This gender-specific effect disappeared in the model predicting young adult deviance. When deviant peer association was measured in the ninth grade rather than the eighth grade the inverse effect of self-rejection on deviant peer associations for female adolescents disappeared. We attribute the loss of this effect to the increase in self-confidence that accompanies development during the adolescent years particularly among the early maturing females. We had interpreted the inverse effect of self-rejection on deviant peer associations in terms of a diffidence or fear of consequences that might accompany the adoption of deviant patterns such as association with deviant peers. The fear of consequences is attenuated as the female adolescent by the ninth grade gains a certain confidence in her own competence to negotiate social reality.

In the model predicting early adolescence, self-rejection had significant positive effects on disposition to deviance for both males and females although the effect was greater for females. However, in the model predicting adult deviance, the gender-related disparity was no longer observed. The effect was positive and significant but was invariant across genders.

Perhaps changes occurring in females' life circumstances between the eighth and the ninth grade attenuate the loss of motivation to conform and motivation to deviate that is consequent to the experience of self-rejection in normative membership groups. It is possible that physical maturation, for example, provides the female adolescent with an alternative basis for self-esteem that obviates the need to attenuate ties with the conventional order. The end result is that the effect of self-rejection on disposition to deviate between the seventh and the eighth grade is attenuated between the seventh and the ninth grade for females while the effect remains relatively constant for male adolescents.

## Early Deviance

The model predicting ninth-grade deviance effectively accounted for the stability between early deviance and later deviance for female adolescents.

However, a significant stability effect was observed for males. This stability effect is no longer noted when accounting for long-term deviance, that is, deviant behaviors performed in young adulthood. This merely reflects an attenuation of the relationship between early deviance (and the mediating linkages) and later deviance over time.

The stronger effect for female adolescents than for male adolescents of early deviance on deviant peer associations observed in the model predicting ninth-grade deviance was replicated in the model predicting young adult deviance. However, because deviant peer association was measured in the ninth grade in the later model, rather than in the eighth grade in the model predicting ninth-grade deviance, some attenuation occurred (to nonsignificance for males) in the effect of seventh-grade deviance on later deviant peer association. The unique effect of early deviance on later deviant peer associations for female adolescents continues to be interpreted in terms of early deviance being incongruent with female-specific role expectations and so being more likely to signal deviant identities to deviant peers. Hence, the deviant peers are more likely to recruit and accept females who perform such acts than males who perform such deviant acts. For males, the performance of these acts may be regarded as role congruent and not necessarily as a signal of a deviant identity.

The relative gender-specific effects of early deviance on self-rejection were observed in both models with female adolescents displaying a greater effect of early deviance on self-rejection. However, the stronger effects observed for subjects who were present during all four waves (seventh grade, eighth grade, ninth grade, and young adulthood) may reflect a more conforming segment of the population than those who were present only for the first three waves. The fact that they were locatable in young adulthood may indicate that initially they had a greater investment in the conventional structure. Therefore, engaging in early deviance would have a much more adverse affect on their self-attitudes that were internalized in the course of the conventional socialization process.

When disposition to deviance was measured in the eighth grade there was no effect for either gender of early deviance (measured in the seventh grade) on disposition to deviance in the eighth grade. However, for the model predicting young adult deviance, when disposition to deviance was measured in the ninth grade rather than the eighth grade, the seventh-grade deviance had a direct gender-specific effect on ninth-grade disposition to deviance such that only for males was early deviance positively and significantly related to disposition to deviance. We interpret this effect as the exacerbation of deviant attitudes occasioned by life-course transitions into adulthood.

At this point, males have to make a number of decisions regarding affiliation with conventional institutional structures, such as the decision to go on in school, the decision to participate in sports, the decision to enter one or another academic track, and so forth. It is at this time that early deviants (reflecting in part affiliation with subcultural groups) who define deviant acts as acceptable have to make a conscious decision to oppose the conventional social order and to remain "loyal" to the contranormative subculture. Further, it should be noted that this effect is independent of the effect of early deviance on self-rejection. That is, the early deviance is syntonic with the attitudes reflected in the disposition to deviance measures.

It would seem that at this stage in the life course those who have earlier engaged in deviance first become aware of the social distance between the attitudes of their group and the attitudes of the more inclusive social world. The awareness this distance, again, is occasioned by the requirement that they consciously make decisions regarding their relationship with the conventional world. Since there was no cost in reduced self-esteem for the early involvement in deviance, continuing expression of deviance-proneness is accomplished at little emotional cost.

# IV

# SUMMARY AND CONCLUSIONS

In Chapter 8 we present an overview of our findings and evaluate the viability of the guiding theoretical framework. While the models in large measure were compatible with this framework, a number of instances were noted in which the theoretical model was conditioned by constructs reflecting social differentiations (according to gender and race/ethnicity) and stage in the life course. These findings suggest the basis for further elaborations of the model in terms of specification of mediating constructs, suppressor variables, moderators of the relationships, and novel constructs that increase the explained variance of deviant behavior. By way of illustrating the stimulus value of the theoretical orientation and logic of procedure guiding the early studies, a number of recent studies that built on the early studies are summarized.

# 8

# The Study of Deviant Behavior
*Retrospect and Prospect*

The theoretical statements, methods, and empirical analyses reported in this volume are not presented as the state of our current understanding of the causes of deviant behavior, but rather are presented as a template for a useful logic of procedure for increasing our understanding of deviant behavior. Starting with a guiding theoretical framework and a methodological approach, we estimated a series of models using a systematic elaboration strategy to decompose hypothesized linear relations, increase explained variance, uncover suppressor effects, and determine scope conditions for the hypothesized models.

We reported the guiding theoretical statement, methodological approach, and series of analyses as a case study demonstrating the influences of our logic of procedure in increasing our understanding of deviant behavior. The tests of the usefulness of our procedures are twofold. First, our findings, by and large, are congruent with the integrative theory of deviant behavior that guided our analyses. Second, the early analyses provided a basis for incorporating the results of new analyses that were stimulated by the earlier findings. We consider in turn: (1) the compatibility of the early findings with a guiding integrative theory and (2) a review of recent studies that build on earlier analyses.

## Summary and Evaluation

Guided by an integrative theory of deviant behavior, we estimated a series of increasingly elaborated models that validated the theoretical framework by demonstrating the theoretically anticipated decomposition of linear relationships, increased explained variance of deviant behavior, countervailing effects, and conditions under which linear effects were observed. Initially we estimated the series of increasingly elaborated theoretically informed models for a sample of seventh graders tested three times at annual intervals. The most inclusive model then was estimated separately for males and females and for African-American, Mexican-American, and white-Anglo subjects separately in order to consider the conditions under which the linear relationships would hold. Finally, we considered the moderating influence of stage in the life course on the linear relationships by contrasting models estimating deviant behaviors as young adults with models estimating deviant behaviors as adolescents. We first contrasted the models for white-Anglo subjects explaining young adult and adolescent deviant behavior, respectively. We then separately contrasted for male and female subject models explaining young adult and adolescent behavior, respectively.

### The Most Inclusive Adolescent Model

Consistent with theoretical expectations, the association of negative self-feelings with perceptions of rejection and failure in family and school (self-rejection) leads to the loss of motivation to conform to, and motivation to deviate from, conventional expectations (disposition to deviance). Self-rejection is in part the consequence of failure to approximate conventional expectations (deviance at Time 1). The disposition to deviate is the result not only of earlier self-rejection but also of the negative social sanctions that were elicited by earlier deviant behavior. Negative social sanctions further alienate the individual from the normative order (disposition to deviance).

Both the disposition to deviance and the stigma associated with earlier social sanctions increase the likelihood of association with deviant peers. Net of these direct positive effects of dispositions to deviance and social sanctions on associations with deviant peers, self-rejection at Time 1 has a direct inverse influence on deviant peer associations. Presumably, self-rejection, net of its indirect (via disposition to deviance) effect on deviant peer association, increases the person's motivation to conform to and be accepted by normative groups. One manifestation of the exacerbation of the need for acceptance is the attempt to avoid deviant activities, including association with deviant peers. In addition, it is possible that the inverse association between self-rejection and deviant peer associations may reflect avoidant tendencies on the part of individuals who have a history of rejection and failure experiences.

Deviant peer associations, the results of rejection of conventional norms, the stigmatization of negative social sanctions, and the attractiveness of deviant subjects to deviant peers have a direct effect on later deviant behavior. Presumably, deviant peer associations provide the opportunities, the social definitions of the situation, and social support for engaging in deviant behavior. Deviant peer association provides the strongest direct effect on deviant behavior. However, independent of this effect, social sanctions and earlier deviant behavior have direct positive effects on deviance. Social sanctions increase the need of the individual for self-justification of the deviant behavior that is accomplished through the repetition of the act. Although the intervening effects of social sanctions and deviant peer associations accounted for most of the stability of the deviant behavior, some of the stability coefficient has yet to be decomposed.

## Moderating Influences of Gender

The inclusive adolescent model tended to be applicable in explaining both male and female deviant behavior. Of 11 causal effects where the effect was significant for the males and/or females, the effects were statistically significant and in the same direction for both categories in nine instances. However, the significant difference between the genders in strength of causal effects suggested the validity of theoretically informed assumptions regarding the conditions under which the linear model will be viable. For example, deviant behavior is more likely to lead to informal stigmatization and to attractiveness to deviant peers where the deviant behavior is role incongruent. Assuming that deviant behavior, as we have measured it, is more role incongruent for females than for males, we would expect (as we observed in fact) that the positive effects of early deviance on self-rejection and association with the deviant peers would be significantly stronger for females than for males.

Another condition for the viability of the linear model is that the subjects define conformity to the expectations of others as a salient self-evaluative criterion. Where the acceptance by others is more salient, the failure to achieve acceptance would be more likely to eventuate in loss of motivation to conform to, and acquisition of motivation to deviate from, normative expectations. On the assumption that females are more likely to be socialized to highly regard conformity to the expectations of parents and teachers than are males, we would expect to find (as we in fact observed) that the positive effect of self-rejection on disposition to deviance would be stronger for females than for males.

A condition for anticipating a positive effect of deviant peer associations on later deviance is an emotional investment in and disposition to be influenced by such associations. On the assumption that females have a stronger need to affiliate, we would expect (as we in fact observed) that the effect of deviant peer associations on deviant behavior would be greater for females than for males.

These findings are illustrative of those that support theoretical expectations regarding the conditions under which the inclusive theoretical model is viable. However, it remains for future research to confirm that the putative correlates of gender that are asserted to mediate the moderating influences of gender in fact mediate these influences.

## Moderating Influences of Race/Ethnicity

Of the 12 causal paths in which one or more racial/ethnic categories of subjects manifested significant effects, 11 paths were significant for the white-Anglo subjects and 8 were significant for the African-American and Mexican-American subjects. However, even where significant effects in the same direction were observed in multiple groups, the magnitudes of the effects frequently were significantly different among the groups. The findings testify both to the generality of the model and to the validity of theoretical specification of moderators that define scope conditions for the general linear model.

While deviant behavior is generally expected to elicit negative social sanctions, the strength of this relationship should be contingent on the degree of role incongruence represented by the deviant behavior. If it may be assumed that the deviant behavior is less prevalent, and therefore more role incongruent, among the white-Anglo subjects, it is to be expected that the tendency for deviant behaviors to elicit negative social sanctions would be stronger among the white-Anglo subjects. This too was actually observed. Although the effect was significant for all three groups, the effect of early deviant behavior on negative social sanctions was stronger for the white-Anglo subjects.

The effect of earlier deviance on disposition to deviance, net of the alienating effect of consequent negative social sanctions, is contingent on the identification with subcultures that have less of a stake in the dominant subculture, are more likely to reinforce motivation to deviate from conventional expectations, and are less likely to reinforce motivation to conform to the normative expectations. On the assumption that deviant behavior reflects a greater degree of subcultural reinforcement in minority groups, we would expect the effect of early deviance on disposition to deviance (again, net of the intervening alienating effect of negative social sanctions) to be significantly stronger for minority group subjects than for white-Anglo subjects. This was observed to be true. The direct positive minority group effects of early deviance on later disposition to deviance were appreciably greater than the effects for white-Anglo subjects.

The countervailing inverse effect of self-rejection on later deviance that was hypothesized in the general model is thought to be contingent on the earlier internalization of conventional norms. Under this condition, the disposition to engage in deviance stimulated by self-rejection is to a degree counterbalanced by the residual commitment to conventional norms that inhibits the acting out of deviant dispositions. On the assumption that the white-Anglo subjects are most likely to have internalized conventional norms, we hypothesized and observed the countervailing inverse effect of self-rejection on deviance uniquely in this group of subjects.

The hypothesized and observed effect of being the object of negative social sanctions on association with deviant peers is believed to be contingent on the difficulty of identifying deviant actors whom the deviant peers would find attractive and recruit into their groups. Where it is difficult to identify deviant actors in the absence of visible negative social sanctions, the presence of such sanctions would be associated with increased association with deviant peers. In the more diffuse white-Anglo category, visible negative sanctions would serve the identifiability function. Hence, the direct effect of negative social sanctions on deviant peer associations is significant among white-Anglo subjects. However, for the African-American and Mexican-American youth, deviant peer networks may be apparent due to socioeconomic-related environmental and other ethnicity-based structural conditions that render official sanctions as superfluous in identifying other deviants. Hence, for these subjects, no significant effects of negative social sanctions on deviant peer associations were observed.

Independent of the indirect effects of negative social sanctions on later deviance via disposition to deviance and deviant peer associations, we hypothesized a direct effect of negative social sanctions on later deviance. This effect was said to reflect the need to restore self-esteem by reevaluating a previously stigmatized deviant status. This effect is contingent on the inability to cope with stigmatizing effects for conventional means, as well as on the absence of increased exposures of stigma associated with the deviant adaptations. Because minority groups are least able to cope with the stigma of official sanctions via conventional means and are less likely than conventional groups to experience stigma in their immediate environments for engaging in deviant adaptations, it is to be expected that the effects of negative social sanctions on deviant behavior would be stronger for these groups than for white-Anglo subjects, as we observed.

These illustrative findings provide some support for the theoretical expectations regarding the contingencies for linear relationships. However, future research must determine unequivocally that race/ethnicity truly reflects the conditions that they have been interpreted as reflecting. Further, a number of other findings have been observed to vary by race/ethnicity. After the fact, many of the findings are interpretable as compatible with the guiding theoretical framework. Nevertheless these interpretations are made with caution in view of the fact that they were unanticipated.

### *Stage in the Life Course as a Moderator: White-Anglo Subjects*

A comparison of the general theoretical models as an explanation of adult deviance and as an explanation of adolescent deviance reveals important similarities and differences. On the one hand, nine significant structural effects in the adolescent model were also observed in the adult model. However, some effects observed in the adolescent model were not observed in the adult model. Arguably the more interesting of these is the effect of deviant peer associations on later deviance, observed uniquely in the adolescent model.

On theoretical grounds it is expected that the effect of deviant peer associations on deviant behavior depends in large part on the centrality of peer associations in the lives of the subjects. As the subjects mature from adolescence to young adulthood, a number of circumstances arise that decrease the salience of peer associations (whether deviant or conventional) in the lives of the subjects. The focus on the school and neighborhood as major areas of the life space during adolescence provides opportunities for peer associations that are no longer provided as the individual matures and ceases to focus on the school and neighborhood. As the youths mature they take on new responsibilities in the formation of families and in the workplace. These new obligations attenuate both the opportunities to engage in peer associations and the salience of the associations.

In view of these observations, it is to be expected that deviant peer associations in adolescence would predict deviant behavior in adolescence, but not in young adulthood. In fact, we observed this to be the case. However, as we shall shortly observe, these effects were also contingent on the gender of the subjects.

### Stage in the Life Course as a Moderator: Interaction with Gender

As in the model predicting adolescent deviance, when predicting adult deviance there are many more similarities than dissimilarities between the genders. Nevertheless, the pattern of dissimilarities between males and females varies according to whether we are predicting young adult or adolescent deviance. That is, gender and stage in the life course interact as moderators of the general linear model. We illustrate this conclusion with some theoretically relevant findings.

The influence of deviant peer associations on deviant behavior is contingent on the salience of conformity to deviant peers in relationship to the centrality of other role obligations. Assuming that the need for peer approval during adolescence is greater for females than for males, and that with maturation the salience of alternative roles, particularly those relating to marriage and family, increases to a greater extent for females (while males are better able to sustain deviant peer associations into young adulthood), it would be expected that during adolescence the effect of deviant peer associations on deviant behavior would be stronger for women than for men, but during young adulthood prior deviant peer associations would have a weaker effect on deviant behavior for females than for males. This was precisely the pattern that was observed. Indeed, in the adult model the effect of prior deviant peer associations on deviant behavior was statistically significant only for male subjects.

The degree to which being the object of negative social sanctions is a more or less permanent stigma is contingent on the perceived role incongruence of this experience. Insofar as females are more greatly stigmatized by the experience of formal sanctions, we would expect that females would be less likely to be readmitted to conventional society and so would be more likely to redefine their deviant status in more favorable terms. They would identify with the deviant roles over a longer time. On these assumptions we would expect that being the object of negative social sanctions would have a uniquely positive effect on deviant behaviors for females in the young adult model. Consistent with this finding, in the young adult model the effect of negative social sanctions on disposition to deviance is significantly greater for females than for males, a relationship that would be expected if females were more stigmatized by virtue of being the object of negative social sanctions.

The strategy of estimating increasingly elaborated theoretically informed models on a longitudinal data set to decompose linear relations, uncover suppressor effects representing countervailing processes, increase explained variance, and establish scope conditions for the general model by specifying theoretically indicated moderating constructs in general, produced a series of models that increased our understanding of deviant behavior. The analyses have highlighted the theoretically anticipated mechanisms through which deviant behavior is initiated or escalated.

The strategies that we followed, as well as the theoretical framework that has guided the analyses, may be viewed as a model for conducting a series of analyses intended to increase our understanding of specified phenomena. Additionally, the procedures we followed, the theoretical framework, and the early analyses provide a basis for systematically building on the current state of our knowledge in order to elaborate our understanding of deviant behavior.

## Building on Past Studies

The usefulness of the theoretical framework, methodology, and resulting early estimations of theoretically informed models in stimulating further elaborations of our understanding of deviant behavior may be illustrated by more recent studies that: (1) decompose linear effects observed in earlier studies by interpolating the theoretically indicated mediating constructs and (2) specify moderating variables that define the conditions under which the linear relations will be observed.

### Mediating Variables

*Self-Rejection.* In earlier analyses (Kaplan & Johnson, 1991; Kaplan et al., 1988), being the object of negative social sanctions was hypothesized and observed to influence disposition to deviate (loss of motivation to conform to, and acquisition of motivation to deviate from, conventional expectations), and to directly affect deviant behavior. In each case the hypothesis rested on the untested premise that being the object of negative social sanctions increased feelings of self-rejection. Theoretical premises derived from the integrative theory of deviant behavior suggest that being the object of negative social sanctions in response to deviant behavior affects self-rejection that in turn has independent effects on attitudes toward conventional society and attitudes toward deviant behaviors and identities. Self-rejection leads to the loss of motivation to conform to, and the genesis of motivation to deviate from, conventional expectations (disposition to deviance), and independently, to the positive reevaluation of, and identification with, deviant identities and behaviors. These premises are tested by estimating an elaborated model that specifies self-rejection as mediating and decomposing the previously hypothesized and observed direct effects of negative social sanctions on disposition to deviance and deviant behavior. The hypothesized effects were observed, thus lending greater credibility to positions that focus on the mediating role of self-rejection in relationships between negative social sanctions and continuity or amplification of deviance (Kaplan & Fukurai, 1992).

*Coping Styles.*   In another elaboration, consistent with the theoretical position that interprets deviant patterns as attempts to cope with self-devaluing experiences in conventional groups, a model was proposed in which the relationships between self-rejection and specific forms of deviant behavior were mediated by coping styles (attack and avoidance) with which the deviant patterns were functionally compatible. Self-rejection at Time 1 was hypothesized and observed to influence both avoidance and attack coping styles measured at Time 2. Also as expected, avoidant coping at Time 2 was related specifically to drug use at Time 3, and attack coping style at Time 2 was related specifically to violence and theft at Time 3. In addition to supporting the position that deviant behaviors serve, or are expected to serve, self-protective and self-enhancing functions, the findings contribute to understanding why one rather than other patterns of deviance is adopted (Kaplan & Peck, 1992).

### Moderating Influences

Arguably, the major limitation in a number of long-term theoretically informed studies is the failure to test for the scope conditions that are implicit or explicitly stated in the outlines of the guiding theoretical frameworks. A number of the more recent analyses were carried out to test the validity of the integrative theory's premises regarding the conditions under which hypothesized linear relationships will be observed. The analyses used either: (1) ordinary least squares (OLS) regression with interaction terms or multiple groups or (2) structural equation models.

*Regression Models.*   A significant feature of the theory relates to the conditions under which deviant behavior has self-enhancing as opposed to self-derogating outcomes. Based on the premise that having weak ties to the conventional order is a precondition for experiencing reduced self-derogation through deviant adaptations, the hypothesis was tested that participation in social protest activities in the seventh grade has self-enhancing outcomes in the ninth grade and in young adulthood where the subjects in the seventh grade express alienation from the conventional social order. However, participation in social protest activities in the seventh grade is expected to have self-devaluing consequences in the ninth grade and young adulthood where the subjects in the seventh grade do not express alienation from the conventional social order. The result of OLS multiple regression analyses with interaction terms were consistent with the hypothesis. As predicted, among subjects who rejected the idea that one can get ahead by working hard, seventh-grade social protest was inversely related to self-derogation, and among subjects who affirmed the idea that one can get ahead by working hard, social protest activities related to higher subsequent levels of self-derogation (Kaplan & Liu, 2000).

Consistent with the theoretical orientation, we observed positive main effects of participation in social movements and denial that children like the subject can get ahead by working hard on later self-derogation. The assumption that ordinary individuals will think less positively of themselves when they fail to conform to the standards of their membership group is consistent with the observation in the multiple regression models that participation in social movements is positively related to later self-derogation scores (controlling on earlier self-derogation). Similarly, consistent with the premise that perceived inability to satisfy one's needs in the context of the conventional social order anticipates self-derogation, is the observation in the multiple regression models that denial of the statement that children like the subject can get ahead if they work hard is positively related to later self-derogation.

More significantly, however, we observed the predicted effect of the interaction between social movement participation and denial that children like the subject can get ahead by working hard on lower levels of self-derogation. Among subjects who indicated that children like the subject can get ahead by working hard, participation in social protest activities in the seventh grade was positively related to self-derogation scores. Presumably, the belief that working hard is associated with rewards reflects an internalization of conventional norms and identification with the membership groups that adhere to these norms. Among individuals who have internalized conventional norms, participation in activities that question the validity of the conventional normative structure should be associated with negative attitudes toward oneself. Participation in social protest activities reflects deviation from conventional norms. Insofar as individuals who internalize these norms judge themselves according to the degree that they approximate the normative standards, failure to do so by engaging in social protest activities would lead to self-devaluation.

In contrast, for subjects who deny that individuals can get ahead by working hard, participation in social protest activities has salutary consequences for their self-attitudes: the greater the degree of participation in social protest activities, the lower the level of future self-derogatory attitudes. This was the case whether the later self-derogatory activities were measured in the ninth grade or as young adults, although the effect was more apparent in later adolescent years. The decrease in self-derogation that followed participation in social movements (controlling on earlier self-derogation) for subjects, who believed that it was not possible to get ahead even with working hard, may be accounted for by any number of mechanisms. It is likely that subjects who believe that it is not possible to get ahead by working hard have lower levels of perceived self-efficacy. Participation in social protest activities perhaps testifies to the individual's capability of controlling his own destiny, albeit outside of conventional parameters.

At the same time, participation in social protest activities reflects affiliation with a group that conforms to different standards than the ones the person was presumably unable to approximate (as reflected in the belief that even with hard work, children like him will not be able to get ahead). By adopting and conforming to the normative standards of the new reference group the person is enabled to evaluate himself positively by virtue of conforming to the now-valued standards (including participation in social protest-related activities). Further, by engaging in contranormative activities, subjects who believe that they cannot get ahead even by working hard express their contempt for the normative activities according to which they must judge themselves to be failures. By rejecting the validity of the standards, these subjects reject the bases for self-derogatory judgments (Kaplan & Liu, 2000).

In another series of analyses we estimated models that specify theoretical conditions under which subjects escalate drug use (Kaplan & Johnson, 1992). Stepwise regression analyses predicted escalation of use from nine circumstances surrounding initial use among a subset of the population who had ever engaged in illicit drug use (other than marijuana). The analyses were conducted separately for males and females and within each grouping of males and females for individuals who were high and low, respectively, on each of the 12 variables characterizing the subjects' personal and social circumstances at the time of initial test administration.

For three of the independent variables, the effects on escalation of drug use were gender specific. For males, increased experiences of potency following initial drug use were associated with escalation of drug use at a later point in time. For males, the initiation of drug use following anger at significant others was associated with escalation of drug use at a later point in time. For female subjects, the weakening of interpersonal ties as a result of initial drug use was positively associated with the escalation of drug use.

The association between the circumstances surrounding initial use and escalation of use for either males or females was contingent on the characteristics of the individual and his environment in the seventh grade. Thus, under conditions of high self-derogation but not under conditions of low self-derogation, the experience of increased potency occasioned by initial drug use was found to be influential on the escalation of drug use. External locus of control serves as a moderating variable for a number of antecedents of escalation of drug use for males, but not for females. This is congruent with the understanding that the masculine identity in our society is much more concerned with issues of autonomy and dependence than is the feminine identity.

The meaning of the moderating variables is influenced by their interaction with gender. For males, initial drug use in response to anger at significant others had significant effects on escalation of drug use only for individuals who were high on a tendency toward avoidance (measured in the seventh grade). This suggests that, for those individuals who are avoidant, others' feelings of anger would be more distressful than for individuals who are less avoidant. Drugs, insofar as they assuage angry feelings, would be more positively reinforcing for high-avoidance than low-avoidance individuals. On the other hand, for females, only those who were low on a need to avoid were positively reinforced by drug use in response to anger. For women, the higher motivation to maintain interpersonal relationships (reflected in low tendencies to avoid) is gratified by drug use in response to the experiences of anger at significant others. For men, the motivation among high-avoidance subjects is to reduce the feelings of anger; for women the motivation is to maintain the relationships (Kaplan & Johnson, 1992). Again, the general theoretical framework appears valid in a number of respects.

*Structural Equation Models.*   Recent analyses illustrate the use of structural equation modeling to test theoretically informed hypotheses regarding moderators of the effects of: (1) negative self-feelings on deviant behavior and (2) deviant behavior on negative self-feelings.

Informed by the general theory of deviant behavior, it was hypothesized that the positive effect of negative self-feelings on later deviant behavior would be observed only for youths who are not characterized by a deviant identity. Data from a second-generational panel of youths tested during early adolescence and retested 3 years later ($N = 1041$) were used to estimate the structural equation models. As hypothesized, for youths without a deviant identity, negative self-feelings had both direct and indirect (via contemporary deviant behavior) positive effects on later deviant behavior. For youths characterized by deviant identities, however, no overall effect of negative self-feelings on deviant behavior was observed due to the operation of countervailing effects. Countering the indirect positive effects of negative self-feelings (presumably reflecting alienation from the conventional order) were inverse direct effects of negative self-feelings on later deviant behavior (presumably reflecting alienation from the deviant identity stemming from its association with concomitant negative self-feelings) (Kaplan & Lin, 2000).

The findings provided direct empirical support for the significance of at least one of the theoretical conditions that are believed to moderate the relation between negative self-feelings and deviant behavior, in particular, nondeviant identity. Informed by general theory of deviant behavior, it was hypothesized that the experience of negative self-feelings would dispose youth to adopt deviant patterns of behavior. It was further expected that this effect would be observed only among participants who were categorized as not having a deviant identity, that is, who were conventional. It was reasoned that if people develop negative self-feelings in the course of conventional group experiences, they would be alienated from the normative system (that is, lose motivation to conform) and would seek alternative (deviant) responses for which they might assuage the stressful self-feelings.

However, according to the general theory, it was predicted that this positive effect of negative self-feelings would not be observed for participants who were classified as having a deviant identity. It was reasoned that, for those individuals, countervailing processes would be at work. On the one hand, deviant identities connote alienation from the conventional world and therefore were expected to have the potential to contribute to continuation of deviant adaptations. On the other hand, the development of negative self-feelings while having a deviant identity suggests that an attenuation of ties to the deviant identity also should occur, and thus that adoption of conventional patterns of behavior would become more likely as an attempt to assuage self-rejecting feelings. These countervailing tendencies were expected to be reflected in a near-zero relation between self-feelings and deviant behavior.

The results of the analyses supported the theoretical models. For the sample as a whole, negative self-feelings predicted deviant behavior. However, further analysis revealed that the subgroup of participants who were classified as not having a deviant identity accounted for this overall effect. For these youth, negative self-feelings were indicated to have both direct and indirect (via contemporary deviant behavior) positive effects on later deviant behavior. However, for youth classified as deviant, the overall effect of negative self-feelings on deviant behavior was nonsignificant; specifically, a direct inverse effect was counterbalanced by an indirect (via contemporary deviant behavior) positive effect. Deviant identity thus appears to moderate the influence of self-feelings on deviant behavior, at least during the period of adolescence that was the focus of the present research (Kaplan & Lin, 2000).

The influence of deviant behavior on self-derogation was also hypothesized to be contingent on the presence of other theoretically indicated conditions, in particular, stage in the life course, gender, and race/ethnicity. Specifically, we examined the effectiveness of the disposition to engage in aggressive strategies of coping with (that is, reducing) self-derogation. We expected that for social identities in which a salient cause of self-derogation is the perceived barrier against self-assertiveness, empowerment, or taking action on one's own behalf, the adoption of aggressive dispositions would be self-enhancing. If the source of self-derogation for females and Mexican-Americans is perceived to be the social disempowerment of these identities, then the adoption of aggressive stances by persons characterized by these identities will result in the reduction of self-derogation. If the perceived disempowerment is experienced more intensely at earlier stages in the life course, then the reduction in self-derogation consequent on the adoption of aggressive behaviors will be associated with earlier stages in the life course (Kaplan & Halim, 2000).

Similarly, we expected that for social identities in which the adoption of aggressive dispositions is deplored, the adoption of such strategies would increase rather than decrease self-derogation. If females, particularly during adulthood, view aggression as inappropriate and are negatively sanctioned for their disposition to aggressively respond to self-devaluing circumstances, then they will experience exacerbation of their self-derogation following adoption of aggressive coping dispositions.

These expectations were tested using data from a panel tested at three points during the life course (early adolescence, young adulthood, and the second half of the fourth decade of life). The basic model specified effects of self-derogation on aggression at each point in time, stability effects of self-derogation and aggression between adjacent stages of the life course, and lagged effects of aggression at an earlier point in time on self-derogation at later points in time.

This model was estimated for males and females separately, and for white-Anglo, African-American, and Mexican-American subjects separately. We expected that gender and race/ethnicity would moderate the model in accordance with the expectation specified above. In general, the results of estimation of the structural equation models were congruent with our expectations. As expected, for females only, aggression in early adolescence anticipated decreases in self-derogation in young adulthood, and aggression increased self-derogation between the third and fourth decades of life. For white-Anglo and African-American subjects, aggression in early adulthood was related to increased self-derogation in later adulthood, but for Mexican-American subjects, early adult aggression decreased self-derogation in later adulthood. The results are interpretable in terms of self-enhancing implications of aggression for disempowered groups and in terms of subcultural differences in acceptability of aggressive adaptations to stress at different stages in the life course.

This volume describes a series of analyses using panel data that are informed by an integrative theory of deviant behavior. The analyses estimate models that are systematically elaborated by the introduction of new constructs. Each new construct increases the amount of explained variance, decomposes linear relations in terms of theoretically indicated mediating variables, exposes suppressor effects, or defines the theoretical conditions that moderate the linear relationships.

We report the results of our early research labors not only for their historic interest or for their usefulness in increasing our understanding of deviant behaviors, but as a case study of our logic of procedure that has contemporary significance for the investigation of deviant behavior. The usefulness of our early research agenda as a template for current investigations of deviant behavior is suggested by both the compatibility of our findings with a guiding integrative theoretical framework and the stimulus value of the theory and early analyses for specifying models that are increasingly precise and inclusive in the range of explanatory variables that increase explained variance, specify countervailing influences, mediate linear relationships, and define the scope of conditions for viable linear relations. The continuing interplay between the integrative theory and the results of the analyses promises to bring us ever closer to our goal of a full understanding of the direct, indirect, and conditional antecedents and consequences of deviant behavior at different stages of the life course.

# References

Ageton, S., & Elliott, D. S. (1974). The effects of legal processing on delinquent orientations. *Social Problems, 22,* 87–100.

Akers, R. L. (1977). *Deviant behavior: A social learning perspective.* Belmont, CA: Wadsworth.

Akers, R. L. (1985). *Deviant behavior: A social learning approach* (3rd ed.). Belmont, CA: Wadsworth.

Akers, R. L. (2000). *Criminological theories: Introduction, evaluation and application.* Los Angeles: Roxbury Publishing.

Akers, R. L., Krohn, M. D., Lanza-Kaduce, L., & Radosevich, M. J. (1979). Social learning and deviant behavior: A specific test of a general theory. *American Sociological Review, 44,* 636–655.

Bachman, J. G. (1970). *Youth in transition* (Vol. 2). Ann Arbor, MI: Institute for Social Research.

Bachman, J. G., O'Malley, P. M., & Johnston, J. (1978). *Youth in transition* (Vol. 6). Ann Arbor, MI: Institute for Social Research.

Becker, H. S. (1963). *Outsiders: Studies in sociology of deviance.* New York: Free Press.

Bentler, P. M., & Bonett, D. G. (1980). Significance tests and goodness of fit in the analysis of covariance structures. *Psychological Bulletin, 88*(3), 588–606.

Bernstein, I., Kelley, W., & Doyle, P. (1977). Societal reaction to deviants: The case of criminal defendants. *American Sociological Review, 42,* 743–755.

Brennan, T., Huizinga, D., & Elliott, D. S. (1978). *The social psychology of runaways.* Boston: Heath.

Briar, S., & Piliavin, I. (1965). Delinquency, situational inducements, and commitment to conformity. *Social Problems, 13,* 34–45.

Burgess, R. L., & Akers, R. L. (1966). A differential association–reinforcement theory of criminal behavior. *Social Problems, 14,* 128–147.

Bynner, J. M., O'Malley, P. M., & Bachman, J. G. (1981). Self-esteem and delinquency revisited. *Journal of Youth and Adolescence, 10,* 407–444.

Cameron, M. O. (1964). *The booster and the snitch: Department store shoplifting.* New York: Free Press.

Clayton, R. R., & Voss, H. C. (1981). *Young men and drugs in Manhattan: A causal analysis* (Research Monograph 39). Rockville, MD: National Institute on Drug Abuse.

Cloward, R. A., & Ohlin, L. E. (1960). *Delinquency and opportunity.* New York: Free Press.

Cohen, A. K. (1955). *Delinquent boys.* Glencoe, IL: Free Press.

Cohen, A. K., & Short, J. (1966). Juvenile delinquency. In R. K. Merton & R. A. Nisbet (Eds.), *Contemporary social problems* (2nd ed., pp. 84–135). New York: Harcourt, Brace & World.

Cohen, J. M. (1977). Sources of peer group homogeneity. *Sociology of Education, 50,* 227–241.

Coleman, L. M. (1986). Stigma: An enigma demystified. In S. C. Ainlay, G. Becker, & L. M. Coleman (Eds.), *The dilemma of difference: A multidisciplinary view of stigma* (pp. 211–232). New York: Plenum Press.

Conger, R. (1976). Social control and social learning models of delinquent behavior: A synthesis. *Criminology, 14*(1), 17–40.

Cressey, D. R. (1953). *Other people's money.* New York: The Free Press of Glencoe.

Duncan, O. D. (1969). Some linear models for two-wave, two-variable panel analysis. *Psychological Bulletin, 72,* 177–182.

Elliott, D. S., Huizinga, D., & Ageton, S. (1985). *Explaining delinquency and drug use.* Beverly Hills: Sage.

Elliott, D. S., & Voss, H. L. (1974). *Delinquency and dropout.* Boston: Heath.

Farrell, R. A. (1987). *Psychological dimensions to an elaboration of deviance theory.* The Albany Conference on Theoretical Integration in the Study of Deviance and Crime: Problems and Prospects. Albany: State University of New York at Albany.

Farrington, D. P. (1977). The effects of public learning. *British Journal of Criminology, 17,* 112–125.

Feyerherm, W. (1981). Measuring gender differences in delinquency: Self-reports versus police contact. In M. Q. Warren (Ed.), *Comparing female and male offenders* (pp. 46–54). Beverly Hills: Sage.

Figueira-McDonough, J., Barton, W. H., & Sarri, R. C. (1981). Normal deviance: Gender similarities in adolescent subcultures. In M. Q. Warren (Ed.), *Comparing female and male offenders* (pp. 17–45). Beverly Hills: Sage.

Foster, J. D., Dinitz, S., & Reckless, W. C. (1972). Perceptions of stigma following public intervention for delinquent behavior. *Social Problems, 20,* 202–209.

Ghodsian, M., Fogelman, K., Lambert, L., & Tibbenham, A. (1980). Changes in behavior ratings of a national sample of children. *Journal of Social and Clinical Psychology, 19,* 247–256.

Ginsberg, I. J., & Greenley, J. R. (1978). Competing theories of marijuana use: A longitudinal study. *Journal of Health and Social Behavior, 19,* 22–34.

Glaser, D. (1964). *The effectiveness of a prison and parole system.* New York: Bobbs-Merrill.

Gold, M. (1970). *Delinquent behavior in an American city.* Belmont, CA: Brooks/Cole.

Gold, M. (1978). Scholastic experiences, self-esteem, and delinquent behavior: A theory for alternative schools. *Crime and Delinquency, 24,* 290–308.

Gold, M., & Mann, D. (1972). Delinquency as defense. *American Journal of Orthopsychiatry, 42,* 463–479.

Gold, M., & Williams, J. R. (1969). The effect of "getting caught": Apprehension of the juvenile offender as a cause of subsequent delinquencies. *Prospectus, 3,* 1–12.

Goldberger, A. S. (1971). Econometrics and psychometrics: A survey of communalities. *Psychometrika, 36,* 83–107.

Gove, W. R. (1975). *The labeling of deviance: Evaluating a perspective.* New York: Halsted Press.

Hawkins, G. (1976). *The prison: Policy and practice.* Chicago: University of Chicago Press.

Hayduk, L. A. (1987). *Structural equation modeling with LISREL: Essentials and advances.* Baltimore: Johns Hopkins University Press.

Hepburn, J. R. (1977). The impact of police intervention upon juvenile delinquents. *Criminology, 15,* 235–262.

Hewitt, J. P. (1970). *Social stratification and deviant behavior.* New York: Random House.

Hirschi, T. (1969). *Causes of delinquency.* Berkeley: University of California Press.

Hoelter, J. W. (1983). Factorial invariance and self-esteem: Reassessing race and sex differences. *Social Forces, 61*(3), 834–846.

Hollander, E. P. (1958). Conformity, status, and idiosyncrasy credit. *Psychological Review, 65,* 117–127.

Howard, J. A., & Levinson, R. (1985). The overdue courtship of attribution and labeling. *Social Psychology Quarterly, 48,* 191–202.

Jensen, G. F. (1972). Parents, peers and delinquent action: A test of the differential association perspective. *American Journal of Sociology, 78,* 562–575.

Jensen, G. F., & Eve, R. (1976). Sex differences in delinquency: An examination of popular sociological explanations. *Criminology, 13,* 427–448.

Jessor, R., & Jessor, S. L. (1977). *Problem behavior and psychosocial development: A longitudinal study of youth.* New York: Academic Press.

Johnson, R. E. (1979). *Juvenile delinquency and its origins.* London: Cambridge University Press.

Johnson, R. J., & Kaplan, H. B. (1987). Corrigendum: Methodology, technology, and serendipity. *Social Psychology Quarterly, 50,* 352–354.

Johnson, R. J., & Kaplan, H. B. (1988). Gender, aggression and mental health intervention during early adolescence. *Journal of Health and Social Behavior, 29,* 53–64.

Johnstone, J. W. C. (1981). The family and delinquency: A reappraisal. In A. C. Meade (Ed.), *Youth and society: Studies of adolescent deviance* (pp. 25–63). Chicago: Institute for Juvenile Research.

Johnstone, J. W. C. (1983). Recruitment to a youth gang. *Youth and Society, 14,* 281–300.

Jöreskog, K., & Sörbom, D. (1984). *LISREL VI: Analysis of linear structural relationships by the method of maximum likelihood.* Mooresville, IN: Scientific Software.

Jöreskog, K., & Sörbom, D. (1986). *LISREL VI: Analysis of linear structural relationships by maximum likelihood, instrumental variables, and least squares methods* (4th ed.). Mooresville, IN: Scientific Software.

Kandel, D. B. (1978a). Convergence in prospective longitudinal surveys of drug use in normal populations. In D. B. Kandel (Ed.), *Longitudinal research on drug use* (pp. 3–38). New York: Wiley.

Kandel, D. B. (1978b). Homophily, selection and socialization in adolescent friendships. *American Journal of Sociology, 84*(2), 427–436.

Kaplan, H. B. (1972). Toward a general theory of psychosocial deviance: The case of aggressive behavior. *Social Science and Medicine, 6,* 593–617.

Kaplan, H. B. (1975a). Increases in self-rejection as an antecedent of deviant response. *Journal of Youth and Adolescence, 4,* 281–292.

Kaplan, H. B. (1975b). *Self-attitudes and deviant behavior.* Pacific Palisades, CA: Goodyear.

Kaplan, H. B. (1975c). Sequelae of self-derogation: Predicting from a general theory of deviant behavior. *Youth and Society, 7,* 171–197.

Kaplan, H. B. (1976a). Antecedents of negative self-attitudes: Membership group devaluation and defenselessness. *Social Psychiatry, 11,* 15–25.

Kaplan, H. B. (1976b). Self-attitudes and deviant response. *Social Forces, 54,* 788–801.

Kaplan, H. B. (1977a). Antecedents of deviant responses: Predicting from a general theory of deviant behavior. *Journal of Youth and Adolescence, 6,* 89–101.

Kaplan, H. B. (1977b). Increase in self-rejection and continuing/discontinued deviant response. *Journal of Youth and Adolescence, 6,* 77–87.

Kaplan, H. B. (1980). *Deviant behavior in defense of self.* New York: Academic Press.

Kaplan, H. B. (1982). Self-attitudes and deviant behavior: New directions for theory and research. *Youth and Society, 14,* 185–211.

Kaplan, H. B. (1983). Psychological distress in sociological context: Toward a general theory of psychosocial stress. In H. B. Kaplan (Ed.), *Psychosocial stress: Trends in theory and research* (pp. 195–264). New York: Academic Press.

Kaplan, H. B. (1984). *Patterns of juvenile delinquency.* Beverly Hills: Sage.

Kaplan, H. B. (1986). *Social psychology of self-referent behavior.* New York: Plenum Press.

Kaplan, H. B. (1995). Drugs, crime, and other deviant adaptations. In H. B. Kaplan (Ed.), *Drugs, crime, and other deviant adaptations: Longitudinal studies* (pp. 3–46). New York: Plenum Press.

Kaplan, H. B. (1996). Psychosocial stress from the perspective of self theory. In H. B. Kaplan (Ed.), *Psychosocial stress: Perspectives on structure, theory, life-course, and methods* (pp. 175–244). San Diego: Academic Press.

Kaplan, H. B., & Damphousse, K. R. (1997). Negative social sanctions, self-derogation, and deviant behavior: Main and interactive effects in longitudinal perspective. *Deviant Behavior, 18*(1), 1–26.

Kaplan, H. B., & Fukurai, H. (1992). Negative social sanctions, self-rejection, and drug use. *Youth and Society, 22,* 275–298.

Kaplan, H. B., & Halim, S. (2000). Aggression and self-derogation: Moderating influences of gender race/ethnicity, and stage in the life course. *Advances in Life Course Research, 5,* 1–32.

Kaplan, H. B., & Johnson, R. J. (1991). Negative social sanctions and juvenile delinquency: Effects of labeling in a model of deviant behavior. *Social Science Quarterly, 72,* 98–122.

Kaplan, H. B., & Johnson, R. J. (1992). Relationships between circumstances surrounding initial illicit drug use and escalation of drug use: Moderating effects of gender and early adolescent experiences. In M. Glantz & R. Pickens (Eds.), *Vulnerability to drug abuse* (pp. 299–358). Washington, DC: American Psychological Association.

Kaplan, H. B., Johnson, R. J., & Bailey, C. A. (1986). Self-rejection and the explanation of deviance: Refinement and elaboration of a latent structure. *Social Psychology Quarterly, 49,* 110–128.

Kaplan, H. B., Johnson, R. J., & Bailey, C. A. (1987). Deviant peers and deviant behavior: Further elaboration of a model. *Social Psychology Quarterly, 50,* 277–284.

Kaplan, H. B., Johnson, R. J., & Bailey, C. A. (1988). Explaining adolescent drug use: An elaboration strategy for structural equation modeling. *Psychiatry, 51,* 142–163.

Kaplan, H. B., & Lin, C. (2000). Deviant identity as a moderator of the relation between negative self-feelings and deviant behavior. *Journal of Early Adolescence, 20*(2), 150–177.

Kaplan, H. B., & Liu, X. (2000). Social protest and self-enhancement: A conditional relationship. *Sociological Forum, 14*(4), 595–616.

Kaplan, H. B., Martin, S. S., & Johnson, R. J. (1986). Self-rejection and the explanation of deviance: Specification of the structure among latent constructs. *American Journal of Sociology, 92,* 384–411.

Kaplan, H. B., & Peck, B. M. (1992). Self-rejection, coping style, and mode of deviant response. *Social Science Quarterly, 73*(4), 903–919.

Kessler, R. C., & Greenberg, D. F. (1981). *Linear panel analysis: Models of quantitative change.* New York: Academic Press.

Kim, J., & Rabjohn, J. (1980). Binary variables and index construction. In K. F. Schuessler (Ed.), *Sociological methodology* (pp. 120–159). San Francisco: Jossey–Bass.

Kitsuse, J. I. (1962). Societal reaction to deviant behavior: Problems of theory and methods. *Social Problems, 9,* 247–257.

Klein, M. W. (1974). Labeling, deterrence, and recidivism: A study of police dispositions of juvenile offenders. *Social Problems, 22,* 292–303.

Klemke, L. W. (1978). Does apprehension for shoplifting amplify or terminate shoplifting activity? *Law and Society Review, 12,* 391–403.

Kornhauser, R. R. (1978). *Social sources of delinquency: An appraisal of analytic models.* Chicago: University of Chicago Press.

Krohn, M. D., Skinner, W. F., Massey, J. L., & Akers, R. L. (1985). Social learning theory and adolescent cigarette smoking: A longitudinal study. *Social Problems, 32*(5), 455–472.

Lefcourt, H. M. (1972). Recent developments in the study of locus of control. In B. A. Maher (Ed.), *Progress in experimental research in personality* (Vol. 6, pp. 1–39). New York: Academic Press.

Lemert, E. M. (1951). *Social pathology.* New York: McGraw–Hill.

Lemert, E. M. (1967). *Human deviance, social problems, and social control.* Englewood Cliffs, NJ: Prentice–Hall.

Lemert, E. M. (1972). *Human deviance, social problems, and social control* (2nd ed.). Englewood Cliffs, NJ: Prentice–Hall.

Leonard, E. B. (1982). *Women, crime and society: A critique of theoretical criminology.* New York: Longman.

Link, B. G. (1982). Mental patient status, work, and income: An examination of the effects of a psychiatric label. *American Sociological Review, 47,* 202–215.

Link, B. G. (1987). Understanding labeling effects in the area of mental disorders: An assessment of the effects of expectations of rejection. *American Sociological Review*, *52*, 96–112.

Loeber, R., & Dishion, T. J. (1983). Early predictors of male delinquency: A review. *Psychological Bulletin*, *94*, 68–99.

Long, J. S. (1983). *Confirmatory factor analysis: A preface to LISREL*. Beverly Hills: Sage.

Macoby, E. E., & Jacklin, C. N. (1974). *The psychology of sex differences*. Stanford, CA: Stanford University Press.

Mankoff, M. (1971). Societal reaction and career deviance: A critical analysis and introduction to the political economy of law enforcement. *Sociological Quarterly*, *12*, 204–218.

Mason, K. O., Czajka, J. L., & Arber, S. (1976). Change in U.S. women's sex-role attitudes. *American Sociological Review*, *41*, 573–596.

Matsueda, R. L. (1982). Testing control theory and differential association. *American Sociological Review*, *47*(4). 489–504.

Matsueda, R. L., & Heimer, K. (1987). Race, family structure, and delinquency: A test of differential association and social control theories. *American Sociological Review*, *52*, 826–840.

McCarthy, J. D., & Hoge, D. R. (1984). The dynamics of self-esteem and delinquency. *American Journal of Sociology*, *90*, 396–410.

McClelland, D. C. (1960). *The achieving society*. Princeton, NJ: Van Nostrand.

Meade, A. C., & Marsden, M. E. (1981). An integration of classic theories of delinquency. In A. C. Meade (Ed.), *Youth and society: Studies of adolescent deviance* (pp. 114–128). Chicago: Institute for Juvenile Research.

Meier, R. F., & Johnson, W. T. (1977). Deterrence as social control: The legal and extralegal production of conformity. *American Sociological Review*, *42*(2), 292–304.

Merton, R. K. (1938). Social structure and anomie. *American Sociological Review*, *3*, 672–682.

Messner, S. F., Krohn, M. D., & Liska, A. E. (1989). *Theoretical integration in the study of deviance and crime: Problems and prospects*. Albany: State University of New York Press.

Miller, W. B. (1958). Lower class culture as a generating milieu of gang delinquency. *Journal of Social Issues*, *14*, 5–19.

Morris, R. R. (1965). Attitudes toward delinquency by delinquents, non-delinquents and their friends. *British Journal of Criminology*, *5*, 249–265.

Naffine, A. (1987). *Female crime: The construction of women in criminology*. London: Allen & Unwin.

O'Connor, G. G. (1970). The impact of initial detention upon male delinquents. *Social Problems*, *18*, 194–199.

Palamara, F., Cullen, F. T., & Gersten, J. C. (1986). The effect of police and mental health intervention on juvenile deviance: Specifying contingencies in the impact of formal reaction. *Journal of Health and Social Behavior*, *27*, 90–105.

Pfuhl, E. H. (1986). *The deviance process* (2nd ed.). Belmont, CA: Wadsworth.

Phares, E. J. (1976). *Locus of control in personality*. Morristown, NJ: General Learning Press.

Piliavin, I., Thornton, C., Gartner, R., & Matsueda, R. L. (1986). Crime, deterrence, and rational choice. *American Sociological Review*, *51*, 101–119.

Polk, K., & Halferty, D. S. (1966). Adolescents, commitment, and delinquency. *Journal of Research in Crime Delinquency*, *4*, 82–96.

Pyszczynski, T., & Greenberg, J. (1987). Depression, self-focused attention, and self-regulating preservation. In C. R. Snyder, & C. E. Ford (Eds.), *Coping with negative life events: Clinical and social psychological perspectives* (pp. 105–129). New York: Plenum Press.

Reckless, W. C. (1967). *The crime problem* (4th ed.). New York: Appleton, Century, Crofts.

Reckless, W. C., Dinity, S., & Murray, E. (1956). Self-concept as an insulator against delinquency. *American Sociological Review*, *21*, 744–746.

Robins, L. N. (1966). *Deviant children grown-up: A sociological and psychiatric study of sociopathic personality*. Baltimore: Williams & Wilkins.

Robins, L. N. (1978). Sturdy childhood predictors of adult anti-social behavior: Replications from longitudinal studies. *Psychological Medicine, 8,* 611–622.

Rogosa, D. (1980). Comparing nonparallel regression lines. *Psychological Bulletin, 88,* 307–321.

Rosenberg, F. R., & Rosenberg, M. (1978). Self-esteem and delinquency. *Journal of Youth and Adolescence, 7,* 279–291.

Rozelle, R. M., & Campbell, D. T. (1969). More plausible rival hypotheses in the cross-lagged panel correlation technique. *Psychological Bulletin, 71,* 74–80.

Scheff, T. (1966). *Being mentally ill: A sociological theory.* Chicago: Aldine.

Schwartz, R. D., & Skolnick, J. H. (1962). Two studies of legal stigma. *Social Problems, 10,* 133–142.

Shelden, R. G. (1981). Sex discrimination in the juvenile justice system: Memphis, Tennessee 1900–1917. In M. Q. Warren (Ed.), *Comparing female and male offenders* (pp. 55–72). Beverly Hills: Sage.

Sherman, L. W., & Berk, R. A. (1984). The specific deterrent effects of arrest for domestic assault. *American Sociological Review, 49,* 261–272.

Shoemaker, D. J. (1990). *Theories of delinquency: An examination of explanations of delinquent behavior* (2nd ed.). London: Oxford University Press.

Simmel, G. (1950). *The sociology of Georg Simmel.* Ed. and Trans. K. H. Wolff. New York: Free Press.

Simons, R. L., Miller, M., & Aigner, S. M. (1980). Contemporary theories of deviance and female delinquency. *Journal of Research in Crime and Delinquency, 17,* 42–57.

Sutherland, E. H. (1947). *Principles of criminology* (4th ed.). Philadelphia: Lippincott.

Thompson, E. A., Smith-DiJulio, K., & Matthews, T. (1982). Social control theory: Evaluation of a model for the study of adolescent alcohol and drug use. *Youth and Society, 3,* 303–326.

Thornton, A., & Freedman, D. (1979). Changes in the sex role attitudes of women. *American Sociological Review, 44,* 831–842.

Tittle, C. J. (1980). *Sanctions and social deviance: The question of deterrence.* New York: Praeger.

Tjaden, P. G., & Tjaden, C. D. (1981). Differential treatment of the female felon: Myth or reality? In M. Q. Warren (Ed.), *Comparing female and male offenders* (pp. 73–88). Beverly Hills: Sage.

Veroff, J., & Peele, S. (1969). Initial effects of desegregation on the achievement motivation of Negro elementary school children. *Journal of Social Issues, 25,* 71–91.

Voss, H. L. (1969). Differential association and containment theory: A theoretical convergence. *Social Forces, 47,* 381–391.

Warren, M. Q. (Ed.). (1981). *Comparing female and male offenders.* Beverly Hills: Sage.

Wellford, C. (1975). Labeling theory and criminology: An assessment. *Social Problems, 22,* 332–345.

Wells, L. E. (1978). Theories of deviance and the self-concept. *Social Psychology Quarterly, 41,* 189–204.

Wells, L. E., & Rankin, J. H. (1983). Self-concept as a mediating factor in delinquency. *Social Psychology Quarterly, 46,* 11–22.

Werner, E. E., & Smith, R. S. (1977). *Kauai's children come of age.* Honolulu: University Press of Hawaii.

West, D. J., & Farrington, D. P. (1973). *Who becomes delinquent?* London: Heinemann.

West, D. J., & Farrington, D. P. (1977). *The delinquent way of life.* London: Heinemann.

Wheaton, B., Muthen, B., Alwin, D., & Summers, G. (1977). Assessing reliability and stability in panel models. In D. R. Heise (Ed.), *Sociological methodology* (pp. 84–136). San Francisco: Jossey–Bass.

Wheeler, G. R. (1978). *Counter-deterrence: A report on juvenile sentencing and effects of prisonization.* Chicago: Nelson–Hall.

Williams, J. R. (1976). *Effects of labeling the "drug-abuser": An inquiry* (Research Monograph No. 6). Rockville, MD: National Institute on Drug Abuse.

# Index